THE WORLD OF WORDS

THE World OF Words

Vocabulary for College Students

FOURTH EDITION

Margaret Ann Richek
Northeastern Illinois University

As part of Houghton Mifflin's ongoing commitment to the environment, this text has been printed on recycled paper.

HOUGHTON MIFFLIN COMPANY   Boston   Toronto

Geneva, Illinois   Palo Alto   Princeton, New Jersey

Dedicated to the memories of my father, Seymour Richek, and my stepfather, Milton Markman; and to my husband Perry Goldberg

Sponsoring Editor: Renee Deljon
Associate Editor: Ellen Darion
Associate Project Editor: Elena Di Cesare
Senior Production/Design Coordinator: Carol Merrigan
Senior Manufacturing Coordinator: Marie Barnes

Definitions reprinted by permission from *The American Heritage College Dictionary, Third Edition*. Pronunciation key adapted and reprinted by permission from *The American Heritage College Dictionary, Third Edition*. Copyright © 1993 by Houghton Mifflin Company.

Cover design by Judy Arisman, Arisman Design.
Cover painting by Carlo Carrà, *Interventist Demonstration, 1914*. Private Collection, Milan.

Art Credits: Chapter 1: Courtesy of Ben and Jerry's. Chapter 2: The Bettmann Archive. Chapter 3: AP/Wide World Photos. Chapter 4: Stock Montage; Smithsonian Institution. Chapter 5: Foto Marburg/Art Resource, NY; Stock Montage; Art Resource, NY; Archive Photos. Chapter 6: Stock Montage; Tony Fitzgerald. Chapter 7: Owen Franken/Stock Boston. Chapter 8: UPI/Bettmann Newsphotos. Chapter 9: Culver Pictures. Chapter 10: Ken Robert Buck/ The Picture Cube; Tony Fitzgerald. Chapter 11: Joel Glenn/Image Bank. Chapter 12: Scott Ian Barry.

Library of Congress Catalog Card Number: 95-76982

ISBN: 0-395-71984-4

6789-DH-00 99 98

Contents

Chapter 7   Word Elements: Movement   *201*

Chapter 8   Word Elements: Together and Apart   *231*

Chapter 9   Word Elements: Numbers and Measures   *265*

Chapter 10   Word Elements: Thought and Belief   *296*

Chapter 11   Word Elements: The Body and Health   *324*

Chapter 12   Word Elements: Speech and Writing   *353*

Preface

The World of Words, Fourth Edition, will help students master strategies for becoming independent learners of vocabulary, learn specific words that will be useful in their academic work, and develop a lifelong interest in words. Through a series of carefully paced lessons, students learn three vocabulary development strategies: using the dictionary, using context clues, and using ancient Greek and Latin word elements.

The Fourth Edition of **The World of Words** continues to link students' general knowledge to vocabulary, covering such topics as popular music, sports, and the origins of names. I find that students enjoy these features and begin to see that learning vocabulary *is* relevant to their lives. While reinforcing these links, the text also supplies information that will be useful to students in their academic work. Thus, as the book progresses, students read about science, the classics, and literature.

The word lists and the ancient Greek and Latin word elements have been carefully selected on the basis of their appropriate level and usefulness in students' academic work. Word elements are presented so that students can easily recognize and use them in modern English words. Avoiding complex discussions of infinitive, participial, and stem forms, the text nevertheless provides the spellings of word elements most commonly found in English.

Feedback from students and instructors has enabled me to adapt this book to the needs of today's diverse student population. Instructors will find **The World of Words,** Fourth Edition, suitable for students of many cultural and linguistic backgrounds, including those for whom English is a second language.

Organization

Part 1 concentrates on dictionary skills and context clues; Part 2 stresses word elements (ancient Greek and Latin prefixes, roots, and suffixes). A theme for each chapter (for instance, Words About People, Chapter 1) helps make vocabulary study more meaningful.

Each chapter of **The World of Words** contains these features:

- *Did You Know?* presents interesting word facts to help spark students' interest in vocabulary.

- *Learning Strategy* provides instruction to help students independently learn new words.
- *Words to Learn* presents twenty-four vocabulary words with pronunciations, definitions, and example sentences. Related Words help students see how one base word can be adapted for use in several different ways, and usage notes help students use their new vocabulary words correctly. The Words to Learn are divided into two parts containing twelve words each. Word facts, etymologies, and trivia quizzes provide a context for the words and help students remember the definitions.
- *Exercises* follow each set of Words to Learn; additional exercises are included at the end of each chapter. A wide variety of exercises, including Matching Definitions, Words in Context, Related Words, Companion Words, Writing with Your Words, and Practicing Strategies, provides thorough practice in both the Words to Learn and the Learning Strategy.
- The *Passages* use many of the chapter words in context and gives students practice reading short essays. Each passage is followed by a brief exercise and three discussion questions.
- *Idioms* present the meanings of several widely used English expressions centered around a theme related to the chapter.

New to this Edition

Based on using this text for thirteen years at Northeastern Illinois University and reviewing constructive comments on the Third Edition from users across the country, I have been able to refine those features students found most useful and add the following new features to the Fourth Edition:

- Revision, updating, and frequency tallies of word lists, resulting in the addition of thirty-two new words.
- A feature on the meanings of *idioms* added to each chapter.
- The use of maps throughout the book to clarify geographical concepts and relate them to word learning.
- A new exercise format, "Say It Again," that asks students to match a sentence using several vocabulary words with a paraphrased sentence.
- Revision and updating of example sentences, exercises, and tests.

Support for Instructors

The *Instructor's Test Package* contains a complete testing program, as well as supplementary exercises. An *Instructor's Annotated Edition* provides answers to all exercises and teaching suggestions for each chapter. *Computer Study Modules,* available for Macintosh, and IBM compatible computers, has been updated for this edition.

Acknowledgments

I wish to thank the many people who have contributed ideas, inspiration, and support for this book. The editorial staff of the Houghton Mifflin Company, especially Mary Jo Southern, Melody Davies, Elena Di Cesare, and Jennifer Huber, provided superb skills and a deep understanding of the purposes of this project. Editors Donald Pharr and Judy MacDonald provided invaluable assistance in shaping the manuscript. Research librarian Anthony Krier responded creatively to hundreds of inquiries. Thanks is also due to Perry Goldberg, Sandra Goldberg, Dorothy Genus, Stephen Richek, Jean Richek Markman, Milton Markman, M. J. Hilberger, Rodolfo Rodriguez Santiago, Jose Rodriguez Santiago, Jai Kim, Marina Ulanovskaya, Julia Ulanovskaya, Phyllis Glorioso, Eleanor Zeff, Daniel Zeff, Iris Cosnow, Kate Feinstein, David Lang, Neil Adelman, Edward (Bomba) Marshall, and Erik Simpson. Special acknowledgment is reserved for Jose Luis Gamboa, whose writing exercise appears in the review section for Chapters 1–4. The following reviewers helped to formulate the shape and direction of the manuscript: Susan Blue, Gulf Coast Community College, FL; Michele Freed, Lexington Community College, KY; Patricia B. Gates, Community College of Allegheny County—Boyce Campus, PA; Hattie L. Pinckney, Florence-Darlington Technical College, SC; Stephen J. Pullem, University of North Carolina, NC; Deborah M. Simpson, Jamestown Community College, NY; and Katie Smith, Riverside Community College, CA.

P A R T

1

Dictionary Skills and Context Clues

Did you know that the size of your vocabulary predicts how well you will do in school? This book will improve your vocabulary so that you become a better reader, writer, listener, and speaker. As you master more words, you can improve your performance in all subjects—from astronomy to electronics to marketing to zoology. A larger vocabulary will also help you make a good impression in a job interview. People judge others by the way they communicate, and vocabulary is a key to communication.

This book will help you use words more precisely and vividly. Instead of describing a *friendly* gathering, you will be able to distinguish between a *convivial* party and an *amicable* meeting. Instead of saying that someone gave money to a charity, you may call that person a *philanthropist* or a *benefactor*. Learning these words will also help you understand the speech and writing of others.

As you work through this book, you will improve your vocabulary, first, by learning the words presented in each chapter and, second, by mastering learning strategies that will enable you to learn words on your own. Chapters 1 through 4 will teach you the strategies of using the dictionary and using context clues. In Chapters 5 through 12, you will learn how to use word elements such as prefixes, roots, and suffixes.

Each chapter contains several sections:

Did You Know? highlights interesting facts about English words.
Learning Strategy presents methods that will enable you to learn words independently.
Words to Learn defines, and gives examples of, twenty-four words that appear frequently in magazines, newspapers, and college texts. Each

Words to Learn section is divided into two parts containing twelve words each.

The *Exercises* give you practice with the words and strategies. One set of exercises follows the first part of the Words to Learn section, another set follows the second part, and a final set appears at the end of the chapter.

The *Passage* presents a reading selection that includes several "Words to Learn" from the chapter. It is followed by an exercise that tests your understanding of words used in context and discussion questions that check your comprehension of the passage.

Parts of Speech

Parts of speech are essential to the definition and use of words. In order to master the vocabulary words in this book, you will need to know the part of speech for each word. In addition, if you understand how words can be changed to form different parts of speech, you can multiply your vocabulary by using one word in many different ways.

Nouns, adjectives, verbs, and adverbs are presented in this book.

A **noun** is a person, place, thing, or idea.

Jocelyn is a *nurse.*

San Diego is a beautiful *city.*

Flowers grew in the *garden.*

Liberty and *justice* are precious.

An **adjective** describes, or modifies, a noun.

The *happy* child played in the sun. (*Happy* modifies *child.*)

The dog was *wet.* (*Wet* modifies *dog.*)

A **verb** expresses an action or a state of being.

I *study* vocabulary.

The class *is* interesting.

Verbs may be divided into two categories: transitive and intransitive. A **transitive verb** has an action that is directed toward someone or something. A transitive verb cannot stand alone in a sentence; it needs a direct object to make the sentence complete. In contrast, an **intransitive verb** does not need a direct object.

Transitive verb: Delphine *bought* a computer. (*Computer* is the direct object.)

Intransitive verb: The noise *stopped*. (No direct object is needed.)

Verbs may express past, future, or present action. Past-tense verbs are usually formed by adding the ending *-ed*. In this case, the verb formed with *-ed* is a **past participle.**

Scott *greeted* his friend.

The future tense is often expressed through the use of the helping verb *will*.

I *will shop* in the mall tomorrow.

When we use the present tense, we add an *s* to third-person singular verbs, that is, verbs that have any one person as the subject except *I* or *you*. (Examples of subjects that require third-person singular verbs are *she, Joe,* or *the door.*)

The doctor *sees* patients each morning.

Tucson *grows* rapidly each year.

We often express actions that started in the past and are still taking place by using a form of the helping verb *to be* and adding *-ing* to the end of the main verb. This is called the present progressive tense, and the *ing* form is called a **present participle.**

I *am waiting* for the mail delivery.

The sun *is shining*.

The *-ing* and *-ed* forms of verbs are also used to form other parts of speech. The *-ing* forms of verbs are called **gerunds** when they are used as nouns.

Smoking is forbidden in the theater.

Cuthbert and Ann went *dancing*.

The *-ing* and *-ed* forms of verbs are called **participles** when they are used as adjectives.

The *insulting* man made others feel bad. (In this sentence, the man insults other people.)

The *insulted* man felt bad. (In this sentence, other people insult the man.)

An **adverb** modifies a verb, an adjective, or another adverb. Many adverbs end in *-ly*.

The athlete ran *quickly*. (*Quickly* modifies *ran*, a verb.)

We admired the *brightly* colored mural. (*Brightly* modifies *colored,* an adjective.)

The disease spread *more rapidly* than we had expected. (*More,* an adverb, modifies *rapidly,* another adverb. *Rapidly,* in turn, modifies *spread,* a verb.)

In addition to nouns, adjectives, verbs, and adverbs, parts of speech also include pronouns, prepositions, conjunctions, and interjections.

A **pronoun** replaces a noun.

Brenda locked the door when *she* left.

We will meet *him* at the airport.

A **conjunction** connects words, phrases, or clauses.

Oswaldo bought a suit *and* a tie.

Will Marie go to the movies, *or* will she stay home?

An **interjection** is an exclamatory word that may appear by itself or in a sentence.

Great!

Oh, look at that!

A **preposition** joins a noun or pronoun with another word in a sentence. Prepositions are found at the beginning of prepositional phrases, which usually function as adjectives and adverbs.

I have a love *of* books.

In this sentence, the preposition *of* joins the noun *books* to another noun in the sentence, *love. Of* is the first word in the prepositional phrase *of books.* The entire prepositional phrase functions as an adjective because it modifies the noun *love.*

This sentence shows a prepositional phrase used as an adverb:

The child ran *over* the bridge.

Here, the preposition *over* connects the noun *bridge* to the verb *ran.* The prepositional phrase *over the bridge* functions as an adverb that modifies the verb *ran.*

Words and phrases commonly used as prepositions include *about, above, according to, across, after, against, before, below, beside, by, during, for, from, in, inside, into, like, of, off, on, out, over, through, to, toward, under, until, up,* and *with.*

Since it is often difficult to predict which preposition should be used in a sentence, mastery of these small words can come only with practice.

Therefore, one exercise in this book, "Companion Words," provides practice in using the correct preposition with the words you will learn.

Word Endings and Parts of Speech

A single word can often be changed to form several different related words. These related words have similar meanings, but they usually function as different parts of speech. For example, as shown in the illustration, the word *nation* (a noun) can form *national* (an adjective), *nationally* (an adverb), *nationalize* (a verb), and *nationality* (another noun).

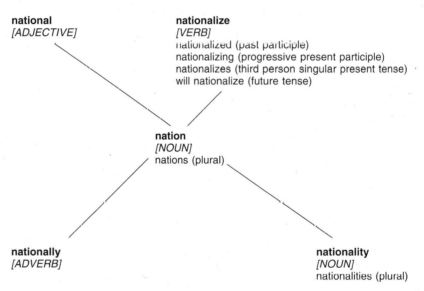

national
[ADJECTIVE]

nationalize
[VERB]
nationalized (past participle)
nationalizing (progressive present participle)
nationalizes (third person singular present tense)
will nationalize (future tense)

nation
[NOUN]
nations (plural)

nationally
[ADVERB]

nationality
[NOUN]
nationalities (plural)

Related words are formed by adding *suffixes*—groups of letters that are attached to the ends of words—to change the part of speech. The following table gives a list of such suffixes and examples of words formed with them.

Suffix	Base word	Suffixed word
	Suffixes that form nouns	
-ance, -ancy	insure, truant	insurance, truancy
-ence	differ	difference
-er	teach	teacher
-ion, -tion	confuse, compete	confusion, competition
-ism	real	realism
-ity	reliable	reliability
-ment	require	requirement

| -ness | happy | happiness |
| -ure | fail | failure |

Suffixes that form adjectives

-able, -ible	wash, reverse	washable, reversible
-al	season	seasonal
-ful	watch	watchful
-ic	angel	angelic
-ous, -ious	fame, space	famous, spacious
-ive	react	reactive
-y	stick	sticky

Suffixes that form verbs

-ate	valid	validate
-ify	simple	simplify
-ize	idol	idolize

Suffix that forms adverbs

| -ly | rapid | rapidly |

When certain suffixes are added to words, they change the pronunciation of the new words that are formed. Some suffixes change the syllable of the word that we stress in speech. An accent mark (′) is used to indicate which syllable of a word receives the main stress. A light accent mark (′) shows that another syllable is also stressed, but not as strongly as the syllable with the darker accent mark. The following examples show the pronunciation changes in a word when these suffixes are added.

When -*ic* or -*tic* is added to a word, the stress moves to the syllable before the -*ic* or -*tic*.

| cha′ os | cha ot′ ic |
| dip′ lo mat | dip lo mat′ ic |

The stress remains on the syllable before the -*ic* or -*tic* even when another suffix is added.

| cha′ os | cha ot′ ic | cha ot′ i cal ly |
| dip′ lo mat | dip lo mat′ ic | dip lo mat′ i cal ly |

When -*ion* or -*tion* is added to a word, the main stress falls on the syllable before the suffix. Sometimes an *a* is added before the -*ion* or -*tion*. Note the light and heavy stresses in these words.

| pro hib′ it | pro′ hi bi′ tion | |
| con demn′ | con′ dem na′ tion | (Note the added *a*.) |

When *-ity* is added to a word, the main stress again falls on the syllable before the suffix.

gul′ li ble   gul′ li bil′ i ty
am′ i ca ble   am′ i ca bil′ i ty

As you can see, when you learn a new word, you will often be able to form a number of different, but related, words simply by adding suffixes. Related words formed in this way are listed with many of the words you will be studying. Since the changes in pronunciation caused by adding *-ic, -ion* (*-tion*), and *-ity* are explained in this section, these changes will not be repeated when related words are introduced in the text. As you work through this book, refer to the table of suffixes and the explanation of pronunciation changes when you meet words with these endings. To find out more about parts of speech and how related words can function in a sentence, you may want to consult a grammar book.

Words About People

Do you know a *frugal* shopper, a person *gullible* enough to believe anything, or an *adroit* athlete? The earth is home to over five billion people, and each of us has a different personality and different interests. The words in this chapter will expand your ability to describe the people around you and to think about yourself. You will find these words useful in school, on the job, and in your daily life.

Chapter Strategy: Using the Dictionary

Chapter Words:

Part 1

adroit	capricious	gullible
aficionado	cosmopolitan	hypocritical
altruistic	disdain	intrepid
ascetic	fraternal	venerable

Part 2

affluent	candid	gauche
alien	dogmatic	novice
amicable	exuberant	renegade
astute	frugal	stoic

Did You Know?

What's in a Name?

Did you know that first names often have meanings? When your parents named you, they may have thought carefully about the meaning that your name would carry. Here are some popular names for women and men, each with its meaning.

For Women

Aisha—life
Alice, Alicia—noble
Barbara—mysterious, foreign
Caroline—strong one
Cynthia—moon goddess
Erica—royal, ever powerful
Helen, Eleanor, Ellen—bright light
Inez—pure
Jennifer—white wave
Jessica—wealthy
Louise—famous warrior maiden
Mary, Maria—bitter
Melissa—bee
Mercedes—merciful
Nicole—victor
Phyllis—green leaf
Rachel—female sheep
Stephanie—crown
Tiffany—godlike in appearance
Ursula—female bear
Yolanda—modest, shy

For Men

Alexander, Alex—protector
Anthony—praiseworthy, beyond compare
Carlos, Charles—masculine, man of the people
David—well loved
Edwin—wealthy friend
George, Jorge—farmer
Henry, Enrico—king of the house
Jason—healer
John, Juan—God's gift
Kevin—kind, gentle, lovable
Michael—godlike
Patrick—noble
Reginald, Ronald—mighty ruler
Robert—famous
Ross—horse
Russell—like a fox, red-haired
Terry—tender
Wayne—wagon maker
William—protector

At times, parents name children in honor of a personal hero. In the 1700s, although the Scots failed to bring Charles Stuart to the throne as their king, many Scottish people remained loyal to him. In tribute to "Bonnie" (handsome) Prince Charlie, one Scot named all fourteen of his sons *Charles*. Similarly, in the 1960s, many parents named their daughters *Jacqueline* after the popular Jacqueline Kennedy, wife of U.S. President John F. Kennedy. In addition, boys were named *Kenyatta* in honor of Jomo Kenyatta, president of Kenya from 1964 to 1978.

In some cultures, religious leaders, rather than parents, name babies. Traditional Buddhist families often ask monks to choose first names. After a name is given, the mother and father may not eat meat for one year.

Middle names may be used to show family ties. In Russia, a "patronymic" middle name contains the father's first name plus -*ovich* (son) or -*ovna* (daughter). Alexander Fekson's son, Gennady, is *Gennady Alexandrovich Fekson;* Alexander's daughter, Sophia, is *Sonya Alexandrovna Fekson.* The most respectful way to address a Russian is to use the first name and patronymic (Sophia Alexandrovna) without the last name.

Many Korean families express their unity by giving all boys of one generation the same middle name. Five names that mean *wood, fire, earth, metal,* and *water* are passed from father to son. If two brothers get the middle name *wood,* their sons are named *fire* and their grandsons are named *earth.* In the sixth generation, the cycle begins again.

Today many English-speaking parents give children hyphenated last (or family) names that contain the family names of both mother and father. This practice is similar to naming customs in Spanish-speaking countries. For instance, one Costa Rican teacher named *Beatrice* has a father whose family name is *Sandino* and a mother whose family name is *Rodriguez.* Beatrice's full name is *Beatrice Sandino-Rodriguez.*

In many Asian countries, family names are actually put first, giving special importance to family relationships. The family name of Chinese leader Mao Tse-tung was *Mao,* not *Tse-tung,* and Americans called him "Chairman Mao."

Learning Strategy

Using the Dictionary

The learning strategies presented in this book will teach you how to figure out the meanings of unknown words on your own. This book presents about five hundred words that you will learn directly from the Words to Learn sections. However, by using techniques from the Learning Strategy sections, you will be able to multiply your vocabulary to include thousands of new words.

This chapter's learning strategy concentrates on the effective use of the dictionary. The dictionary is an important tool for improving your vocabulary, since it is the best source for finding the precise meaning of a word.

There are many different types of dictionaries. The smallest is the pocket or abridged dictionary, usually a paperback, which gives short definitions. The most complete kind is the unabridged dictionary, which includes many unusual words, extensive definitions, and full word histories. You may have seen an unabridged dictionary on a stand in the library. Between these two sizes is the college-level dictionary, which includes enough detail for most college students.

Because a dictionary conveys much information in a small space, learning to use this important tool takes practice. A skillful dictionary user can find not only the meaning of a word but also its pronunciation, its history, and other words related to it.

Here is an entry from a college-level dictionary, the *American Heritage Dictionary, Third College Edition.* Each part is labeled.

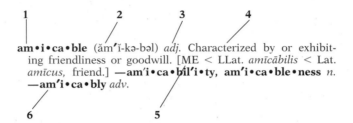

A standard dictionary entry contains the following parts.

1. The word. The entry word is printed in boldface type and divided into syllables.

2. The pronunciation. A key at the bottom of each page of a dictionary shows you how to interpret the pronunciation symbols. (You can also find a key to these symbols on the inside front cover of this textbook.) This key gives a common word that contains the sound represented by that symbol. For example, the symbol ă (which represents the first sound in *amicable*) should be spoken like the sound of *a* in the word *păt.*

   An accent mark (′) follows the syllable that should be stressed when you pronounce a word. In *amicable*, only the first syllable is stressed. If two syllables have accent marks, the syllable with the darker accent mark receives more stress.

   At times, an entry will give two pronunciations for a word. The pronunciation that appears first is the preferred one.

3. The part of speech. The parts of speech you will most often encounter are commonly abbreviated as follows.

n.—noun	*tr. v.*—transitive verb
adj.—adjective	*intr. v.*—intransitive verb
adv.—adverb	

   These parts of speech and their functions are described in the Introduction to Part One.

4. The definition. Since some words have more than one definition, you

must choose the one that best fits the sentence you are reading or writing. Choosing the best definition is often a very difficult task. Be sure to read all of the definitions before you select one.

Dictionaries have different methods of ordering definitions. In the *American Heritage Dictionary, Third College Edition*, published by Houghton Mifflin Company, the most general definition of a word is given first, and the least general is given last. In *Webster's Ninth New Collegiate Dictionary*, published by Merriam-Webster, the oldest definition of a word appears first, and the newest definition last. In the *Random House College Dictionary, Revised Edition*, published by Random House, definitions are ordered from the most commonly used to the least commonly used.

Dictionary definitions usually state only the precise, or *denotative*, meanings of words. But words also have implied, or *connotative*, meanings, which are suggested by the images, ideas, and emotions that we associate with them. For example, the words *skinny* and *slender* have the same denotative meaning, "thin," but they differ in connotative meaning. *Skinny* has negative associations, or connotations, and is an uncomplimentary word; *slender* has positive connotations and is a complimentary word. In the same way, *car* has a neutral connotation; *limousine* connotes an expensive, luxurious auto; and *wreck* connotes an auto that is worthless. Although dictionaries give some hints about connotative meanings, most information is learned simply by observing the ways people use words when they write and speak.

5. The etymology. In this section, the history of a word is traced to its origin. The word *amicable* comes to us in its present form from Middle English. Before this, the word appeared in Late Latin as *amicabilis*, which can be followed back still further to the Latin word *amicus*, meaning "friend." The dictionary includes a complete list of the abbreviations for languages used in etymologies. A few of the most common abbreviations follow.

ME—Middle English, spoken in England from A.D. 1100 to 1500
OE—Old English, spoken in England before A.D. 1100
Fr.—French, spoken in France today
OFr.—Old French, spoken in France from A.D. 800 to 1200
Lat.—Latin, spoken by the Romans in Italy about 2,000 years ago
 (LLat., Late Latin, was spoken at a later time.)
Gk.—Ancient Greek, spoken in Greece about 2,500 years ago

Etymologies are always enclosed in square brackets ([ ]) in a dictionary entry.

6. Related words. Sometimes several forms of a word are listed under one dictionary entry. Related words usually differ from the entry word because they contain *suffixes*, or word endings. Often these suffixes make the related words into different parts of speech. For instance,

under the main entry *amicable* (an adjective), two nouns (*amicability*, *amicableness*) and an adverb (*amicably*) are also listed. A discussion of suffixes and how they change the part of speech can be found in the Introduction to Part One.

While the dictionary entry for *amicable* is relatively simple, some entries are more complex. In the entry below, the word *lock* has many definitions, which are separated according to different parts of speech.

(1)   **lock** (lŏk) *n.* **1.** A device operated by a key, combination, or keycard and used for holding, closing, or securing.   **2.** A section of a waterway closed off with gates, in which vessels in transit are raised or lowered by raising or lowering the water
(5)   level.   **3.** A mechanism in a firearm for exploding the charge.   **4.** An interlocking or entanglement of elements or parts.   **5.a.** *Sports.* A hold in wrestling or self-defense that is secured on a part of an opponent's body.   **b.** A secure hold or grip.   —*v.* **locked, lock•ing, locks.** —*tr.* **1.a.** To fasten the
(10) lock of.   **b.** To shut or make secure with or as if with locks.   **2.** To confine or exclude by or as if by means of a lock: *locked the dog in.*   **3.** To fix in place so that movement or escape is impossible; hold fast.   **4.a.** To sight and follow (a moving target) automatically.   **b.** To aim (a weapon or other de-
(15) vice) at a moving target so as to follow it automatically.   **5.** To engage and interlock securely so as to be immobile.   **6.** To clasp or link firmly; intertwine.   **7.** To bind in close struggle or battle.   **8.a.** To equip (a waterway) with locks.   **b.** To pass (a vessel) through a lock.   **9.** *Print.* **a.** To secure (letter-
(20) press type) in a chase or press bed by tightening the quoins.   **b.** To fasten (a curved plate) to the cylinder of a rotary press.   **10.** To invest (funds) in such a way that they cannot easily be converted into cash.   **11.** *Comp. Sci.* To deny access to the contents of (a file or disk, for example).   —*intr.* **1.** To
(25) become fastened by or as if by means of a lock.   **2.** To become entangled; interlock.   **3.** To become rigid or immobile.   **4.** To pass through a lock or locks in a waterway.   —*phrasal* ***verb.* lock out.** To withhold work from (employees) during a labor dispute.   —*idioms.* **lock horns.** To become em-
(30) broiled in conflict. **lock, stock, and barrel.** To the greatest or most complete extent; wholly. [ME < OE *loc*, bolt, bar.] —**lock′a•ble** *adj.*

The entry shows that *lock* can be used as three parts of speech: noun (line 1), transitive verb (line 9), and intransitive verb (line 24). Sometimes a part of speech has several forms. In the entry above, *lock* has different forms when it is used as a verb (line 9). These forms are (1) *locked*— the past participle, (2) *locking*—the present participle, and (3) *locks*—the third-person singular verb form.

If the entry had been for a verb of more than one syllable, these forms might have been listed without the first syllable. For example, the forms for the verb *answer* are listed in the dictionary as *-swered, -swering,* and *-swers,* with the *an-* simply left out. Entries for nouns list the spelling of irregular plural forms, and entries for adjectives list spellings for comparative forms, such as *prettier* and *prettiest*.

As you look at the definitions within each part-of-speech category of *lock,* you will notice several other features of the dictionary entry. First, two or more closely related definitions may be listed under one number. Definition 5 of *lock* as a noun (line 7) has two parts, 5a and 5b. This is also true of definitions 4, 8, and 9 as a transitive verb (lines 13–22).

Next you will notice that a word or abbreviation in italics, such as *Print.* (line 19) and *Comp. Sci.* (line 23), is included in some definitions. This is called a "label," and it indicates that this definition is used in a special field. For example, the eleventh definition of *lock* as a transitive verb (line 23) is used in computer science.

Other labels give information about the style or use of a definition. For example, the label *Informal* shows that a definition is acceptable in informal speech; *Slang* shows that a word is used only in slang, or very informal usage; and *Nonstandard* indicates that a usage is not commonly accepted. The labels *Obs.* (for "obsolete") and *Archaic* show that a meaning of a word is no longer commonly used. An explanation of labels is given in the front of each dictionary.

A dictionary entry may also include examples of the word being used in phrases or sentences. Sometimes the examples are from everyday use. In addition, if sentences written by well-known authors are quoted, the author's name appears in parentheses after the quotes. (Although *lock* does not give any usage examples, many other words do.)

Finally, toward the end of the entry you may see —*phrasal verb* and —*idioms.* These show how the word is used with other words. A phrasal verb is a phrase that functions as a verb, such as *lock out.* Idioms are common phrases, such as *lock horns* and *lock, stock, and barrel.*

Notice, in the etymology, that the word *lock* comes from Old English and is found later in Middle English. For some words, the etymology deals with the origins of the different word parts contained within the word. Finally, some etymologies refer the reader to other words.

To check your knowledge of the dictionary, read the following definition and then answer the questions below.

> **paw** (pô) *n.* **1.** The nailed or clawed foot of an animal, esp. of a quadruped. **2.** *Informal.* A human hand, esp. a large clumsy one. —*v.* **pawed, paw•ing, paws.** —*tr.* **1.** To strike with the paw or paws. **2.** To strike or scrape with a beating motion. **3.** To handle clumsily, rudely, or with too much familiarity. —*intr.* **1.** To scrape the ground with the forefeet. **2.** To paw someone or something as in rudeness. [ME *pawe* < OFr. *powe.*] —**paw′er** *n.*

1. What three parts of speech does *paw* function as? _____

_____

2. Which definition (including part of speech) is acceptable only in informal speech? _____

3. In which language was *paw* first recorded? _____

Words to Learn

Part 1

1. **adroit** (adjective)   ə-droit′

   skillful; clever

   > The **adroit** politician avoided answering several embarrassing questions.
   >
   > Scottie Pippen's **adroit** moves make him one of the best players in the National Basketball Association.

   ▶ *Related Word*

   adroitness (noun)   The mathematician's mental *adroitness* enabled him to add fifty numbers in his head.

   NOTE: The word *adroit* can refer to quickness of mind or of body.

2. **aficionado** (noun)   ə-fĭsh′ē-ə-nä′dō

   fan; admirer; follower

   > **Aficionados** of spicy food can subscribe to *Chili Pepper* magazine.
   >
   > The football **aficionado** watched two games every Sunday.

   NOTE: An *aficionado* often connotes a fan with great knowledge.

3. **altruistic** (adjective)   ăl′troo-ĭs′tĭk

   dedicated to the good of others; unselfish

   > The **altruistic** doctor willingly treated patients who could not afford to pay.

► *Related Word*

altruism (noun) (ăl′trōō-ĭs′əm) The minister's *altruism* inspired him to run a shelter for abused children.

Many famous comedians have displayed *altruism* toward their communities. The great Mexican comic Cantinflas (1911–1993) built many hospitals for children and personally gave millions of dollars to poor people. The modern U.S. comics Whoopi Goldberg, Billy Crystal, and Robin Williams host a yearly show called *Comic Relief* that raises over ten million dollars to help homeless people.

4. **ascetic** (noun, adjective)   ə-sĕt′ĭk

a person who gives up pleasures and practices self-denial (noun)

Siddartha, the first Buddha, gave up princely wealth to live as an **ascetic.**

avoiding or giving up pleasures (adjective)

The **ascetic** woman lived alone in a room furnished with only a bed.

NOTES: (1) *Ascetics* are often religious people who feel that self-denial and social isolation will bring them closer to God. (2) Be careful! Do not confuse *ascetic* with *aesthetic,* which means "beautiful" or "appealing to the senses." The two words sound almost the same.

Power is usually associated with luxury and wealth. But Mohandas Ghandi, one of the great leaders of this century, proved that an *ascetic* life can be a source of power too. Gandhi led the movement that brought India and Pakistan independence from Great Britain. Gandhi lived simply and even wove the cloth for his clothes. A vegetarian who sometimes fasted to make political statements, Gandhi refused to injure any living thing. Gandhi used nonviolent resistance against oppression. When he and his followers were attacked, they simply refused to fight back. In this way, they maintained personal dignity and showed the justice of their cause. Gandhi was assassinated in 1948, but his principles continue to inspire nonviolent change throughout the world.

5. **capricious** (adjective)   kə-prĭsh′əs

unpredictable; changeable; not based on reason or judgment; fickle

Because of **capricious** enforcement of the law, many speeding drivers did not receive tickets.

The teenager's **capricious** behavior was the first sign of her drug addiction.

▶ *Related Word*
  capriciousness (noun)   The *capriciousness* of the country's transportation system resulted in many late trains and buses.

Caligula, emperor of the Roman Empire in 37–41 A.D., was known for his *capriciousness*. He furnished his favorite horse with a marble stall and a jeweled collar. When his sister died, he declared her a goddess and built a shrine to her. Yet he treated advisers like slaves and provided no explanation when he removed awnings that protected people from the hot sun during public gatherings. His *capricious* nature could be combined with great cruelty, such as when he sentenced people to death for no apparent reason. This puzzling behavior came to an end when he was killed by one of his own guards.

6. **cosmopolitan** (adjective)   kŏz′mə-pŏl′ə-tən

from several parts of the world; international

   Los Angeles has a **cosmopolitan** population.

free from local bias; having a world view

   Covering events in many countries gave the newscaster a **cosmopolitan** view of the world.

▶ *Related Word*
  cosmos (noun)   (kŏz′məs)   The nature of the *cosmos* is still a mystery. (*Cosmos* means "universe.")

The ancient Greek word *cosmos* meant "world." It is said that the Greek philosopher Diogenes was asked to name the city-state of which he was a citizen. He replied, "I am a citizen *(polites)* of the world *(cosmos)*." The word *cosmopolitan* was coined from his reply.

7. **disdain** (verb, noun)   dĭs-dān′

to scorn; to treat as unworthy (verb)

   The rich nobleman **disdained** the poor peasant.
   The politician **disdained** to respond to the insult.

scorn (noun)

> The gang's drug dealing showed **disdain** for the law.

▶ *Common Phrase*
  disdain for

▶ *Related Word*
  disdainful (adjective)   Maria's sloppy clothes showed she was *disdainful* of fashion.

8. **fraternal** (adjective)   frə-tūr'nəl

referring to brothers

> **Fraternal** detectives starred in the television program *Simon and Simon.*

like a brother; very friendly

> Clarence had **fraternal** feelings for the men he had served with in the navy.

▶ *Related Word*
  fraternize (verb)   (frăt'ər-nīz')   Our boss warned us not to *fraternize* on the job. (*Fraternize* means "to socialize.")

The word *fraternity* comes from *frater,* the Latin word for "brother." College *fraternities* are meant to foster brotherly relationships. Other *fraternal* organizations seek to foster friendships or associations in a community or a profession. Examples of these are the Knights of Columbus and the Fraternal Order of Police.

---

9. **gullible** (adjective)   gŭl'ə-bəl

easily deceived; easily cheated

> Martin was **gullible** enough to believe that standing on his head would cure warts.

> The crook tried to sell the Brooklyn Bridge to the **gullible** young man.

▶ *Related Word*
  gullibility (noun)   Marsha's *gullibility* allowed the crook to convince her that the brass ring was really gold.

10. **hypocritical** (adjective)

not sincere; referring to actions that don't match stated beliefs

> The **hypocritical** governor spoke against public waste while using state employees to mow her lawn.

▶ *Related Words*
hypocrisy (noun)   (hĭ-pŏk′rə-sē)   Their *hypocrisy* did not fool us.

hypocrite (noun)   That *hypocrite* told us to give our money to charity, but he gave none at all.

NOTE: The word *hypocrite* comes from a Greek word meaning "actor."

11. **intrepid** (adjective)   ĭn-trĕp′-ĭd

fearless; brave

> The **intrepid** soldier led his men into battle.

The *intrepid* African American Harriet Tubman (1820–1913) led hundreds of slaves to freedom before the Civil War. After her own escape, she went back to slave territory nineteen times to lead others to a new life through a path of secret hiding places called the "Underground Railway." A huge reward was offered for her capture, and, if caught, she certainly would have been killed. However, she braved these dangers to bring more than 300 men, women, and children to freedom.

---

12. **venerable** (adjective)   vĕn′ər-ə-bəl

worthy of great respect because of dignity or age

> The **venerable** grandfather made many decisions for his family.

> The **venerable** church of Notre Dame has stood in Paris since the year 1189.

NOTE: 1. *Venerable* often refers to people or things of great age. 2. Do not confuse *venerable* with *vulnerable*. (*Vulnerable* means "easily injured or hurt.")

▶ *Related Words*
venerate (verb)   vĕn′ə-rāt′   We *venerate* the founders of our country.

veneration (noun)   The tribe's priest gave gold to the temple to show *veneration* of their gods.

Exercises

Part 1

■ Who's Who?

The sentences below begin by naming a type of person. For each example, choose the letter of the word or phrase on the right that defines the type most accurately. Use each choice only once.

1. A venerable person _____ .

2. To disdain is to _____ .

3. An intrepid person _____ .

4. Capricious people _____ .

5. A cosmopolitan person

    _____ .

6. An aficionado _____ .

7. An ascetic _____ .

8. An altruistic person

    _____ .

9. A hypocritical person

    _____ .

10. A gullible person _____ .

a. is sophisticated

b. is brave

c. is not sincere

d. is a fan

e. are brothers or close friends

f. gives up pleasures

g. is easily fooled

h. be scornful

i. is skillful

j. is unselfish

k. change their minds often

l. is worthy of respect

■ Words in Context

Complete each sentence with the word that fits best. Use each choice only once.

a. adroit   e. capricious   i. gullible
b. aficionado   f. cosmopolitan   j. hypocritical
c. altruistic   g. disdain   k. intrepid
d. ascetic   h. fraternal   l. venerable

1. Cats are _____ and can easily walk on top of narrow fences.

2. The _____ explorer traveled without fear in the dangerous country.

3. Darius was a(n) _____ person who volunteered to tutor poor children in reading.

4. Mr. Lopez made many friends when he joined the

   _____ organization in his neighborhood.

5. People felt only _____ for the man who had stolen government money.

6. The music _____ traveled from Los Angeles to New York to see the Metropolitan Opera.

7. The _____ man believed that money grew on trees in the United States.

8. The _____ ten-year-old changed her friends every week.

9. The _____ professor had served her college well for forty years.

10. The _____ lived alone in the mountains and prayed most of the day.

■ *Using Related Words*

Complete each sentence by using a word from the pair of related words above it. You may need to capitalize a word when you put it into a sentence. Use each choice only once.

1. fraternize, fraternal

   Soldiers from the U.S. 82nd Airborne Division developed

   _____ relationships when they served in the Persian Gulf War. Although they later scattered throughout the country, they are able to _____ at yearly reunions.

2. adroit, adroitness

The _____ of the acrobats in the Great Moscow Circus amazes their audience. Pavel Lavrik balances on top of several steel barrels; the Doveiko Acrobats swing through the air from

a steel platform. The final act, an _____ ballet done in the air, is dedicated to the Russians who died in World War II.

3. disdain, disdainful

Clothing may be used to show that we are snobs. Children who wear expensive sneakers made by Nike and Reebok are often

_____ of those who wear cheaper shoes. This

_____ hurts the feelings of children whose families cannot afford costly clothing.

4. hypocritical, hypocrisy

My husband's _____ attitude annoys me. He tells our teenage son and daughter not to smoke, yet he smokes when he is away from home.

I hope he quits smoking soon and ends this _____ .

5. altruism, altruistic

In many fraternities and sororities, being _____ is as important as having fun. As part of his membership in Kappa Alpha Psi, Michael Long is working to help children suffering from cancer. Many fraternities and sororities are leading a movement

toward _____ .

■ Which Should It Be?

To complete the following sentences, choose the letter of the phrase that makes better sense.

1. A popular sportscaster would be _____ .
   a. disdainful of listeners   b. an aficionado of athletics

2. A mayor should be _____ .
   a. capricious in making decisions
   b. adroit in handling sensitive public issues

3. You will know about life in different countries if you are _____ .
   a. a cosmopolitan person   b. an altruistic person

4. A person likely to attend a large party would be _____ .
   a. one who was an ascetic   b. one who fraternized easily

5. A good lawyer would be _____ .
   a. gullible enough to believe any client
   b. intrepid in defending cases

Words to Learn

Part 2

13. **affluent** (adjective)   ăf′loo-ənt

    wealthy; prosperous

    > **Affluent** people can afford many vacations.
    > Enormous oil reserves have made Kuwait an **affluent** country.

    ▶ *Related Word*
    affluence (noun) The immigrant rose from poverty to *affluence*.

14. **alien** (adjective, noun)   ā′lē-ən

    strange; foreign (adjective)

    > The custom of bowing to others is **alien** to most Americans.
    > Cruelty was **alien** to her kind nature.

    a foreigner; a person who is not a citizen (noun)

    > Many **aliens** come to Canada and the United States in search of peace and personal freedom.

    a being from outer space (noun); coming from outer space (adjective)

    > The **alien** creature had seven eyes and three arms.

NOTE: All three meanings have the connotation (or hint) of being unknown or strange.

▶ *Related Words*
alienate (verb)   The man's cruelty *alienated* his friends. (*Alienate* means "to make hostile or unfriendly.")

alienation (noun)   His *alienation* from his family made him unhappy. (*Alienation* means "psychological isolation.")

The popular television series *Star Trek: Deep Space Nine* features a crew of humans and *aliens* working together in outer space. Human commander Banjamin Sisko is assisted by Odo, an alien "shape shifter" who can change his form, but must return to a liquid every 24 hours. Wadzia Das is a Trill, an alien composed of an attractive female joined to the spirit of a 300-year-old brilliant scientist. Quark, a bartender, is a Ferengi, a greedy but amusing alien.

---

15. **amicable** (adjective)   ăm′ĭ-kə-bəl

friendly; peaceful

By settling the labor problem in an **amicable** manner, the boss and the labor leader avoided a strike.

The United States maintains **amicable** relations with Iceland.

NOTE: Amicable indicates a friendly, but not very close, relationship.

▶ *Related Word*
amicability (noun)   The *amicability* of Canada, Mexico, and the United States led to the signing of NAFTA, the North American Free Trade Agreement.

16. **astute** (adjective)   ə-stoot′

shrewd; having good judgment

The **astute** worker knew that being well liked would help her get a promotion.

NOTE: An *astute* person will know what is really important, rather than what people say is important.

▶ *Related Word*
astuteness (noun)   The politician's *astuteness* helped him get on powerful city committees.

Before he became President of the United States, Abraham Lincoln was a successful and widely respected lawyer. However, he was *astute* enough not to reveal his full intelligence. Instead, he talked slowly and told long stories that charmed juries into thinking he was a simple man from the backwoods. His behavior in the courtroom led rival lawyers to underestimate him. Research into the Lincoln law files is currently uncovering the intelligence and sophistication behind the *astute* mask of innocent "country boy."

17. **candid** (adjective)   kăn′dĭd

truthful; frank; honest in giving opinions

> Prince Charles was **candid** to the press about his failed marriage.

> My mother's **candid** opinion of my new dress hurt my feelings.

not posed or rehearsed

> The **candid** photograph caught me with my mouth open and my eyes shut.

▶ *Related Word*
  candidness (noun)   The professor's *candidness* about my essay made me seek help to develop my writing skills.

18. **dogmatic** (adjective)   dôg-măt′ĭk

arrogant in belief; opinionated

> Workers found it hard to suggest new ideas to their **dogmatic** boss.

> The **dogmatic** principal refused to admit girls to the all-boys school.

▶ *Related Word*
  dogmatism (noun)   (dôg′mə-tĭz′əm)   Because of the teacher's *dogmatism*, students feared to present their true opinions.

19. **exuberant** (adjective)   ĕg-zoo′bər-ənt

very enthusiastic; joyfully energetic

> **Exuberant** at seeing his mother after ten years, Hean grabbed her and lifted her into the air.

> Fans applauded the **exuberant** cheerleaders.

▶ *Related Word*

exuberance (noun)   In their *exuberance,* the audience ran onto the stage and began dancing.

20. **frugal** (adjective) $fr\overline{oo}'g\partial l$

thrifty; economical; attempting to save money; sparing

The **frugal** homemaker carefully shopped for low-cost food.

Unfortunately, my husband is **frugal** with compliments.

▶ *Related Word*

frugality (noun)   The parents' *frugality* enabled them to save for their son's college education.

21. **gauche** (adjective) $g\overline{o}sh$

Awkward; lacking in social graces

The **gauche** woman described painful surgery in front of her sick friend.

Our cousin was so **gauche** that he licked his fingers at a formal dinner.

In many languages, words that refer to the right side are positive and words that refer to the left side are negative. Two words in this chapter have their roots in the concepts of "right" or "left." In French, *à droit* means "to the right," and in both French and English *adroit* is a positive word meaning "skillful." *Gauche,* French for "left," means "awkward" or "clumsy" in English.

---

22. **novice** (noun) $n\breve{o}v'\breve{i}s$

beginner; person in a new situation

The expert chef patiently taught the **novice** how to make sauces.

Since the city council member was a political **novice,** he often said foolish things to the press.

23. **renegade** (noun) $r\breve{e}n'\partial\text{-}g\bar{a}d$

traitor; deserter; outlaw

The army offered a reward for the capture of the **renegade.**

The president of the country was a **renegade** who refused to follow international guidelines on nuclear weapons.

For centuries, Spain ruled over much of Mexico, Central America, South America, and what became the southwestern United States. As a result, most countries south of the United States are Spanish speaking. In addition, several million people within the United States speak Spanish. Not surprisingly, many Spanish words have entered American English. Two such words, *aficionado* and *renegade*, are introduced in this chapter. In Spanish, *aficionado* means "fan," in particular, a follower of the popular sport of bullfighting; and *renegado* means "deserter." Other examples of Spanish words found in American English are *corral, desperado, fiesta, patio,* and *rodeo.*

24. **stoic** (adjective, noun)   stô′ĭk

    not affected by pleasure or pain (adjective)

    > The **stoic** child remained still and silent during the painful medical treatment.

    ▶ *Related Word*
    stoicism (noun)   Sulyema's *stoicism* enabled her to bear bad luck without complaining.

    NOTE: In modern English usage, *stoic* is usually associated with pain, bad luck, or misfortune.

    The word *stoic* refers to an Ancient Greek school of philosophical thought founded in 308 B.C. The philosopher Zeno taught that, since the world had been made by gods, it was perfect. Therefore, human beings must accept their fates and should not express either sorrow or joy. The word *stoic* is taken from the covered porch (*stoa* in Greek) where Zeno taught.

Exercises

Part 2

■ *Who's Who*

The following sentences begin by naming a type of person. For each example, choose the letter of the word or phrase on the right that defines the type most accurately.

1. An affluent person is

_____

2. A dogmatic person is

_____ .

3. A candid person is _____ .

4. A stoic person is _____ .

5. An astute person is _____ .

6. A renegade is _____ .

7. A novice is _____ .

8. A frugal person is _____ .

9. An alien is _____ .

10. An amicable person is

_____ .

a. not affected by pain

b. trying to save money

c. awkward, lacking social graces

d. enthusiastic

e. wealthy

f. honest in giving opinions

g. a foreigner

h. a beginner

i. opinionated

j. friendly

k. a rebel

l. shrewd

■ *Words in Context*

Complete each sentence with the word that fits best. Use each choice only once.

a. affluent   e. candid   i. gauche
b. alien   f. dogmatic   j. novice
c. amicable   g. exuberant k. renegade
d. astute   h. frugal   l. stoic

1. The adoring crowd gave the marine a(n) _____ welcome home.

2. The _____ farmer did not complain when cold weather killed his orange trees.

3. The _____ doctor told the patient the truth about her illness.

4. The _____ teenager always seemed to be able to persuade her father to lend her the car.

5. As a freshman, I was a(n) _____ who knew nothing about college life.

6. My _____ father rarely feels he can afford new clothes.

7. The _____ man accidentally insulted his date.

8. Although I am now a(n) _____, I soon hope to become a Canadian citizen.

9. The divorcing man and woman tried to maintain a(n)

    _____ relationship for the sake of their children.

10. Despite much evidence that he was wrong, the _____ jury member refused to change his mind.

■ Using Related Words

Complete each sentence by using a word from the pair of related words above it. You may need to capitalize a word when you put it into a sentence. Use each choice only once.

1. stoic, stoicism

    In 1963, President John F. Kennedy was murdered by an assassin's bullet. His young widow, Jacqueline Kennedy, bore her husand's

    murder in a _____ manner, without showing

    emotion. Her _____ during his funeral made her a heroine to the American people.

2. alien, alienated

    When an immigrant family comes to America, they must often

    adapt to _____ customs. Chroek Tao brought his family from Cambodia to the United States to escape danger and poverty. However, some of Tao's children find his traditional ways to be old-fashioned. Family differences have _____ Tao from some of his children.

3. dogmatic, dogmatism

My aunt has _____ opinions about the proper way to dress and behave. Despite modern trends, she feels that women who leave the house should always wear dresses. She also expects that men will open doors for her and give her their seats on

crowded buses. Her _____ makes her unpopular with the younger members of the family.

4. amicable, amicability

Morocco has a long history of _____ relations with the United States. Only a year after the United States declared its independence in 1776, Morocco recognized the young country.

To further show his _____, Sultan Moulay Suliman presented a lion house to the U.S. consulate in 1821. Located in Morocco, it is now a U.S. National Historic Landmark.

5. astute, astuteness

_____ business leaders realize that their companies must show sensitivity to public opinion by recycling waste products. McDonald's and Arby's restaurants use only recyclable

paper wrappers for food. This shows _____ in recognizing strong public feelings about recycling.

■ *Which Should It Be?*

To complete the following sentences, choose the letter of the word or phrase that makes better sense.

1. A person who tells the truth is _____ .
   a. candid   b. amicable

2. An army general would never trust a _____ .
   a. renegade   b. stoic

3. If your team won the state championship, you would feel _____ .
   a. dogmatic   b. exuberant

4. A(n) _____ person is more likely to influence other people.
   a. astute   b. gauche

5. A(n) _____ person would be likely to spend money freely.
   a. affluent   b. frugal

Chapter Exercises

■ *Practicing Strategies: Using the Dictionary*

Read the definitions, and answer the questions that follow.

> **fab•u•lous** (făb′yə-ləs) *adj.* **1.** Barely credible; astonishing. **2.** Extremely pleasing or successful: *a fabulous vacation.* **3.a.** Of the nature of a fable or myth; legendary. **b.** Told of or celebrated in fables or legends. [ME, mythical < OFr. *fabuleux* < Lat. *fābulōsus* < *fābula*, fable. See FABLE.] —**fab′-u•lous•ly** *adv.* —**fab′u•lous•ness** *n.*

1. What part of speech does *fabulous* function as? _____

2. Which syllable of *fabulous* is stressed in pronunciation?

   _____

3. What adverb is related to *fabulous*? _____

4. In which language did *fabulous* originate? _____

> **bribe** (brīb) *n.* **1.** Something offered or given to a person in a position of trust to influence that person's views or conduct. **2.** Something serving to influence or persuade. —*v.* **bribed, brib•ing, bribes.** —*tr.* **1.** To give, offer, or promise a bribe to. **2.** To gain influence over or corrupt by bribery. —*intr.* To give, offer, or promise bribes. [ME < OFr., piece of bread given as alms.] —**brib′a•ble** *adj.* —**brib′er** *n.*

5. Which three parts of speech does *bribe* function as?

   _____

6. What part of speech does *bribable* function as? _____

7. In total, how many definitions does *bribe* have? _____

> **max•i•mum** (măk′sə-məm) *n., pl.* **–mums** or **–ma** (–mə).
> **1.a.** The greatest possible quantity or degree.   **b.** The greatest
> quantity or degree reached or recorded; the upper limit of varia-
> tion.   **c.** The time or period during which the highest point or
> degree is attained.   **2.** An upper limit permitted by law or
> other authority.   **3.** *Astron.* **a.** The moment when a variable
> star is most brilliant.   **b.** The magnitude of the star at such a
> moment.   **4.** *Math.* **a.** The greatest value assumed by a func-
> tion over a given interval.   **b.** The largest number in a set.   —
> *adj.* **1.** Having or being the maximum reached or attainable.
> **2.** Of, relating to, or making up a maximum. [Lat. < neut. of
> *maximus*, greatest. See **meg-***.]

8. Write the two full plural spellings of *maximum.*

   _____

9. What two parts of speech docs *maximum* function as?

   _____

10. Give the number and the part of speech of the definition of *maximum*

    most often used in astronomy. _____

■ *Practicing Strategies: Using a Dictionary Pronunciation Key*

It takes practice to use a pronunciation key efficiently. For each of the
following words, use the key that is located on the inside of the front
cover of this book to figure out the pronunciation. Try saying each word
out loud several times.

1. accolade   ăk′ə-lād
2. pseudonym   sōō′də-nĭm′
3. cuisine   kwĭ-zēn′
4. epitome   ĭ-pĭt′ə-mē
5. cliché   klē-shā′

■ *Practicing Strategies: Using the Dictionary Independently*

Use a college or unabridged dictionary to research the answers to the
following questions. Be sure to consult a recently published dictionary.

1. In what language was the word *sheriff* first recorded? _____

   _____

2. What is *myrrh*? _____

   _____

3. Which syllable of the word *oxymoron* receives most stress? _____

   _____

4. If you do something *gingerly,* how do you do it? _____

   _____

5. What is a *tupelo*? _____

   _____

■ Companion Words

Complete each sentence with the word that fits best. Choose your answers from the words below. You may use words more than once.

Choices: for, by, of, to, with

1. My professor is an aficionado _____ Civil War history.

2. The custom of eating with one's fingers is alien _____ me.

3. I have fraternal feelings _____ my best friend.

4. Jose has amicable relationships _____ his neighbors.

5. The renegade had disdain _____ the government.

■ Writing with Your Words

This exercise will give you practice in using the vocabulary words in your own writing. Each sentence is started for you. Complete it with an interesting phrase that also indicates the meaning of the italicized word.

1. An *intrepid* mountain climber would _____

_____ .

2. When the *venerable* elder spoke, _____

_____ .

3. The *cosmopolitan* woman _____

_____ .

4. My *gauche* friend _____

_____ .

5. A person might show *disdain* by _____

_____ .

6. A *novice* at driving might _____

_____ .

7. A *capricious* ruler might _____

_____ .

8. Only a *gullible* person would believe that _____

_____ .

9. One custom *alien* to me is _____

_____ .

10. When I am *affluent,* I will _____

_____ .

Passage

Two Real Guys: The Story of Ben and Jerry's Ice Cream

In 1978, they started with a $6,000 investment of personal cash; today their business is worth more than $100,000,000. Along the way, they became known for their sense of humor and their charity. This is the story of Ben Cohen and Jerry Greenfield, the two real guys behind Ben and Jerry's ice cream.

Ben and Jerry met in junior high school and soon **(1)** developed a relationship so close that it was almost **fraternal.** Both **candidly** describe themselves as fat "nerds" who hated sports but loved to eat ice cream. **(2)** Ben, who left college without graduating, was a **renegade.** Once, when he was working in a kitchen, his boss ordered him to get rid of his beard. Instead, he simply shaved a thin line down the middle of his chin and declared that he now had sideburns. Not surprisingly, Ben was fired from a series of jobs, although he did do well at mopping floors. His partner, Jerry, managed to complete college, but was rejected from 40 medical schools.

In 1978, Ben and Jerry decided to start an ice-cream shop in Burlington, Vermont, one of the coldest towns in the United States. **(3)** They completed a mail-order course in ice-cream making for **novices** and applied for a loan from the Merchant's Bank. Dressed in suits for the first time in years, their goal was to impress the **venerable** bankers. After the loan was granted, Ben and Jerry were able to start their business.

The next several months they worked day and night changing an abandoned gas station that lacked heating or adequate plumbing into an ice-cream shop. To save money, they lived in a trailer and existed on an **ascetic** diet of sardines and crackers. **(4)** In their desire to be **frugal,** Ben and Jerry paid construction workers with promises of free ice cream for life, instead of with money.

From the moment the shop opened, customers knew the ice cream was special. Ben, who lacked a strong sense of taste, had to approve each flavor. Because he could not taste mild things, **(5)** he **dogmatically** insisted that the flavors be strong and rich and have lots of crunchy additions. In 1981, *Time* magazine reported that Ben and Jerry's ice cream was among the best in the world.

(6) Customers also loved the shop's **amicable** atmosphere, which featured personalized service, games, and live piano music. In keeping with the company motto, "If it's not fun, why do it?" Ben and Jerry threw a public festival that included an ice-cream eating contest and an award for the longest unbroken apple peel. **(7)** An **exuberant** Jerry, who per-

Ben and Jerry are the two real guys behind a large ice–cream company.

formed magic tricks, smashed a cinder block on Ben's stomach and demonstrated his fire-eating abilities.

Sales were great, but there was not much profit. Since Ben and Jerry **disdained** standard business practices, they failed to keep track of their costs. They often supplied too much ice cream on their cones, or **(8)** lack of **adroit** scooping meant that they did not serve people quickly enough to make money. Their bookkeeping practices were so **capricious** that they often crumpled up checks, put them in their pockets, and forgot them. To help produce a profit, Ben and Jerry hired professional management staff and started to sell ice cream to grocery stores.

Despite Ben and Jerry's need to focus on the business, the fun continued as they created many imaginative and delicious flavors. **(9)** Two **aficionados** of the Grateful Dead rock group suggested the ice cream Cherry Garcia, a combination of chocolate and cherry named after star Jerry Garcia. Ben and Jerry's rich-tasting New York Super Fudge Chunk combined white and dark chocolate chunks with three kinds of nuts. Their best seller, Chocolate Chip Cookie Dough ice cream, contained raw cookie dough. Publicity also continued to be creative, as when Ben and Jerry crossed the United States in the summer of 1986 in a "Cowmobile" and gave away free ice-cream samples. In 1994, they hired Spike Jones to direct a humorous ad campaign for a new "Smooth" ice cream, without chunks.

Ben and Jerry's Homemade Inc. continued to grow in size and profits. Despite their new **affluence,** however, Ben and Jerry remained true to their original values. Formality continued to be **alien** to the company style, for everyone from factory workers to bosses wore jeans, participated in Elvis Presley look-alike contests, and received three pints of ice cream per day. As another worker benefit, 5% of company profits were distributed to all employees. Since recycling was important to Ben and Jerry, the company bought 200 pigs—one of them named after Ben and another one after Jerry—to eat ice-cream waste. (Unfortunately, the pigs refused to eat mint ice cream.)

Ben and Jerry also became famous for their **altruism.** When they sold their first public stock nationally, they announced a policy of "linked-prosperity," meaning that the company would use profits to support important causes. **(10)** The announcement turned out to be **astute,** for their **altruism** encouraged more people to buy their ice cream. Projects sponsored by Ben and Jerry's Homemade Inc. have included a New York "partnershop" that funds a drug counseling center and homeless shelter, efforts to preserve the Brazilian rain forests, and a Mexican cooperative company that supports poor peasants. From 1991 to 1994, the company focused all of its charitable efforts on "Sav-a Child," a campaign to improve the lives of children. Each year, 7.5% of profits before taxes were donated to charity.

Ben and Jerry's is now a **cosmopolitan** company that sells ice cream throughout the United States and Europe. Its stock is publicly traded, and it employs over 600 people. Yet the heart of the company remains in the two real guys, Ben and Jerry, who, rich or poor, remain true to their values and to their community.

■ *Exercise*

Each numbered sentence below corresponds to a sentence in the Passage. Fill in the letter of the choice that makes the sentence mean the same thing as its corresponding sentence in the Passage.

1. Ben and Jerry developed a relationship that was almost _____ .
   a. hateful   b. acceptable   c. wonderful   d. brotherly

2. Ben was a _____ .
   a. failure   b. rebel   c. tease   d. fan

3. They completed a mail-order course for _____ .
   a. beginners   b. skillful people   c. foreigners   d. poor people

4. In their desire to be _____ , the partners paid with promises of free ice cream for life.
   a. friendly   b. thrifty   c. scornful   d. excited

5. He _____ insisted that the flavors be strong and rich.
   a. stubbornly   b. happily   c. truly   d. sometimes

6. Customers also loved the shop's _____ atmosphere.
   a. happy   b. excited   c. friendly   d. rich

7. A(n) _____ Jerry performed magic tricks and smashed a cinder block on Ben's stomach.
   a. easily fooled   b. very stupid   c. truthful   d. excited

8. Lack of _____ scooping meant that they did not serve people quickly enough.
   a. deep   b. skillful   c. generous   d. enough

9. Two _____ of the Grateful Dead suggested the ice cream Cherry Garcia.
   a. singers   b. old people   c. heros   d. fans

10. The announcement of "linked-prosperity" turned out to be _____ .
    a. helpful   b. shrewd   c. charitable   d. friendly

■ Discussion Questions

1. Give two examples of the informality of Ben and Jerry's Homemade, Inc.

2. Describe three factors that contributed to the success of Ben and Jerry's company. Defend your answers.

3. Name another company that is involved in charitable efforts and describe these efforts.

◀ ENGLISH IDIOMS

Color

Each chapter in this book gives the meaning of some English idioms. Idioms are groups of words that have special meanings, which are different from the usual meanings of the words. Since the passage in this chapter is about Ben and Jerry, two colorful (or lively and interesting) characters, the idioms for Chapter 1 are about colors.

Some color idioms have negative meanings. *Feeling blue* means feeling depressed or bad, and *yellow-bellied* means cowardly.

The color words green and rose are used in idioms that have positive meanings. A person with a *green thumb* has a talent for gardening. People who look at the world *through rose-colored glasses* see things as much better than they really are.

Idioms containing the words black and red are used in business. A firm that is *in the red* is losing money, but one that is *in the black* is profitable.

During ancient Roman holidays, rival groups of young men would compete to see who could cover the most statues with red wine. Not surprisingly, the statue of Bacchus, god of wine, was particularly popular as a target. Today, when people go out for the evening to have a good time, they *paint the town red*.

2

Words in the News

Even on a remote mountain top, we are never more than a few seconds away from the news. A touch of a radio button brings us the latest reports of international events, accidents, sports scores, and gossip about our favorite stars. Television transports images from thousands of miles away into our living rooms; we learn about the weather throughout the world, and in our own backyards. Daily newspapers give us in-depth political analysis, advice columns, and tips on daily living. News from the "information superhighway" is brought into home and office computers through modems. This chapter presents many words that will help you better understand the news.

Chapter Strategy: Context Clues of Substitution

Chapter Words:

Part 1

accord	consumer	intervene
attrition	corroborate	media
bureaucracy	diplomacy	pacify
catastrophe	entrepreneur	Third World

Part 2

apprehend	ludicrous	radical
chaos	ominous	liberal
defer	supplant	conservative
epitome	thrive	reactionary

Did You Know?

How Many Ways Can a Team Win or Lose?

If you read the sports pages of the newspapers, you know how cleverly they are written. Many sportswriters are masters of the English language, who express game results in exciting ways that make fans read on eagerly. Every day, football, basketball, baseball, or hockey games are reported in newspapers; day after day, sportswriters make their reports sound fresh and enthusiastic.

How do they do it? After all, most of the events are basically the same:

1. The game is played.
2. One team or player wins.
3. The other team or player loses.

Because sportswriters have had to report wins and losses over and over again, they have developed clever synonyms (words that mean the same thing) for the words *win* and *lose.*

Let's look at some of the many ways to say *win* with examples taken from newspaper sports pages.

A's *beat* Yankees.

49ers *top* Broncos.

And here are some examples of ways to say *lose.*

Ohio State *is canned* by Michigan.

Nuggets *falter* in overtime.

Sportswriters vary their expressions depending on the amount of winning (or losing) points. For example, the connotations of these synonyms for *win* show that the victors won by a big score, really "killing" their opponents.

Purdue *crushes* winless Northwestern.

Giants *stun* Expos.

Iowa State *rips* number 4 Kansas.

On the other hand, the connotations of these words show that the winners barely got by.

Nebraska *struggles past* Baylor.

Chiefs *edge* Redskins.

Sometimes the name of a team is used in an imaginative way. The headlines that follow are *metaphors,* or figurative uses of names.

Flyers *soar past* Islanders. (Something that flies can soar.)

Flat Bulls *give* Rockets *a lift.* (Rockets are said to "lift off" when they begin to fly.)

Pirates *slice up* Cubs. (The Pirates take their swords and "slice up" the Cubs.)

49ers *shear* Rams. (A ram is a sheep; sheep get sheared.)

At other times, rhyme is used.

Bears *sack the Pack.*

Hornets *shake, bake* Bulls. (The food product Shake and Bake has seasoned crumbs for coating chicken and pork.)

Hoosiers *fake, shake, break* Illini.

Sometimes a short headline tells much about a game. What do you think happened in these games?

1. Bruins' rally on ice from 2 down stuns Rangers 4–3.

2. Iowa State surprises Minnesota in overtime.

3. Bulls surprise Bucks, end road slump.

(*Answers:*   1. The Bruins were losing 3–1, but, to the Rangers' surprise, the Bruins ended up winning the ice hockey game 4–3.   2. Minnesota, not Iowa State, was expected to win. The game was tied at the end, so it went into overtime. Iowa State won.   3. The Bulls had been playing away from their home town and had been losing games. Surprisingly, they won this game, which was also away from home.)

Learning Strategy

Context Clues of Substitution

Using *context clues* is a powerful strategy that can help you to figure out the meaning of unknown words. *Context* refers to the group of words or paragraphs surrounding a word. When you use context clues, you use the words that you do know in a sentence to make an intelligent guess about the meaning of an unknown word.

You may think that it is not a good strategy to guess at words. After all, it is better to know the answer on a test than just to guess. However, intelligent guessing is a very important strategy to use when you are reading. English has so many words that even the best readers cannot know them all. Good readers often use context clues, or intelligent guesses, when they meet unfamiliar words.

Context clues have two important advantages for you:

1. You do not have to interrupt your reading to go to the dictionary.

2. Using context clues allows you to rely on your own common sense. Common sense is your best learning tool.

You probably use context clues already. For example, context clues are the only way to choose the correct meaning for words that have more than one meaning, such as *cold*. You must use context clues to figure out what the word *cold* means in the following sentences.

a. She greeted him in a *cold* manner.

b. A cough and a stuffed nose are signs of a *cold*.

c. Alaskan winters are quite *cold*.

In which sentence does *cold* mean

1. a low temperature?

2. a type of illness?

3. unfriendly?

(*Answers:*   1. c   2. b   3. a)

Let's turn to a more difficult word. What are the meanings of the word *concession* in these sentences?

a. He bought some food at the hot-dog *concession*.

b. Because the country wanted peace, the leaders made a *concession* of land to the enemy.

In which sentence does *concession* mean

1. something that is surrendered or given up?

2. a business that sells things?

(*Answers:*   1. b   2. a)

Context clues and the dictionary are natural partners in helping you to determine the meaning of unknown words. Context clues usually give you an approximate meaning for a word and allow you to continue your reading without interruption. After you have finished reading, you can look up the word in a dictionary. Why not use the dictionary first? People usually remember words they figured out for themselves far better than those they simply looked up in a dictionary.

You may be wondering exactly how to figure out unknown words that you find in your reading. Many people find the following steps helpful:

1. As you are reading, try to pinpoint words you do not know. This advice sounds almost silly, but it isn't. Many people lose the opportunity to learn words simply because they let unknown words slip by. Don't let this happen to you. Try to capture difficult words!

2. Use context clues to make an intelligent guess about an unknown word's meaning. The strategies you will learn here and in the following chapters will help you do this. Remember that context clues will often give you an approximate—not an exact—meaning.

3. Write down the word and later check it in a dictionary. This step will tell you whether you guessed correctly and will give you a more exact definition of the word.

How does a person learn to make these "intelligent guesses"? In this book, we will present three different methods: substitution in context (in this chapter), context clues of definition (in Chapter 3), and context clues of opposition (in Chapter 4).

Substitution in context is perhaps the most useful way to determine a word's meaning. To use this strategy, simply substitute a word or phrase that makes sense in place of an unknown word. The word you substitute will usually be an approximate definition for the unknown word. Here are some examples.

> Ron's two brothers were hitting each other, but Ron would not join the *fray*. (Since people often hit each other in a fight, the word *fight* is a good substitution and provides an approximate meaning.)

> The *indigent* student could not afford books or school supplies. (A person who cannot afford things necessary for school is poor, and the word *poor* may substitute for *indigent*.)

Of course, context clues of substitution cannot be used all the time. Some sentences simply do not provide enough context clues. For example, in the sentence "Jane saw the *conger*," it would be impossible to find a good substitution for *conger*. (A conger is a type of eel.) However, since most sentences do provide context clues, substitution in context will help you much of the time.

Two additional examples are given below. Try using context clues of substitution to make intelligent guesses about the meanings of the italicized words. To do this, take out the unknown word and substitute a word you know that seems to make sense in the sentence.

1. The famous star was *inundated* with letters from fans.

2. Carmen *entreated* her sick grandfather to sit down and rest.

(*Possible answers:*   1. overloaded, flooded   2. begged)

Now try using the substitution strategy to make intelligent guesses about the meanings of some words to be studied in this chapter.

Each of the following sentences contains a word that will be presented in the Words to Learn section. Read the sentence and use a context clue of substitution to make an intelligent guess about the meaning of the italicized word.

1. The outdated computer was *supplanted* by a new model.

   Supplanted means _____ .

2. The rise in prices made us *defer* buying a home until next year.

   Defer means _____ .

3. The two countries reached a final *accord* that enabled them to stop fighting.

   Accord means _____ .

(*Answers:*   1. replaced   2. delay   3. agreement)

Words to Learn

Part 1

1. **accord** (noun, verb)   ə-kôrd′

   agreement; harmony (noun)

      An international **accord** controls nuclear weapons.

      We are in **accord** with your proposal to increase money for education.

to give or grant (verb)

The judge **accorded** Mrs. Mozzi $500 in damages.

▶ *Common Phrases*
in accord with

reach an accord

2. **attrition** (noun)   ə-trĭsh′ən

slowly wearing down; wearing away

The two countries gradually weakened each other in the war of **attrition.**

Since the company reduced its staff by a process of **attrition,** people who quit or retired were not replaced.

Hawaii's land has been gradually worn away by the continuous *attrition* caused by the waves that pound against its shores. Thousands of years ago, Hawaii was one continuous piece of land, but water has slowly covered much of it, and today only eight islands remain. Known for its comfortable climate and breathtaking scenery, Hawaii is a favorite tourist spot. In 1959 it became the fiftieth of the United States; the only one not a part of North America.

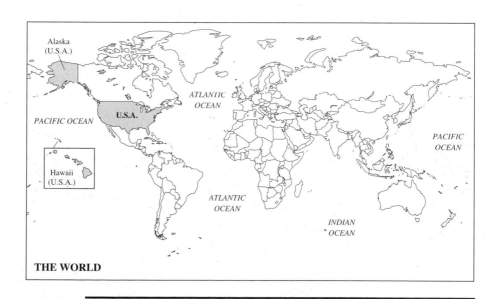

THE WORLD

3. **bureaucracy** (noun)   byŏŏ-rŏk′rə-sē

government by appointed officials

> The newly elected mayor promised to reform the inefficient city **bureaucracy.**

> My health insurance benefit was delayed because it had to be approved by several levels of **bureaucracy.**

NOTE: Bureaucracy is usually a negative word that refers to a government involving too many officials and too much delay. Perhaps because members of a bureaucracy are *appointed*, rather than *elected*, they often are more concerned with following rules than with getting things done.

▶ *Related Words*

bureaucratic (adjective)   The college changed its *bureaucratic* registration procedures.

bureaucrat (noun)   For twenty years, the *bureaucrat* made four copies of every letter he received.

Bureaucracy is often associated with the term *red tape* in sentences such as "There is too much bureaucratic red tape." In the 1700s, red tape was actually used to bind piles of English government documents. Since the government was bureaucratic and inefficient, *red tape* came to refer to excessive and silly official routines.

---

4. **catastrophe** (noun)   kə-tăs′trə-fē

a great disaster

> The bubonic plague of the 1400s was a **catastrophe** that killed one-third of all people in Europe.

> The ten-year civil war was a **catastrophe** for the economy of the small country.

▶ *Related Word*

catastrophic (adjective)   kăt′ə-strŏf′-ĭk)   The Exxon *Valdez* oil spill had *catastrophic* effects on Alaskan wildlife.

5. **consumer** (noun)   kən-sōō′mər

a buyer

> Shop owners try to please **consumers.**

▶ *Related Words*

consume (verb)   The athlete *consumed* three bottles of Gatorade. (*Consume* usually refers to eating and drinking.)

consumption (noun)   (kən-sŭmp′shən)   A person's *consumption* of food should be light during the evening. (*Consumption* may refer to eating and drinking, as well as to buying.)

Conspicuous *consumption* means making unneeded purchases in order to impress other people.

6. **corroborate** (verb)   kə-rŏb′ə-rāt′

to confirm; to make more certain

Five eyewitnesses **corroborated** the police report.

Notes on doors **corroborated** the radio announcement that school had been canceled due to bad weather.

▶ *Related Word*
corroboration (noun)   The existence of the legendary Loch Ness monster has not received scientific *corroboration*.

7. **diplomacy** (noun)   dĭ-plō′mə-sē

official relationships among nations

When **diplomacy** fails to settle disputes between nations, they may go to war.

tact; politeness

Jantima's great **diplomacy** enabled her to criticize others without hurting their feelings.

▶ *Related Words*
diplomat (noun, person)   John C. Munjo is the *diplomat* serving as United States ambassador to Pakistan.

diplomatic (adjective)   In 1993, Israel established *diplomatic* relations with Russia.

The United States has an enormous network of diplomats stationed in other countries. These diplomats represent U.S. interests, help U.S. citizens who travel abroad, and grant visas to foreigners who wish to visit the United States. Diplomatic work is sometimes dangerous. From 1979 to 1980, the Iranian government held over 100 U.S. diplomatic employees captive for 444 days.

People in the U.S. diplomatic corps work in embassies, which are considered U.S. land. Foreigners who need protection from their own governments may "ask for asylum" by fleeing to a U.S. Embassy, where other governments have no official control.

---

8. **entrepreneur** (noun)   ŏn′trə-prə-nûr′

a person who organizes and runs a business

> The Chinese-American **entrepreneur** An Wang built Wang Laboratories into one of the largest computer firms in the United States.

▶ *Related Word*
> **entrepreneurial** (adjective)   My *entrepreneurial* brother-in-law started with one fruit stand and now runs a nationwide business.

In the twentieth century, *entrepreneurs* have emerged from many backgrounds. African American *entrepreneur* John H. Johnson founded the enormous Johnson Publishing Company in 1942. Berry Gordy developed Motown Record Corporation (now Motown Industries), the Detroit-based company that revolutionized rock music with such singers as the Supremes and Marvin Gaye. Cuban-born Roberto C. Goizueta is the CEO of Coca-Cola. Many women have also become successful *entrepreneurs*. Both Estee Lauder and Mary Kay Ash have founded major firms in the cosmetics industry, and Debbi Fields is the force behind Mrs. Fields' cookies.

---

9. **intervene** (verb)   ĭn′tər-vēn′

to act in a matter involving others; to interfere

> Concerned citizens **intervened** to prevent the historic building from being torn down.

> I **intervened** in the argument between my two friends.

▶ *Related Word*
> **intervention** (noun)   In 1953, the United Nations' *intervention* ended North Korea's invasion of South Korea.

NOTE: To *intervene* can also mean to come between points of time, as in "Two years intervened between the skating competitions."

10. **media** (plural noun, adjective)   mē′dē-ə

means of communication, especially TV, radio, and newspapers (plural noun)

> Many analysts believe that the **media** play a decisive role in electing the President of the United States.

> Reporters turned the terrible crime into a **media** event.

referring to the media (adjective)

> A political candidate must have good **media** coverage to win an election.

NOTES: (1) *Medium* is the singular form of the plural noun *media*. (2) These two words can also refer to the tools of artists, as in "The artist's main *medium* was oil, but she also used watercolor."

11. **pacify** (verb)   pas′ə-fī′

to calm; to establish peace

> Mothers can often **pacify** crying infants.

> Political reforms helped to **pacify** the country's angry farmers.

NOTE: Pacify can also mean to establish peace by conquering, as in "The army *pacified* the rebels."

In 1513, after crossing many miles of Central American jungle, the Spanish explorer Vasco Núñez de Balboa found himself faced by a large body of calm water. He chose the Spanish word for *peaceful* as a name for his discovery. In English it is now called the Pacific Ocean.

---

12. **Third World** (noun, adjective)   thûrd wûrld

economically underdeveloped countries of Asia, Africa, and Latin America (noun)

> The **Third World** must fight problems of poverty and disease.

referring to countries of the Third World (adjective)

> Many **Third World** countries are developing important industries.

Exercises

Part 1

■ Matching Words and Definitions

Check your understanding of words in the news by matching each word with the letter of its definition. Use each choice only once.

1. corroborate _____

2. pacify _____

3. catastrophe _____

4. entrepreneur _____

5. media _____

6. bureaucracy _____

7. consumer _____

8. Third World _____

9. accord _____

10. attrition _____

a. government by appointed officials

b. underdeveloped countries

c. to act in a matter involving others

d. to confirm; make more certain

e. person who runs a business

f. disaster

g. wearing away

h. official relationships among nations

i. means of communication

j. buyer

k. to calm

l. agreement

■ Words in Context

Complete each sentence with the word that fits best. Use each choice only once.

a. accord
b. attrition
c. bureaucracy
d. catastrophe

e. consumer
f. corroborate
g. diplomacy
h. entrepreneur

i. intervene
j. media
k. pacify
l. Third World

1. The police had to _____ to stop the fight.

2. To _____ his angry wife, the man washed the dishes.

3. To _____ the fact I found in one encyclopedia, I looked in another.

4. Water changes stone <u>to</u> sand by a process of _____ .

5. The five-hundred-point drop in the stock market average was a(n) _____ for investors.

6. The economies of many _____ countries are beginning to develop.

7. Since we are in _____ with each other, we can easily make a decision.

8. People who use _____ when they deal with others are usually well liked.

9. People in the _____ often took several days to approve forms.

10. Many talk shows appear on the _____ .

■ *Using Related Words*

Complete each sentence by using a word from the group of related words above it. You may need to capitalize a word when you put it into a sentence. Use each choice only once.

1. bureaucratic, bureaucracy

Texan Calvin Graham won medals for bravery in World War II, but navy officials expelled him and took away his medals when they discovered he was only 12 years old! Graham spent the last years of his life asking the military _____ to return his medals. But _____ agencies move slowly.

The last medal, a Purple Heart, was returned only after his death.

2. diplomatic, diplomacy, diplomat

African American Ralph Bunche (1904–1971) had a distinguished

career as a writer and as a _____ in the United

Nations. In 1949, his _____ and intelligence en-
abled him to bring about peace in the Middle East. In 1950, he was
the first African American to be awarded the Nobel Prize for
peace. By the time of his retirement, he held the highest

_____ rank of any U.S. citizen in the United
Nations.

3. consumption, consumers

In the past several years, _____ of liquor has decreased. Campaigns by groups such as MADD (Mothers Against

Drunk Driving) have convinced _____ that if people drank less, there would be fewer automobile accidents.

4. entrepreneurial, entrepreneurs

An _____ spirit has helped to build the economies of many countries. Clothes worn throughout the world
have been manufactured by firms in South Korea. Korean

_____ have helped their economy to grow.

5. intervened, intervention

Because many animal species are in danger of becoming extinct,

zoos have _____ to save them. Animals that have

been helped by the _____ of zoo preservation programs include the Madagascar tortoise, the okapis (a relative of
the giraffe), and a rare type of Asian leopard.

■ *Reading the Headlines*

This exercise presents five headlines that might appear in newspapers. Read each headline and then answer the questions that follow. (Remember that small words, such as *is, are, a,* and *the,* are often left out of newspaper headlines.)

CONSUMERS CORROBORATE THAT NEW CAR IS DANGEROUS

1. Are consumers selling the car? _____

2. Were consumers the first to discover the danger? _____

THIRD WORLD COUNTRY PACIFIES REBEL FORCES

3. Is the country economically developed? _____

4. Is there now peace? _____

TRANSPORTATION SYSTEM RUN BY BUREAUCRACY IS A CATASTROPHE

5. Is transportation run by elected officials? _____

6. Is the transportation system working well? _____

TWO COUNTRIES REACH ACCORD NOT TO INTERVENE IN WAR OF ATTRITION

7. Will the countries interfere? _____

8. Will the war be over quickly? _____

DIPLOMATIC ENTREPRENEUR TAKES CONTROL OF MEDIA COMPANY

9. Is the entrepreneur polite? _____

10. Is the company involved in communication? _____

Words to Learn

Part 2

13. **apprehend** (verb)   ăp′rĭ-hĕnd′

    to arrest or take a criminal into custody

    > The police **apprehended** the escaped convicts.

    to understand mentally; to grasp

    > Scientists only vaguely **apprehend** the origin of the universe.

    ▶ *Related Words*
    apprehension (noun) The *apprehension* of the criminal calmed the neighborhood's fears. I had *apprehensions* about the test. (In the first sentence, *apprehension* means "arrest"; in the second sentence, it means "fear.")

    apprehensive (adjective)   I am *apprehensive* about the test.

    NOTE: The related word *apprehension* can mean "an arrest," "a mental understanding," or "fear." *Apprehensive* always means "fearful."

14. **chaos** (noun)   kā′ŏs′

    a state of total disorder or confusion

    > A power failure left the city in **chaos.**

    > In a single day, the five active children reduced the orderly room to **chaos.**

    ▶ *Related Word*
    chaotic (adjective)   The countryside became *chaotic* as people rushed to escape from the bombs.

15. **defer** (verb)   dĭ-fûr′

    to delay

    > Thu decided to **defer** her visit to Vietnam until after her graduation from college.

    to show respect; to submit to the wishes of another

    > When boarding a bus, you should **defer** to elderly people by letting them on first.

    > I **deferred** to my father's wishes and attended college.

    ▶ *Common Phrase*
    defer to

► *Related Words*

deference (noun) (dĕf′ər-əns) He showed his *deference* by bowing to the king. (*Deference* means "respect.")

deferential (adjective) The lawyer was *deferential* to the judge.

16. **epitome** (noun) ĭ-pĭt′ə-mē

a defining example; the best example; a symbol

Albert Einstein, the physicist who discovered the principle of relativity, is often considered the **epitome** of a genius.

Many consider Al Capone to be the **epitome** of a gangster. (In this sentence, *epitome* is used in a negative sense.)

► *Related Word*

epitomize (verb)   Rising 630 feet into the air, the graceful Gateway Arch has come to *epitomize* the city of St. Louis.

NOTE: The final *e* of *epitome* is pronounced.

17. **ludicrous** (adjective) lo͞o′dĭ-krəs

absurd; ridiculous; outrageous

It is **ludicrous** to think that unborn babies can be taught to read.

The fat, middle-aged singer looked **ludicrous** playing a young lover in the opera.

18. **ominous** (adjective) ŏm′ə-nəs

warning of bad things; threatening evil

The **ominous** black clouds warned us of a thunderstorm.

The rising number of crimes committed by teenagers is an **ominous** sign for our society.

19. **supplant** (verb) sə-plănt′

to replace

No other pet could ever **supplant** the girl's first puppy in her affections.

In the future, "smart money" plastic cards may entirely **supplant** cash.

In most of the world, electric lights have **supplanted** oil lamps and candlelight.

Jim Thorpe (1888–1953) *epitomizes* a great athlete. A Native American descended from the Sauk and Fox tribes, Thorpe first excelled in football at the Carlisle Indian School. After winning two Olympic events, Thorpe played baseball as an outfielder for six years. He then became one of the early stars of football and the first president of the American Professional Football League. Thorpe also excelled in swimming, hockey, lacrosse, basketball, and boxing. In 1950, U.S. sportswriters and broadcasters selected Thorpe as both the greatest American athlete and the greatest football player of the first half of the twentieth century.

20. **thrive** (verb)   thrīv

to grow vigorously; to prosper

Protected by strong national laws, rain forests have **thrived** in Costa Rica.

Many athletes **thrive** on competition.

The next four words—*radical, liberal, conservative,* and *reactionary*—refer to political opinions that range from left to right.

LEFT _____ *RIGHT*

radical   liberal   conservative   reactionary

Radical and liberal politicians are called *left-wing* because they sat on the left side (or wing) of the semicircular seating of the French National Assembly of 1789. Other European assemblies have continued this custom. Radical politicians want swift reforms that will benefit poor people, minorities, and others without political power. Liberal politicians favor the extension of rights and privileges through gradual reform.

Conservatives and reactionaries are spoken of as *right-wing* because they sat on the right wing of the French National Assembly. Conservative politicians favor tradition and oppose change. They want to protect business interests, religion, and the traditional family. Reactionary politicians oppose change so strongly that they often want to return to the way things used to be.

Three of these words also have nonpolitical meanings.

---

21. **radical** (adjective)   răd′ĭ-kəl

favoring great change; extreme

China went through a **radical** social revolution during the 1950s and 1960s.

Radical politicians favored distributing all farmland to the peasants.

Leshan's new business suit was a **radical** departure from the jeans and T-shirt he usually wore.

▶ *Related Word*
   radical (noun)   The *radical* thought that revolution would solve the problems of his country. (*Radical* means a person who holds radical beliefs.)

22. **liberal** (adjective)   lĭb′ər-əl

favoring gradual progress and reform

Liberal politicians favor providing health care for everyone.

favoring liberty; tolerant

> Because my parents' rules for curfew were **liberal,** I could stay out later than my friends.

plentiful; generous in amount

> We ate **liberal** quantities of the delicious white-chocolate cake.

▶ *Related Words*
> **liberal** (noun)   The *liberal* voted for increased legal aid for the poor. (*Liberal* means a person who holds liberal beliefs.)
>
> **liberalize** (verb)   Students wanted to *liberalize* college rules to allow greater freedom on campus.

23. **conservative** (adjective)   kən-sûr′və-tĭv

favoring traditional beliefs and actions; traditional

> The **conservative** senator favored prayer in schools.
>
> Coming from a **conservative** background, Fatimah was surprised to see couples kissing on the street.
>
> George's gold earring was a strange contrast to his **conservative** business suit.

cautious or moderate

> We gave a **conservative** estimate that there were twenty thousand people at the rally; there may have been more.

▶ *Related Words*
> **conservative** (noun)   Senator Ruggles, a **conservative,** voted against increasing taxes to fund welfare payments. (*Conservative* means a person who holds conservative beliefs.)
>
> **conserve** (verb)   It is important to *conserve* trees by recycling newspapers. (*Conserve* means "to save.")

24. **reactionary** (adjective)   rē-ăk′shə-nĕr′ē

opposing progress in an extreme way

> The **reactionary** politician wanted to separate boys from girls in all schools.

▶ *Related Word*
> **reactionary** (noun)   The *reactionary* wanted to take away the vote from eighteen-year-olds. (*Reactionary* means a person who holds reactionary beliefs.)

NOTE: Reactionary usually has a negative connotation.

Exercises

Part 2

■ *Matching Words and Definitions*

Check your understanding of words in the news by matching each word with the letter of its definition. Use each choice only once.

1. ominous _____

2. ludicrous _____

3. thrive _____

4. defer _____

5. liberal _____

6. conservative _____

7. reactionary _____

8. radical _____

9. supplant _____

10. apprehend _____

a. favoring gradual progress and reform

b. ridiculous

c. to replace

d. to arrest

e. favoring traditional beliefs

f. to delay

g. opposing progress in an extreme way

h. threatening evil

i. confusion

j. to grow

k. best example

l. favoring great change

■ *Words in Context*

Complete each sentence with the word that fits best. Use each choice only once.

a. apprehend   e. ludicrous   i. radical
b. chaos   f. ominous   j. liberal
c. defer   g. supplant   k. conservative
d. epitome   h. thrive   l. reactionary

1. This _____ change will affect the entire organization of our hospital.

2. Superman, who symbolizes heroism, is the _____ of a comic book hero.

3. The _____ wanted gradual reforms.

4. The _____ principal, who had traditional values, asked that children dress neatly and not play music in the halls.

5. The _____ sign read "Danger, keep out!"

6. My father decided to _____ quitting smoking until next year.

7. Children usually _____ in a warm, loving home.

8. Compact disc players may soon _____ cassette players.

9. It is _____ to think that an ant could lift up an elephant.

10. There was _____ on the busy street when all the traffic lights broke down.

■ *Using Related Words*

Complete each sentence by using a word from the group of related words above it. You may need to capitalize a word when you put it into a sentence. Use each choice only once.

1. apprehend, apprehended, apprehensive

   Soon after he robbed a house, the man was _____

   by the police. He was _____ about the possibility of going to jail for his crime. So, during his trial, he tried

   to _____ all of the complex rules of the legal system.

2. conserve, conservatives

   Political _____ often feel that it is important to provide opportunities for business. They state that while it is good

   to _____ forest land and the wilderness, it is economically more important to allow the oil and forestry industries to develop.

3. chaotic, chaos

The 1994 Los Angeles earthquake left the city in _____ for several days, as water supplies, electric power, and road systems all failed to operate. The Red Cross and other charitable agencies helped to improve the _____ situation.

4. defer, deference, deferred

Although I wanted to buy a car in the fall, my father asked me

to _____ my purchase. Out of _____

to him, I _____ buying a car for a year.

■ *Reading the Headlines*

This exercise presents five headlines that might appear in newspapers. Read each headline and then answer the questions that follow. (Remember that small words, such as *is, are, the,* and *a,* are often left out of newspaper headlines.)

LUDICROUS MOVIE IS THE EPITOME OF BAD TASTE

1. Is the movie silly? _____

2. Is the movie an example of bad taste? _____

LIBERALS SUPPLANT RADICALS IN PARLIAMENT

3. Are liberals taking the places of radicals? _____

4. Do radicals want fewer changes than liberals? _____

LAWS PUT FORWARD BY CONSERVATIVES THRIVE IN SENATE

5. Do the people putting forward the laws want great changes in

the structure of society? _____

6. Are senators voting to pass most of these laws? _____

REACTIONARY LAW RESULTS IN SCHOOL CHAOS

7. Is the law opposed to progress? _____

8. Is the situation calm? _____

DEFERRING MEETING IS AN OMINOUS SIGN FOR SOLUTION TO PROBLEM

9. Will the meeting be held when it was scheduled? _____

10. Do things look good for solving the problem? _____

Chapter Exercises

■ *Practicing Strategies: Context Clues of Substitution*

In each of the following sentences, one difficult word is italicized. Using context clues of substitution, make an intelligent guess about the meaning of the word as it is used in this sentence. Your instructor may ask you to look up these words in your dictionary after you've finished the exercise.

1. The rotten food gave off a *noisome* odor.

    Noisome means _____ .

2. *Corpulent* people often become healthier after they lose weight.

    Corpulent means _____ .

3. The child was so *contrite* about losing the money that we found it easy to forgive him.

    Contrite means _____ .

4. We have a *surfeit* of food, so please take some home.

    Surfeit means _____ .

5. The road was *truncated* when several miles were closed down.

    Truncated means _____ .

6. The *parsimonious* millionaire bought a cheap used car.

   Parsimonious means _____ .

7. On the exam, Antonio made a *grievous* error which lowered his grade from an A to a D.

   Grievous means _____ .

8. Eating fruits and vegetables, visiting the doctor regularly, and exercising have a *salubrious* effect.

   Salubrious means _____ .

9. The desert is a *desiccated* place where it is difficult to find water.

   Desiccated means _____ .

10. Injuries to their two best players had a *deleterious* effect on the football team.

    Deleterious means _____ .

■ Practicing Strategies: New Uses of Familiar Words in Context

Context clues can often help you determine the meaning of words used in unusual ways. Make an intelligent guess about the meaning of the italicized word or phrase in each of the following sentences.

1. Neslihan wanted to *air* her opinions in public.

   Air means _____ .

2. He couldn't vote because he was a few months *shy of* eighteen.

   Shy of means _____ .

3. After spending the day at the library, they *repaired* to the restaurant.

   Repaired means _____ .

4. President Jackson was alone *save for* a few friends.

   Save for means _____ .

5. In her anger, she *stormed* out of the room.

   Stormed means _____ .

■ *Companion Words*

Complete each sentence with the word that fits best. Choose your answers from the words below. You may use each word more than once.

Choices: to, with, on, of, in, by, about

1. Wars _____ attrition ruin nations.

2. The radioactivity had catastrophic effects _____ children.

3. He showed his deference _____ opening the door for his grandmother.

4. I am apprehensive _____ visiting my doctor.

5. I am in accord _____ your opinion.

6. Michael Jordan is the epitome _____ a great basketball player.

7. Nobody dared to intervene _____ the fistfight.

8. I defer _____ my superiors.

9. Monica thrived _____ healthy food.

■ *Writing with Your Words*

This exercise will give you practice in writing effective sentences that use the vocabulary words. Each sentence is started for you. Complete it with an interesting phrase that also indicates the meaning of the italicized word.

1. A *bureaucracy* _____

    _____.

2. I would like to *supplant* required courses with _____

    _____.

3. To *pacify* an upset child, I might _____

_____ .

4. A *diplomatic* person would _____

_____ .

5. My career will *thrive* when _____

_____ .

6. The *entrepreneur* _____

_____ .

7. Two things a *liberal* would favor are _____

_____ .

8. I would favor a *radical* change in _____

_____ .

9. I am in *accord* with the government on _____

_____ .

10. I cannot *apprehend* how _____

_____ .

Passage

How Advertising Persuades Us

Advertising, the art of persuading **consumers** to buy products, has become a multibillion-dollar business. Every day the **media** carry thousands of advertisements.

One of the most important goals of advertising is the development of brand loyalty. Companies want to make **consumers** loyal to one type of soap, vegetable, or other product, despite the fact that this brand may be no different from any other. **(1)** Advertisers try to persuade **consumers** not to allow any other brand to **supplant** a favorite one. If the local store runs out of "Silky Soap" or "Best Beans," advertisers hope that people will actually **defer** making a purchase.

Cigarettes are an excellent example of how brand loyalty is developed. Advertisers try to give each brand a different personality. **(2)** For instance, Virginia Slims cigarettes have come to **epitomize** one view of a liberated woman. A corner of one widely used advertisement shows a woman of the early 1900s being pointed at angrily by a group of **reactionary** men. **(3) Chaos** has erupted, for they have **apprehended** her in the act of daring to smoke! In the center of the page, a confident modern woman is displayed with a Virginia Slims cigarette in her hand. The caption reads "You've come a long way, baby!"

In contrast, Marlboro cigarettes have a male image. The "Marlboro Man" disdains an easy lifestyle, preferring to put on his boots and cowboy hat and ride his horse into the wilderness. His only luxury is, of course, a pack of Marlboro cigarettes.

Sometimes advertisers try to change the image of an entire product rather than a specific brand. An example of this is the prune. Sales in the prune industry had been declining for many years before producers sought the help of market researchers. **(4)** A survey revealed that people's image of the prune was a marketing **catastrophe.** Some people associated it with boardinghouse food, others with medicine. Still others reported that the black color of the prune reminded them of witchcraft. **(5)** Advertisers needed to change this image **radically. (6)** New ads suddenly appeared showing the prune as a healthy, delicious, candy-like dessert, best eaten in **liberal** quantities. Beautiful women and athletic youngsters sang the virtues of the pretty prune. Slogans cried out: "Prunes help bring a glow to your face." In recent years the raisin industry has improved its product's image by featuring animated raisins that dance to the popular song "I Heard It Through the Grapevine."

Ads often feature sports stars, for many campaigns have **corroborated** players' ability to boost sales. Some athletes lend their names to products; "Air Jordan" athletic shoes are named for basketball star Michael Jordan. **(7)** Another player, Shaquille O'Neal, has been **accorded** the trademark "Shaq" to use for two hundred different types of items. **(8)** However, athletes sometimes appear in ads that seem **ludicrous,** as when hockey star Wayne Gretsky lacks enough money for a long-distance call and has to call "collect."

Performing artists can also sell products. **(9)** The **entrepreneurial** country music star Jimmy Dean is known for a successful brand of sausages. Actor Paul Newman contributes all profits from his brand of foods to charity.

In a new trend, artists who have died "appear" (through old film segments) in modern ads. **(10)** When 1950s actor James Dean "lived" again long enough to endorse Jack Purcell sneakers, sales of the shoes **thrived.** James Cagney, Humphrey Bogart, and Louis Armstrong were shown in a nightclub scene for Diet Coke. Through the **intervention** of modern technology, a modern-day model changed into the glamorous, but dead, Marilyn Monroe to advertise Chanel No. 5 perfume.

The exporting of U.S. television programming has meant that these commercials are seen around the world, in **Third World** countries as well as in **affluent** ones. Thus, people in many different places have become familiar with U.S. products and lifestyles.

■ *Exercise*

Each numbered sentence below corresponds to a sentence in the Passage. Fill in the letter of the choice that makes the sentence mean the same thing as its corresponding sentence in the Passage.

1. Advertisers try to persuade consumers not to allow any other brand

   to _____ a favorite one.
   a. cheapen   b. outsell   c. replace   d. harm

2. The Virginia Slims cigarette advertisement has come to _____ one popular, if simplified, view of a liberated woman.
   a. help   b. replace   c. fight   d. symbolize

3. _____ has erupted.
   a. Horror   b. Truth   c. Warfare   d. Disorder

4. The image of the prune was a _____ .
   a. help   b. lesson   c. reality   d. disaster

5. Advertisers needed to change this image _____ .
   a. in a slight way
   b. in a positive way
   c. in an extreme way
   d. in a healthy way

6. Ads showed the prune as a healthy dessert, best eaten in _____ quantities.
   a. large   b. small   c. medium   d. limited

7. Shaquille O'Neal has been _____ a trademark.
   a. given   b. denied   c. helped   d. warned about

8. Sometimes athletes appear in ads that seem _____ .
   a. changed   b. confused   c. bad   d. ridiculous

9. _____ Jimmy Dean is known for a brand of sausage.
   a. Handsome   b. Businesslike   c. Wealthy   d. Friendly

10. Sales of the shoes _____ .
    a. fell   b. delayed   c. grew   d. returned

■ *Discussion Questions*

1. What image were advertisers trying to give to the prune?

2. Do you think the cigarette ads described contain stereotypes of males and females? Defend your answer.

3. Describe a current advertisement, and discuss the emotions it appeals to.

◆ **E**NGLISH **I**DIOMS

The Media and Communication

Although news sometimes comes to us *by word of mouth,* or through personal contact, we get most of our news from the media. On our way home, for example, we may *lend an ear to,* or listen to, the radio. If a reporter giving the news is not clear, we may not be able to *make heads or tails of,* or understand, what is being said. At other times, we may *see eye to eye with,* or agree with, a reporter's opinion.

On many television news broadcasts, people announcing the weather *ham it up,* or joke and overact. This may *rub us the wrong way,* or annoy us.

Increasingly, television talk shows have dealt with sex and violence. This practice has *raised eyebrows,* or shocked, some members of the public. On the other hand, talk shows have *brought to light,* or made public, many important issues.

Yellow journalism refers to newspaper reporting that concentrates on shocking and sensational news, such as brutal murders and scandals. The term comes from the "Yellow Kid," the first comic strip in the United States, which was printed in yellow ink to attract attention. Because the newspaper containing the strip, the *New York World,* was known for its shocking news, *yellow paper* or *yellow journalism* came to mean shocking and sensational reporting.

3

Words for Feeling, Expression, and Action

Have you ever yawned at a *bland* speech, heard the roar of a *boisterous* crowd, or been *elated* at winning a prize? English has many vivid words that we can use to describe how we feel, how we express ourselves, and how we act. This chapter will present words that you can use to describe your own behavior and the thoughts and actions of others.

Chapter Strategy: Context Clues of Definition

Chapter Words:

Part 1

bland	confrontation	emulate
boisterous	dynamic	enigma
clarify	elated	skeptical
concise	emphatic	thwart

Part 2

appall	condemn	flaunt
articulate	contemplate	harass
belligerent	contend	prohibit
chagrin	elicit	undermine

Did You Know?

How Do Cars Get Their Names?

The process of naming cars shows how expression, feeling, and action can relate to one another. A car's name is an important part of its image. Every year, in Detroit and other centers of car production, auto makers spend millions of dollars researching car names that will appeal to the consumer. By using words that express speed, power, or glamour, manufacturers hope to give you positive feelings about their cars. These feelings translate into actions when you decide to buy one.

Larger cars get names that suggest powerful images.

Grand Prix refers to a series of international sports car competitions held in Europe.

El Dorado is Spanish for "the Land of Gold." European explorers searched in the Americas for El Dorado, a city said to be so rich that its ruler coated his body with gold.

Thunderbird was, according to Native American legend, a birdlike god of storm that caused thunder by flapping its wings and lightning by blinking its eyes.

Royalty and titles are also suggested.

Dodge *Dynasty*—a set of kings from one family

Mercury *Grand Marquis* and Chrysler *Le Baron*—*marquis* and *baron* are French titles of nobility

Ford *Crown Victoria*—named after Victoria, the famous queen of Great Britain (England) in the 1800s

Cars named for animals often suggest speed or fierceness.

Jaguar

Mercury *Cougar*

Dodge *Viper*—a poisonous snake

Other names give images of combat.

Buick *LeSabre*—French for "the sword"

Dodge *Cutlass*—the curved sword used by pirates

Dodge and Plymouth *Conquest*—to overcome by force

Astrological signs have also made an appearance.

Ford *Taurus*—the sign of the bull
Dodge *Aries*—the sign of the ram

Four-wheel-drive or utility vehicles often express adventure on unknown paths.

Nissan *Pathfinder*
Ford *Explorer*

Perhaps reflecting the age of high technology, many new luxury cars have letters and numbers in their names.

Mitsubishi 3000GTS
Acura NSX
Audi 5000 Turbo Quattro
Nissan 300 ZX
Mazda RX7

Finally, the names of famous and romantic places are often used for cars. The map below shows parts of the world that gave their names to seven automobiles: Chrysler *New Yorker* (a U.S. city and state), Dodge *Monaco* (a country), Mercury *Capri* (an island that is part of Italy), Cadillac *Seville* (a city in Spain), Mitsubishi *Montero* (a city in Bolivia), Dodge *Dakota* (after the U.S. states of South Dakota and North Dakota), and Dodge *Daytona* (a city in the U.S. state of Florida).

Car manufacturers think long and hard before they assign a name to a new product. Most names are designed to create an image—and thus to increase car sales.

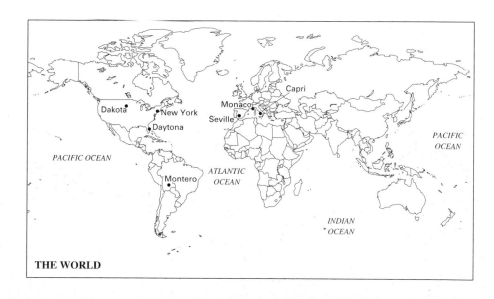

THE WORLD

Learning Strategy

Context Clues of Definition

The learning strategy in this chapter will focus on *context clues of definition*. Often, words that you don't know will actually be defined for you as they are used in sentences. Sometimes a sentence provides a *synonym* (a word that means the same thing or nearly the same thing) for the unknown word. For example, look at the word *effervescent* as it is used in a sentence.

> Coca-Cola is an *effervescent,* or bubbly, beverage.

The word *effervescent* means? . . . bubbly. Thus, *bubbly* is a synonym for *effervescent*.

Clues of definition are quite easy to use if you can recognize them. These clues include the following:

1. Words or phrases set off by commas, dashes, or parentheses:

   > The man's altruistic, *unselfish,* motives caused him to donate money to charity.

   > The man's altruistic—*unselfish*—motives caused him to donate money to charity.

   > The man's altruistic *(unselfish)* motives caused him to donate money to charity.

2. Direct definition:

   > She thought his motives were altruistic, *which means unselfish.*

   > She thought his motives were altruistic, *that is to say, unselfish.*

3. Indirect definition:

   > He was an altruistic person *who often acted out of unselfish motives.*

4. The use of *or, and,* or *also:*

   > The man's altruistic, *or unselfish,* motives pleased his family.
   > (The use of commas with *or* is an extra hint signaling that a context clue of definition is being used.)

   > The man's altruistic *and unselfish* motives pleased his family.
   > (Sometimes, however, words joined by *and* and *or* do not mean the same thing. Examples are "The man was lazy and dishonest" and "People shouldn't be lazy or dishonest.")

5. Words signaling agreement, such as *therefore, likewise, in the same way, as well as,* and *similarly:*

> The man was altruistic; *therefore, he donated money to charity and did volunteer work with children.*

As you can see, the word *altruistic,* which you learned in Chapter 1, has been defined in each sentence. Many sentences use the synonym *unselfish.* Others provide a longer definition through examples, such as *donated money to charity* and *did volunteer work with children.*

Three more examples of context clues of definition are given on the following page. Can you make an intelligent guess about the meaning of each italicized word?

1. The margin of the leaf was *sinuated,* and indented curves ran along the edge. (An *and* clue is used.)

2. The king took *draconian* measures against the rebels, and their supporters were also punished severely. (*And* and *also* clues are used.)

3. In 776 B.C. the first Olympic games were held in *Olympia,* a city in Greece. (A following phrase is set off by a comma.)

(*Answers:*   1. having indented curves   2. severe   3. a city in Greece)

Now try using context clues to figure out the meanings of some words you will be learning in this chapter.

1. The police thought the party was too *boisterous,* or noisy.

   Boisterous means _____ .

2. The teenager tried to *emulate* rock-star Madonna's clothes as well as to imitate her singing.

   Emulate means _____ .

3. The French philosopher Pascal was a *skeptical* thinker who doubted many accepted beliefs.

   Skeptical means _____ .

(*Answers:*   1. noisy   2. copy; imitate   3. doubting)

Words to Learn

Part 1

1. **bland** (adjective)   blănd

nonirritating

> The mayor's **bland** responses calmed the angry crowd.
>
> Vanilla pudding is a **bland** food.

dull

> The speech was so **bland** that I fell asleep.
>
> A **bland** shopping mall, where all stores looked the same, replaced the colorful and varied shops on the city street.

2. **boisterous** (adjective)   boi′stər-əs

noisy; rowdy; rough

> The **boisterous** crowd shouted and banged on their seats when a rival team stepped onto the field.

▶ *Related Word*
boisterousness (noun)   The audience's *boisterousness* made it difficult to hear the music.

3. **clarify** (verb)   klăr′ə-fī′

to make clear or sensible

> We asked the teacher to **clarify** her expectations for the research paper.

▶ *Related Word*
clarification (noun)   My sister gave us *clarification* of the confusing directions.

4. **concise** (adjective)   kən-sīs′

short; clear but using few words

> Most students prefer a **concise** definition of a word to a more lengthy one.
>
> Computer manuals should give **concise** explanations.

5. **confrontation** (noun)   kŏn′frŭn-tā′shən

hostile meeting; direct fight

> There have been many deadly **confrontations** between Armenians and Azerbaijanis.

> To avoid a **confrontation** with her parents, Jane took the ring out of her nose when she went home.

▶ *Related Word*
  confront (verb)   (kən-frŭnt′)   A strong person is able to *confront* problems. (*Confront* means "to meet.")

6. **dynamic** (adjective)   dī-năm′ĭk

energetic; forceful

> The **dynamic** salesman gave ten presentations in one day.

> Oprah Winfrey's **dynamic** personality has made her a national star.

fast moving; fast changing

> Prices change quickly in Moscow's **dynamic** economy.

▶ *Related Word*
  dynamics (noun)   Child psychologists often study family *dynamics*. (Here, *dynamics* means changes in social forces.)

NOTE: Dynamics can also refer to physical forces.

The word *dynamite* is related to *dynamic,* since both are formed from the Greek root *dyne,* meaning "power." Dynamite, a powerful explosive, was invented by the Swedish scientist Alfred Nobel in the mid 1800s. Nobel decided to find a positive use for the riches this destructive force had brought him, so he created prizes for peace, literature, medicine, physics, and chemistry. Today these Nobel Prizes are among the most prestigious in the world.

---

7. **elated** (adjective)   ĭ-lāt′əd

thrilled; very happy

> Michael was **elated** when he won the twenty-million-dollar lottery.

8. **emphatic** (adjective)   ĕm-făt′ĭk

strong; definite; done with emphasis

> The blind student was **emphatic** in her determination to get a college degree.
>
> The Los Angeles Dodgers scored an **emphatic** victory over the Chicago Cubs.

▶ *Related Word*
  emphasis (noun)   The employer placed great *emphasis* on promptness.

9. **emulate** (verb)   ĕm′yə-lāt′

to try to equal or excel through imitating; to imitate

> Competitors have tried to **emulate** Southwest Airline's success in providing low-cost service.

▶ *Related Word*
  emulation (noun)   Its wise political and economic policies make the African country of Botswana worthy of *emulation*.

10. **enigma** (noun)   ĭ-nĭg′mə

something unexplainable or puzzling

> The Pascagoula River, a Mississippi waterway that makes strange humming sounds, is an **enigma** to scientists.
>
> John was an **enigma** to his coach, who could not understand how the overweight, injured tennis player won every game.

▶ *Related Word*
  enigmatic (adjective)   We couldn't explain Alma's *enigmatic* behavior.

11. **skeptical** (adjective)   skĕp′tĭ-kəl

doubting; tending to disbelieve

> The jury members were **skeptical** of the witness's truthfulness.
>
> **Skeptical** people make good scientists because they demand proof of everything.

► *Common Phrase*
skeptical of

► *Related Words*

skeptic (noun)   *Skeptics* do not believe that universal health care will benefit the United States.

skepticism (noun)   The doctor's *skepticism* about using herbs as medicine disappeared when they cured his patient's malaria.

12. **thwart** (verb)   thwôrt

to prevent from happening

The guards **thwarted** the prisoner's plans to escape.

Mickey's efforts to score in the basketball game were **thwarted** by an alert guard.

Poverty can **thwart** a student's wish to finish college.

Exercises

Part 1

■ Definitions

The following sentences deal with feelings, thoughts, and expressions. Complete each statement by choosing the letter of a word or phrase from the right-hand column. Use each choice only once. This exercise continues on page 80.

1. If we feel skeptical, we

   are _____ .

2. To emulate is to _____ .

3. Dynamic is _____ .

4. Boisterous means _____ .

5. An emphatic statement

   is _____ .

a. energetic

b. imitate

c. thrilled; very happy

d. prevent from happening

e. short

f. definite; strong

g. dull

h. hostile meeting

i. doubtful

6. A bland story is _____ .

7. A concise statement

 is _____ .

8. Elated is _____ .

9. To thwart is to _____ .

10. An enigma is a(n) _____ .

j. puzzle

k. noisy

l. make clear

■ *Words in Context*

Complete each sentence with the word that fits best. Use each choice only once.

a. bland   e. confrontation   i. emulate
b. boisterous   f. dynamic   j. enigma
c. clarify   g. elated   k. skeptical
d. concise   h. emphatic   l. thwart

1. If you tell my brother about the party, you will _____ our plans to surprise him.

2. I am _____ of her claims that she can see through walls.

3. I was _____ to find that I was elected president of my class.

4. The _____ woman swam three miles every day before going to work.

5. I seek to _____ my father's success as a musician.

6. The _____ report she gave took only three minutes.

7. We asked our accountant to _____ the instructions on our tax form.

8. The _____ party was so noisy that the neighbors called the police.

9. The _____ of the two enemies resulted in a fistfight.

10. Ishmael had a _____ manner and never became excited.

■ *Using Related Words*

Complete each sentence by using a word from the group of related words above it. You may need to capitalize a word when you put it into a sentence. Use each choice only once.

1. enigma, enigmatic

   In 1591, English explorers returning to the new colony of Roanoke, Virginia, found that everyone had vanished. Their disappearance

   was an _____ . The initials "CRO" carved into a

   doorpost was the only clue to this _____ event. Were they killed? Did they wander away? To this day, no one knows.

2. skeptics, skeptical

   Where is the tomb of Genghis Khan, the legendary thirteenth-century Mongolian ruler? Businessman Maury Kravitz thinks he knows and has started a search. But scholars remain

   _____ . These _____ point out that the only clues are in a 700-year-old book that is known to be inaccurate. They think Mr. Kravitz's search will be in vain.

3. confront, confrontations

   Alcoholics may deny that they drink too much and therefore refuse

   to stop. Should their families _____ them? Some

   psychologists recommend surprise _____ at which family members demand that an alcoholic face the truth.

4. emphatic, emphatically

   Baseball umpires' calls must be _____ so that the public can understand them. Calls that are not

   _____ made may not be clear to a large crowd. Therefore, umpires make gestures to indicate their calls.

5. boisterous, boisterousness

Every sports team enjoys the _____ roars of fans cheering them on. But enthusiasm can turn to tragedy if

_____ becomes aggression. In 1985, thirty-eight fans were crushed at a soccer game when a concrete wall collapsed. This incident started when British fans threw rocks and bottles at Italians in the audience.

■ *True or False?*

Each of the following statements uses at least one word from this section. Read each statement and then indicate whether you think it is probably true or probably false.

_____   1. Boisterous laughter is loud.

_____   2. Dynamic movements are slow.

_____   3. Emphatic views are stated in a weak fashion.

_____   4. A concise statement contains too many words.

_____   5. We would be skeptical that a high school dropout could emulate the career of a famous scientist.

_____   6. An enigma puzzles people.

_____   7. You would be elated if your plans for a vacation were thwarted.

_____   8. A confrontation is usually pleasant.

_____   9. Chili peppers taste bland.

_____   10. A good textbook should clarify important concepts.

Words to Learn

Part 2

13. **appall** (verb)   ə-pôl′
      horrify; fill with horror, dismay, or shock

The public was **appalled** when police found fourteen children living in a filthy, roach-infested apartment.

The writer was **appalled** by his niece's bad grammar.

▶ *Related Word*
  appalling (adjective)   The violence on city streets is appalling.

NOTE: Appall can refer to very serious matters, such as murder or starvation, or simply annoying things, such as manners.

14. **articulate** (adjective) är-tĭk′yə-lĭt;   (verb) är-tĭk′-yə-lāt′

skilled in using language; clearly and well expressed (adjective)

An **articulate** person often has a well-developed vocabulary.

The **articulate** Palestinian Hanan Ashrawi served as chief spokeswoman for her people to the United Nations.

to express clearly and distinctly (verb)

Jose **articulated** his reasons for a raise so well that his boss gave him one immediately.

▶ *Related Word*
  articulation (noun)   The singer's *articulation* was so clear that we could understand every word.

Are animals *articulate*? Scientists have tried to determine whether chimpanzees can learn language. Lacking human vocal organs, chimpanzees cannot *articulate* sounds, yet some have acquired elements of human language. One animal, Washoe, learned 160 sign-language words and used them to communicate with other chimpanzees. Some chimps can create sentences and form new words. Washoe called a watermelon a "candy drink" and a swan a "water bird."

---

15. **belligerent** (adjective)   bə-lĭj′ər-ənt

hostile; engaged in warfare

The two **belligerent** countries bombed each other's territory.

The minor disagreement between drivers turned into a **belligerent** shouting match.

▶ *Related Word*
  belligerence (noun)   Shop owners in the city closed for one day to protest the *belligerence* of local gangs.

Belligerent comes from the Latin words *bellum*, "war," and *gerere*, "to carry on." *Bellum* is also the root of the word *rebellion*, a war waged against a ruling power. The United States gained its independence in a rebellion against Great Britain that lasted from 1775 to 1783.

16. **chagrin** (noun)   shə-grĭn′

embarrassment or humiliation caused by failure or disappointment

> To Jodi's **chagrin,** at her sixteenth birthday party her mother showed everyone her baby pictures.
>
> To my **chagrin,** I spilled spaghetti sauce all over my boyfriend's mother.

▶ *Common Phrase*
  to my (your/his/her/our/their) chagrin

17. **condemn** (verb)   kən-dĕm′

to express strong disapproval of

> Animal rights activists **condemn** the cruel treatment of laboratory animals.

to give a punishment; to find guilty

> The judge **condemned** the criminal to five years in prison.
>
> His lack of education **condemned** him to a low-level job.
>
> The decayed old building was **condemned** by the city inspectors. (In this case, *condemn* means "decide to destroy.")

▶ *Common Phrase*
  condemn to

▶ *Related Word*
  condemnation (noun)   kŏn′dĕm-nā′shən   The United Nations issued a *condemnation* of modern-day slavery.

18. **contemplate** (verb)   kŏn′təm-plāt′

to think about carefully

> I like to **contemplate** what the world would be like if there were no war.
>
> When Mario **contemplated** taking a vacation with his four children, he realized he would have to rent a large car.

▶ *Related Word*

contemplation (noun)   Each day, the priest took time for religious *contemplation*.

19. **contend** (verb)   kən-tĕnd′

to fight; to compete

Greeks from Sparta, Athens, and many other cities **contended** in the ancient Olympic games.

Born in poverty, Julio Cesar Chavez became one of the world's leading boxing *contenders*. This champion fighter is now considered a Mexican national hero. He states that "When I fight, the eyes of all Mexico are upon me." Although famous in Spanish-speaking countries, Chavez is not as well-known in America. He *contends* this is because he does not speak English. If he learns the language, Chavez is expected to accept one of the many film roles that have been offered to him.

to put forth a point of view

> When Lucy **contended** that women were more intelligent than men, her boyfriend became angry.

▶ *Related Words*

contender (noun, person)   Three *contenders* entered the race.

contention (noun)   Jason's *contention* was that men were smarter than women.

contentious (adjective)   A *contentious* person often starts fights. (*Contentious* means "tending to argue.")

NOTE: The phrase *contend with* means "to cope with." Effie had to *contend with* a class of naughty children.

20. **elicit** (verb)   ĭ-lĭs′ĭt

to draw forth (a response)

> The hilarious comedy *Living Single* **elicits** laughter from television audiences.

> Mouth-to-mouth resuscitation finally **elicited** a response from the child who had stopped breathing.

▶ *Related Word*

elicitation (noun)   The *elicitation* of laughter requires skill.

21. **flaunt** (verb)   flônt

to display obviously or showily

> The star **flaunted** her wealth by buying a huge mansion and a private jet.

> Brazilians proudly **flaunted** their flag after their soccer team won the 1994 World Cup.

NOTE: Be careful not to confuse *flaunt* (to display) with *flout* (to disregard or ignore).

22. **harass** (verb)   hə-răs′ or hăr′əs

to annoy or attack repeatedly

> The class bully **harassed** boys who wouldn't fight back.

> Photographers **harassed** Princess Diana by secretly taking pictures of her private moments.

1. Because Alphonse was _____ , he was often asked to give speeches.

2. To my _____ , my five-year-old child told some of our family secrets to strangers.

3. The horrors of the brutal war will _____ the public.

4. The _____ nation invaded its neighbor's territory.

5. Smoking cigarettes can _____ a person's health.

6. A tragic play may _____ an audience's tears.

7. Do not _____ people until you are sure that they have acted wrongly.

8. Laws _____ drivers from drinking too much alcohol.

9. Dogs often _____ cats by chasing and barking at them.

10. The other students became jealous when the girl began to _____ her good grades.

■ Using Related Words

Complete each sentence by using a word from the group of related words above it. You may need to capitalize a word when you put it into a sentence. Use each choice only once.

1. contemplated, contemplation

_____ can sometimes lead to scientific breakthroughs. It is said that Sir Isaac Newton (1642–1727) discovered

the principle of gravity as he _____ an apple falling from a tree.

2. contended, contender, contention, contentious

The great African American athlete Jesse Owens _____
in the Olympic Games of 1936. These games, held in Germany,
were attended by the racist leader, Adolf Hitler. It was Hit-

ler's _____ that the white "Aryan" race was supe-

rior to all others and that no black _____ could
win. However, Owens earned four gold medals in running events.

This outcome was so _____ that Hitler refused to
attend the award ceremonies. Owens, who died in 1978, remains
a symbol of black athletes' struggle for equality.

3. prohibition, prohibit

The durian, an unusual fruit, is popular in Thailand. Although its
taste is wonderful, its terrible smell reminds people of garbage. Be-

cause of the odor, some hotels and airlines _____

the fruit. However, this _____ has not affected the
popularity of this delicious but strange-smelling food.

4. undermining, undermine

Pollution from car exhaust is _____ air quality
and causing smog in places like Los Angeles and Mexico City.
Because these two cities are located in valleys, car emis-
sions become trapped. Since poor air quality can seriously

_____ health, efforts are being made to build
more public transportation and to limit car use.

■ *True or False?*

Each of the following sentences uses at least one word from this section.
Read each statement and then indicate whether you think it is probably
true or probably false.

_____   1. Bosses should be prohibited from harassing employees.

_____   2. People would be likely to condemn you for undermining the
interests of close family members.

____   3. You would be chagrined if the person you were with talked loudly during a quiet scene in a movie theater.

____   4. We take immediate action when we contemplate.

____   5. A contender drops out of a contest.

____   6. If you flaunt a diamond ring, people will not notice it.

____   7. A disabled child often elicits sympathy from adults.

____   8. A belligerent person would be likely to start a fight.

____   9. We would be appalled by the sight of starving people.

____   10. An articulate person never talks.

Chapter Exercises

■ *Practicing Strategies: Context Clues of Definition*

In each of the following sentences, a difficult word is italicized. Using context clues of definition, make an intelligent guess about the meaning of the word as it is used in this sentence. Your instructor may ask you to look up these words in your dictionary after you have finished the exercise.

1. The *vestige*, or small remaining part, of the fossil revealed the impression of a bird's wing.

    Vestige means _____ .

2. Judge Learned Hand, a *paragon* of virtue, set an example of goodness in every moment that he lived.

    Paragon means _____ .

3. The billionaire's *avarice*, his incredible greed, knew no bounds.

    Avarice means _____ .

4. The judge showed *clemency* to criminals by treating them with mercy.

    Clemency means _____ .

5. The child's *dyslexia*—serious reading disorder—was being investigated by a team of psychologists and teachers.

Dyslexia means _____ .

6. The plans were *clandestine,* and almost no one knew about them.

Clandestine means _____ .

7. The two close friends held a *tête-à-tête,* that is to say, a private conversation.

Tête-à-tête means _____ .

8. Ira was a *buffoon* in class, as well as a person who was always trying to amuse people at home.

Buffoon means _____ .

9. President Calvin Coolidge was a *taciturn* person who seldom talked to others.

Taciturn means _____ .

10. He *prevaricated,* which, put more plainly, means he lied.

Prevaricated means _____ .

■ *Practicing Strategies: Using the Dictionary*

Read the following definition and then answer the questions below it.

torch (tôrch) *n.* **1.a.** A portable light produced by a burning stick of resinous wood or burning material wound about the end of a stick of wood; a flambeau. **b.** *Chiefly British.* A flashlight. **2.** Something that serves to illuminate, enlighten, or guide. **3.** *Slang.* An arsonist. **4.** A portable apparatus that produces a very hot flame by the combustion of gases, used in welding and construction. —*tr.v.* **torched, torch•ing, torch•es.** *Slang.* To cause to burn or undergo combustion. [ME *torche* < OFr. < VLat. **torca,* alteration of Lat. *torqua,* var. of *torquēs,* torque < Lat. *torquēre,* to twist. See **terkʷ-*.**]

1. Which two parts of speech does *torch* function as?

_____

2. Which common word in the dictionary key contains a vowel pronounced like the *o* in *torch*? _____

3. In which language was *torch* first recorded? _____

4. Give the number and part of speech of the definition that best fits this sentence: "Gandhi's courage was a *torch* for the people of India."

_____

5. Give the number and part of speech of the definition mostly used in

Britain. _____

■ *Companion Words*

Complete each sentence with the word that fits best. Choose your answers from the words below. You may use each word more than once.

Choices: to, of, by, into, over, from

1. Our plans for the picnic were thwarted _____ rain.

2. We asked for clarification _____ the assignment.

3. Many great artists were condemned _____ lives of poverty.

4. The public was appalled _____ the rising murder rate.

5. The timing of earthquakes remains an enigma _____ scientists.

6. _____ my chagrin, my girlfriend kissed me in front of my boss.

7. People are prohibited _____ eating in the theater.

8. I am skeptical _____ the wisdom of your decision.

9. He undermined his health _____ eating junk food.

■ *Writing with Your Words*

This exercise will give you practice in writing effective sentences that use the vocabulary words. Each sentence is started for you. Complete it with an interesting phrase that also indicates the meaning of the italicized word.

1. The *belligerent* neighbors _____

   _____ .

2. A person who *contemplates* divorce _____

   _____ .

3. Sam *flaunted* his expensive new watch by _____

   _____ .

4. I would be *elated* if _____

   _____ .

5. My plans for getting a good job would be *thwarted* if _____

   _____ .

6. If someone *harassed* me, I would _____

   _____ .

7. I am *skeptical* that _____

   _____ .

8. It is an *enigma* to me how _____

   _____ .

9. It is *appalling* that _____

   _____ .

10. I would feel *chagrin* if _____

   _____ .

Passage

Jackie Robinson, Baseball Hero

Fifty years ago, a quiet man made baseball history. In 1947, Jackie Robinson became the first African American to play major league baseball in the twentieth century. **(1)** He bravely faced **appalling** persecution **(2)** and helped **undermine** racial prejudice in America. Jackie Robinson "broke the color line."

Before Robinson signed with the Brooklyn Dodgers, blacks had been **prohibited** from playing in major league baseball. Although many black players were as good as, or better than, white major league players, blacks were **condemned** to receive almost no national attention.

(3) When the Dodgers' management decided to sign Robinson, they issued a purposely **bland** announcement: "The Brooklyn Dodgers today purchased the contract of Jackie Roosevelt Robinson from the Montreal Royals." The baseball world reacted strongly. Some applauded the move to end discrimination. Others predicted disaster. How could a black succeed in white baseball? Some critics **contended** that Robinson would never be able to live peacefully with white teammates or tolerate the insults of fans. **(4)** Still others were **skeptical** of Robinson's ability as a baseball player.

All the doubters were wrong.

(5) The Dodgers' general manager, Branch Rickey, had *contemplated* the problem before making his choice. Rickey ensured Robinson's success in the major leagues by advising him in how to respond to **harassment.** "Hey," he would say, impersonating a hotel clerk. "You can't eat here." He imitated a prejudiced white ballplayer and charged into Robinson, saying, "Next time get out of my way, you bastard." Robinson was puzzled: "Are you looking for a Negro who is afraid to fight back?" Replied Rickey, "I'm looking for a ballplayer with guts enough not to fight back. Those **boisterous** crowds will insult you, **harass** you, do anything to make you start a fight. And if you fight back, they'll say, 'Blacks don't belong in baseball.'"

Of all the struggles Jackie was to have, the hardest one would be to keep calm in the face of insults. Nobody would be able to **elicit** an outburst of temper from Jackie Robinson. This fiercely competitive man, who had refused to sit in the back of an army bus, found the ultimate courage—the courage to be quiet.

In the 1947 season, Robinson was to face **harassment** that would have defeated a lesser man. **(6)** Roars of "Go home!" and "Kill him!" were heard from **belligerent** crowd members. Robinson was hit in the head by more "beanballing" pitchers than any other player in the major leagues. Sometimes it became too much for his friends. Robinson's teammate, Pee Wee Reese, once challenged some **harassers** by telling them to "take on somebody who could fight back." **(7)** But Robinson himself avoided **confrontations** and never **articulated** his grievances publicly.

Robinson claimed revenge in another way. To the amazement of his critics, he succeeded brilliantly in the major leagues. **(8)** Although he never **flaunted** his skill, it was apparent that he was a marvelous ballplayer. For his first year in the majors, he had a batting average of .297, the team high, and was named Rookie of the Year. In his ten years in baseball, his superior playing helped his team win the pennant six times. He must have been **elated** when he was elected the first black member of the Baseball Hall of Fame.

Robinson is perhaps best remembered for his daring base stealing. Sleepy pitchers had to beware, for Robinson could steal a base at a moment's notice. As he ran from base to base, he confused defense players into making mistakes and losing control of the ball. **(9)** A fellow player gave a **concise** description of Robinson as "a hard out." He stole home base eleven times! Although many have tried to **emulate** him, this feat has never been equaled.

In his later years Robinson became ill with diabetes. Although he left baseball, he never stopped fighting for a just society. He championed civil rights and made investments to help build good housing in slum areas.

Jackie Robinson's name lives on in history. We all owe a debt to a brave man who bore the troubles of a prejudiced society. **(10)** No one could **thwart** the ambitions of this great baseball player and great man.

■ *Exercise*

Each numbered sentence below corresponds to a sentence in the Passage. Fill in the letter of the choice that makes the sentence mean the same thing as its corresponding sentence in the Passage.

1. He bravely faced _____ persecution.
   a. terrible   b. shocking   c. violent   d. frightening

2. He helped _____ racial prejudice in America.
   a. delay   b. increase   c. weaken   d. strengthen

3. The Dodgers' management issued a purposely _____ announcement.
   a. exciting   b. short   c. long   d. dull

4. Still others were _____ of Robinson's ability as a baseball player.
   a. confident   b. doubtful   c. hopeful   d. talking

5. The Dodgers' general manager, Branch Rickey, had _____ the prob-

lem before making his choice.
a. planned for   b. thought about   c. met with   d. argued about

6. Roars were heard from _____ crowd members.
a. adoring   b. ridiculous   c. excited   d. hostile

7. But Robinson himself avoided _____ .
a. attention   b. fights   c. competitions   d. praise

8. Although he never _____ his skill, it was apparent that he was a marvelous ball player.
a. showed off   b. fully understood
c. wondered about   d. succeeded with

9. A fellow player gave a(n) _____ description of Robinson as "a hard out."
a. short   b. silly   c. excellent   d. emotional

10. No one could _____ the ambitions of this great man.
a. aid   b. prevent   c. know   d. accomplish

■ Discussion Questions

1. What was Robinson's greatest skill as a baseball player?

2. Why do you think Robinson's refusal to lose his temper was important?

3. In 1955, Rosa Parks refused to obey a law that required blacks to sit in the back of a bus. How is Robinson's struggle similar to her act, and how is it different?

◀ ENGLISH IDIOMS

Feelings and Actions

Many English idioms express feelings and actions. Some expressions deal with confusion. *To drive wild* and *to drive to the wall* mean to cause someone to become frantic or crazy. People who are *at loose ends* are unsettled and lack a clear direction for their lives. Such people may also have many *loose ends,* or undone things to finish.

Other idioms deal with preciseness. When we *hit the nail on the head,* we get something exactly right.

When teachers tell students *don't sweat* an exam, they mean don't worry about it. However, most students will improve their grades if they *hit the books,* or study. Computers, which are always improving, help us to study. If your old computer *can't hold a candle* to your new computer, your new computer is much better than your old one.

To *bury the hatchet* means to make peace. The early English settlers of the American colonies often fought and then made peace with Native American tribes. To symbolize that fighting had stopped, both sides buried a hatchet in the ground. In 1680, Samuel Sewall wrote that since the hatchet was a very important weapon for the Native Americans, this ceremony was more meaningful to them than any written agreement could be.

4

Other Useful English Words

In this chapter you will find a variety of words that college students like you have identified as useful to know. These words were collected from textbooks, newspapers, magazines, and similar materials. Students reported seeing the words many times and felt they were important to learn. You, too, should find them valuable additions to your vocabulary.

Chapter Strategy: Context Clues of Opposition

Chapter Words:

Part 1

accolade	cryptic	meticulous
augment	indulge	obsolete
chivalrous	jeopardize	perpetual
complacent	mandatory	zealous

Part 2

accelerate	cultivate	pinnacle
adulation	euphemism	procrastinate
chronological	mammoth	successive
copious	mitigating	withstand

Did You Know?

How Does English Get New Words?

What language is the second most widely spoken in the world? What language is used for international communication in business and science?

What language has the most words? The answer to all three questions is English!

English is not the most widely spoken native language in the world. (Mandarin Chinese holds that position.) However, when we add people who speak English as a first language to people who speak it as a second language, it emerges as the world's most popular language. About 775 million people spoke English in 1985, and the number is constantly growing. English is now the international language of science, technology, and business. Japanese and German companies, for instance, train many employees in English. People doing research often find that international scientific journals are published in English.

In keeping with the large number of people who speak English, many experts estimate that it has more words than any other spoken language. The complete *Oxford English Dictionary, Second Edition,* consists of twenty volumes, and it is available on compact disc for use on a computer.

The vocabulary of English grows continually as new inventions, discoveries, and customs emerge. Publications such as *Barnhart's Dictionary of New English Words* help us catalogue additions to our language.

Where do new words come from? Some are from comic strips. The creators of the Buck Rogers comic strip first used *zap* to describe the sound of a fictional "paralysis gun." Today the word means to kill, defeat, or destroy. Tad Dourgan (1877–1929), another cartoonist, introduced such terms as *hot dog* and *dumbbell.*

Computer science has given English such terms as *software* (computer program), *modem* (long-distance communication system), *microprocessor* (small computer), and *user friendly.* Whether you are a member of a *TAFY* (technologically *a*dvanced *f*amily) or you are a *digerati* (a person highly skilled in working with digital, or computer, data), computers have probably affected the language you use.

Radio and television have inspired many new words. A large handheld radio is called a *boom box* because of its booming sound. Do you often like to just relax and watch television? If you do this several hours a day, you might be called a *couch potato.* Your exercise might be limited to *channel surfing* (rapidly changing channels by using a remote control) or watching *feevee* (channels available only to those who pay a fee).

Ancient Greek and Latin word parts are also used to create new words. A person who is interested in the latest forms of stereo equipment is an *audiophile.* This word is formed from the Latin verb *audire* (to hear) and the ancient Greek noun *philos* (love). People who are afraid of eating high-fat food may be said to suffer from *cholesterophobia,* a word formed from *cholesterol* and *phobia* (the ancient Greek noun for *fear*).

One new word can be formed from two old ones. Since traffic is often heavy in the Los Angeles area, people spend several hours a day in cars. Some treat their cars as miniature homes, furnishing them with expensive stereos, facilities for dressing, and telephones. The new word *carcoon* has been coined to describe this. *Carcoon* is composed of *car* and *cocoon*. Similarly, a newly built *tunnel* joins France and England by going beneath the English *channel*. Thus, it is called the *chunnel*.

English has also borrowed words from other languages. *Cotton* comes from Arabic; *pajamas* from Urdu, a language of India and Pakistan; and *tea* from Chinese. *Chocolate* and *tomato* came from languages spoken by the Aztecs, who lived in Mexico. The Algonquin Indians, of the northeastern United States, gave us *raccoon*. *Potato* came from the Taino, native inhabitants of the West Indies. *Banana* came from Africa. *Piano* is from Italian, *boss* from Dutch, *ranch* from Spanish, and *hamburger* from German. (In fact, the hamburger was named for the German city of Hamburg.) A word for a video game entered English within the last ten years. The game, named for a 100-year-old company in Kyoto, Japan, is called *Nintendo*.

Finally, English speakers expand the language by using old words in new ways. Many English words have gradually changed their meanings over the centuries. *Husband* once meant "master of the house." *Lady* meant "kneader of bread." The common word *nice*, which has been in English since 1100, has gone through several changes of meaning. In its long career it has meant foolish or stupid, sexy, strange, lazy, and shy. None of these meanings is in common use today.

Learning Strategy

Context Clues of Opposition

This chapter's learning strategy presents *context clues of opposition*. These clues give the opposite definition or sense of the word you are trying to understand. A simple opposition clue is *not*. Take the following example:

> The food was *not* hot, but *cold*.

Hot is, of course, the opposite of *cold*. Clues of opposition can be used for more difficult words.

> Since it was something not usual or normal in nature, it was considered an *anomaly*. (An anomaly is something not usual or normal, a "freak.")

Often a clue of opposition will provide an *antonym*, or a word opposite in meaning. In the first example, *hot* is an antonym of *cold*. Clues of opposition are easy to use if you become familiar with opposing structures in sentences. Some of the common structures are as follows.

1. The use of *not* and *no*.

    Peggy was *not happy,* but despondent.

2. Words signaling opposition. These include *but, nevertheless, despite, rather than, regardless of the fact, unless, if not,* and *although.*

    Peggy was despondent *despite* the fact that her sister was *happy.*

3. Words with negative senses. Certain words have a negative meaning, such as *merely, mere, barely, only, rarely, never, hardly, nowhere,* and *nothing.*

    Peggy was despondent and *rarely* felt happy.

4. Words containing negative prefixes, such as *anti-, un-, dis-, non-,* and *in-.* For example, when the prefix *un-* is added to *happy,* it forms *unhappy,* which means the opposite of *happy.*

    Peggy was despondent and felt *unhappy.*

From these examples, it is clear that *despondent* means "sad" or "depressed." In the examples, the antonym of *despondent (happy)* is given as a context clue.

Three examples of context clues of opposition are given below. Can you guess at the meaning of the italicized words? Remember that context clues of opposition, like all context clues, may give only the general sense of a word.

1. He was not shy and was, in fact, an *extrovert.* (A *not* clue is used.)

2. There was so much *enmity* between James and Harold that they refused to speak to each other. (A word with a negative sense is used.)

3. Although Kristin thought the candidate was *despicable,* her friend thought he was wonderful. (A word signaling opposition is used.)

(*Answers:* 1. a person who socializes easily and is outgoing 2. hatred 3. worthless, bad)

Some words that you will study in this chapter are used in the following sentences, which contain clues of opposition. Try to make an intelligent guess about the meaning of each italicized word.

1. The *meticulous* person rarely made a careless error. (A word with a negative sense is used.)

    Meticulous means _____ .

2. We were unable to understand the *cryptic* message. (A negative prefix is used.)

    Cryptic means _____ .

3. Because the course was *mandatory*, we could not choose whether to take it. (A *not* clue is used.)

Mandatory means _____ _____ _____ .

(*Answers:* 1. careful 2. puzzling 3. required)

Words to Learn

Part 1

1. **accolade** (noun)   ăk′ə-lād′

   praise, honor, award

   > The hero received **accolades** from the press.

   > In 1994, Vince Gill was awarded the **accolade** of Country Music Entertainer of the Year.

   The word *accolade* comes from a ceremony during the Middle Ages in which a warrior was made a knight. The king gave the knight an accolade (an embrace) and dubbed him (tapped him on the shoulder with a sword). *Accolade* is related to chivalrous, word 3 in this section.

   ---

2. **augment** (verb)   ôg-mĕnt′

   to increase

   > Congress is expected to **augment** assistance for poor families.

   ▶ *Related Word*
   augmentation (noun)   Advertising often results in considerable *augmentation* of a store's sales.

3. **chivalrous** (adjective)   shĭv′-ăl-rəs

   having qualities of honor, including courtesy, loyalty, and generosity

   > A **chivalrous** man would never insult a woman.

   > The **chivalrous** knight used his body to shield his master from attack.

   ▶ *Related Word*
   chivalry (noun)   Sir Lancelot followed the code of *chivalry*.

Chivalry was the code of conduct for European knights of the Middle Ages. A true knight was brave, loyal, and fair. Knights were also faithful Christians, showing mercy to the defeated and loyalty to their overlord, or master. In the tradition of courtly love, a knight dedicated poems to his lady and fought tournaments in her name. However, this idealized passion involved worship from afar and rarely resulted in marriage. Chivalrous gestures, such as opening doors for women, are out of favor in today's society, but in the Middle Ages they represented an improvement in women's lives.

4. **complacent** (adjective)   kəm-plā′sənt

overly self-satisfied

> After achieving straight A's, Rick became **complacent** and stopped studying.

> In today's competitive television market, no program can be **complacent** about its ratings.

NOTE: Complacent is a somewhat negative word.

▶ *Related Word*
complacency (noun) The *complacency* of the company enabled its competitors to succeed.

5. **cryptic** (adjective)   krĭp**′**tĭc

puzzling; mysterious in meaning

> Nancy's **cryptic** smile left us unsure of her feelings.
>
> The **cryptic** note we found in the attic said "Treasure is all around you."

6. **indulge** (verb)   ĭn-dŭlj**′**

to pamper; to yield to desires

> People often **indulge** in daydreams while relaxing.
>
> After **indulging** in five pieces of chocolate cake, nine-year-old Julia felt sick.

▶ *Common Phrases*
   indulge in

   indulge oneself (*Indulge* often uses a reflexive pronoun, such as *myself, yourself,* or *herself.*)

7. **jeopardize** (verb)   jĕp**′**ər-dīz**′**

to risk loss or danger

> Don't **jeopardize** your safety by approaching animals that might attack you.
>
> Marcus **jeopardized** his savings by putting them in a risky investment.
>
> One computer virus can **jeopardize** an entire system.

▶ *Related Word*
   jeopardy (noun)   The soldier's loud whispering put the secret attack in *jeopardy.*

8. **mandatory** (adjective)   măn**′**də-tôr**′**ē

required; commanded

> English 101 was **mandatory** for college graduation.
>
> It is **mandatory** for all residents of the United States to register births and marriages.

▶ *Related Words*
   mandate (noun)   (măn**′**dāt**′**)   The government issued a *mandate* returning land to the Cherokee nation. (*Mandate* means "command.")

   mandate (verb)   The government *mandates* taxes.

NOTE: *Mandate* can also refer to the unspoken wishes of the people who have elected an official, as in "The governor felt he had a clear *mandate* to veto the bill."

9. **meticulous** (adjective)   mə-tĭk′yə-ləs

extremely careful; concerned with details

> Finely woven Turkish silk rugs are created with **meticulous** care.

> A computer programmer must be **meticulous,** for even a small mistake can ruin many hours of work.

▶ *Related Word*
meticulousness (noun)   Accountants value *meticulousness* in keeping business records.

10. **obsolete** (adjective)   ŏb′sə-lēt′

no longer in use; outmoded; old-fashioned

> The sword, horse, and chariot have become **obsolete** in modern warfare.

> The word *thou* is an **obsolete** way of saying "you."

▶ *Related Words*
obsolescent (adjective)   (ŏb′sə-lĕs′ənt)   Few people wanted to buy the *obsolescent* computer. (*Obsolescent* means "becoming obsolete.")

obsoleteness (noun)   No one questions the *obsoleteness* of the quill pen.

11. **perpetual** (adjective)   pər-pĕch′o͞o-əl

lasting forever; eternal

> Religion teaches that God is **perpetual.**

continuous

> The disorganized office was in a **perpetual** state of confusion.

▶ *Related Words*
perpetually (adverb)   The mother was *perpetually* worried about her children.

perpetuate (verb)   (pər-pĕch′o͞o-āt′)   In my heart, I *perpetuate* the memory of my dead father.

In the shadow of the Bear Paw Mountains, south of Chinook, Montana, lies a field *perpetually* dedicated to the Nez Perce tribe and their chief, Joseph. Forced from their lands in 1877, 200 warriors, accompanied by women, children, and elderly people, fled from the enormous forces of the U.S. Army. The Nez Perce repeatedly outfought and outwitted the army. Only after a flight of some 2,000 miles did they finally surrender. The Montana field *perpetuates* the memory of their bravery and endurance.

12. **zealous** (adjective)   zĕl′əs

extremely dedicated or enthusiastic

> The **zealous** piano student practiced eight hours each day.

▶ *Related Word*
zeal (noun)   (zēl)   In her *zeal* to be a perfect mother, Crystal sometimes forgot to take care of her own needs.

The first *zealots* were religious Jews who fought against Roman rule. After Romans destroyed the second Jewish temple in 70 A.D., the Zealots retreated to the ancient mountaintop fortress of Masada. There, 1,000 people held off a Roman force of 15,000 for more than two years. Preferring death to defeat, the Zealots committed suicide when they realized they could not win.

NOTE: Zealot can still mean a person dedicated to religion.

Exercises

Part 1

■ Matching Words and Definitions

Check your understanding of useful words by matching each word in the left-hand column with a definition from the right-hand column. Use each choice only once.

1. cryptic _____

2. indulge _____

3. mandatory _____

4. zealous _____

5. perpetual _____

6. augment _____

7. obsolete _____

8. accolade _____

9. meticulous _____

10. complacent _____

a. overly self-satisfied

b. having qualities of honor

c. award

d. yield to desires

e. to risk loss or danger

f. mysterious in meaning

g. dedicated or enthusiastic

h. very careful

i. no longer used

j. to increase

k. lasting forever

l. required

■ Words in Context

Complete each sentence with the word that fits best. Use each choice only once.

a. accolade   e. cryptic   i. meticulous
b. augment   f. indulge   j. obsolete
c. chivalrous   g. jeopardize   k. perpetual
d. complacent   h. mandatory   l. zealous

1. Too much sun can _____ your health by causing skin cancer.

2. The farm workers tried to be _____ about separating the good strawberries from the spoiled ones.

3. The Earth is in _____ motion as it constantly rotates on its axis.

4. I would like to _____ myself by taking a vacation.

5. When the champion boxer became _____ and did not train for the fight, he was defeated.

6. We could not break the _____ code the spies had used.

7. The _____ man followed his religion enthusiastically.

8. U.S. General Colin Powell (Ret.) received the _____ of the Purple Heart for wounds he received in combat.

9. It is _____ for drivers to have a valid license.

10. In a famous _____ gesture, Walter Raleigh laid his cloak over a puddle so that Queen Elizabeth I could keep her feet dry.

■ *Using Related Words*

Complete each sentence by using a word from the group of related words above it. You may need to capitalize a word when you put it into a sentence. Use each choice only once.

1. meticulously, meticulousness

Which object in the solar system has been most _____ mapped and photographed? The answer is not the Earth, but the Moon. In 1994, the spaceship *Clementine* orbited the Moon for three months, taking millions of photos. Scientists analyzed the

photos with great _____ to gather as much information as possible. In contrast, since the Earth is largely under
water, it is much more difficult to map than the Moon is.

2. jeopardy, jeopardized

A few years ago, the Shoemaker-Levy comet whizzed by Jupiter,
spitting out fragments that made large holes in the planet's surface.

Could the Earth also be _____ by a comet? Scien-

tist Brian Marsden says that if we were in _____ ,
we would know several years in advance, enabling us to plan the
comet's destruction.

3. chivalry, chivalrously

In Poland, a country with a deep respect for tradition, a school of

_____ located in Castle Golub-Dobrzyn teaches
sword fighting, honor, loyalty, and courage. Men are required to

treat ladies _____ by bowing to them and kissing
their hands.

4. obsolescent, obsolete

The invention of the transistor in the 1950s enabled scientists to
miniaturize many appliances and tools. Radios built with tubes be-

came completely _____ . Smaller and more powerful radios replaced them. Twenty-five years ago, room-sized
computers built with tubes were still in use, but were already

_____ . Today, a computer with more memory
than the earlier version can fit on a desktop.

5. mandatory, mandate

The new mayor interpreted his large victory as a _____

for conservation. Within a year, recycling was _____
for all residents.

■ *True or False?*

Each of the following statements contains at least one word from this section. Read each statement and then indicate whether you think it is probably true or probably false.

———   1. An obsolete invention is widely used.

———   2. Indulging in too much alcohol can jeopardize a person's health.

———   3. Complacent employees are hard workers.

———   4. We would be upset if the crime rate augmented.

———   5. Cryptic messages are easily understood.

———   6. A zealous worker would be likely to receive the accolade of employee of the month.

———   7. Perpetual care will end soon.

———   8. A chivalrous person is polite.

———   9. You need not pay a mandatory tax.

———   10. A meticulous housekeeper dusts everything.

Words to Learn

Part 2

13. **accelerate** (verb)   ăk-sĕl′ə-rāt′

    to speed up; to go faster

    > The fax machine and E-mail have **accelerated** communication.

    > The discovery of large oil deposits **accelerated** Mexico's economic development.

    ▶ *Related Words*
      acceleration (noun)   Exposure to too much sun can cause *acceleration* of the aging process.

accelerator (noun)   The race car driver pressed the *accelerator* to the floor.

14. **adulation** (noun)   ăj′o͝o-lā′shən

extreme admiration or flattery

> The bride looked at the groom with **adulation** as she said, "I do."

> Nelson Mandela, the first Black president of South Africa, received the **adulation** of the 50,000 people who gathered at his inauguration.

▶ *Related Words*
adulate (verb)   Teenagers of the past *adulated* Rudolph Valentino and Frank Sinatra.

adulatory (adjective)   (ăj′o͝o-lə-tôr′ē)   Tony's *adulatory* comments flattered his boss.

15. **chronological** (adjective)   krŏn′ə-lŏj′ĭ-kəl

arranged in order of time

> John's résumé listed his work experience in **chronological** order.

▶ *Related Word*
chronology (noun)   (krə-nŏl′ə-jē)   The scholarly book gave a *chronology* of World War II battles.

16. **copious** (adjective)   kō′pē-əs

plentiful; abundant

> The student's **copious** lecture notes filled ten pages.

NOTE: Copious cannot be used to refer to a single large thing. We cannot say "a copious piece of cake." We can, however, refer to "copious notes," "a copious amount of sand," and "copious supplies."

17. **cultivate** (verb)   kŭl′tə-vāt′

to grow deliberately; to develop

> On the Basilan Islands of the Philippines, farmers **cultivate** seaweed.

> The violin teacher carefully **cultivated** the talents of his students.

The poor student **cultivated** a relationship with his rich aunt, whom he hoped might help him pay his college tuition.

▶ *Related Words*

cultivated (adjective)   John was a *cultivated* person who knew much about art and classical music. (*Cultivated* often describes people who are cultured and have interests in art, classical music, books, etc.)

cultivation (noun)   John's musical *cultivation* impressed us.

Corn, or maize, is the most important product *cultivated* in the Americas. Canned foods, candy, and soap are all made from its products. When Christopher Columbus first saw corn in Cuba, he remarked on the meticulous efficiency of its cultivation. Early Americans developed modern corn over thousands of years, interbreeding it with grass to increase the size of the cobs. Modern scientists at the International Center for Improvement of Maize and Corn, in Mexico, are making a new "lysine" corn that contains an important protein absent in traditional varieties.

---

18. **euphemism** (noun)   yoo′fə-mĭz′əm

a positive word or phrase substituted for a negative one

"Relaxed fit" is a **euphemism** referring to clothes designed for overweight people.

▶ *Related Word*

euphemistic (adjective)   "Discomfort" is a *euphemistic* word for pain.

Euphemisms are used frequently. A bank recently announced that it was "rightsizing" itself by "lowering payroll costs through reducing head count." In other words, it was firing people.

Do you know what these common euphemisms stand for?

1. She *stretched the truth a bit.*

2. We watched an *encore telecast.*

3. He was *laid to rest.*

4. I bought a *pre-owned* car.

(*Answers:*   1. lied   2. rerun   3. buried   4. used)

19. **mammoth** (adjective)   măm′əth

huge; very large

> Each day, one hundred thousand visitors shop, eat, play golf, ride roller coasters, and even get married in Minnesota's **mammoth** Mall of America.

> Effective handling of garbage has become a **mammoth** problem.

20. **mitigating** (adjective)   mĭt′ə-gāt′ĭng

making less severe or intense; moderating

> Because high altitude has a **mitigating** effect on heat, mountain air is cool.

> Tony admitted he was late, but offered the **mitigating** circumstance that his car had a flat tire on the way.

▶ *Related Word*
   mitigate (verb)   Grandmother *mitigated* her harsh words with a wink.

21. **pinnacle** (noun)   pĭn′ə-kəl

top; highest point

> The Keck telescope, the largest in the world, is located at the **pinnacle** of Mauna Kea in Hawaii.

> At the **pinnacle** of his career, the TV news anchor earned more than a million dollars per year.

22. **procrastinate** (verb)   prō-krăs′tə-nāt′

to delay; to put off

> I always manage to **procrastinate** when it is time to study.

> For almost a year, the bride **procrastinated** writing thank-you notes for the gifts she had received.

▶ *Related Words*
   procrastinator (noun)   In honor of a common fault, "National *Procrastinator*'s Week" takes place each March.

23. **successive** (adjective)   sək-sĕs′ĭv

following one after another without interruption

My family has lived on the same farm for six **successive** generations.

▶ *Related Word*

succession (noun)   I had a *succession* of classes from nine to three.

The prince's *succession* to the throne was greeted with much celebration. (*Succession* can mean the inheritance of a crown or title.)

24. **withstand** (verb)   wĭth-stănd′ (past tense: **withstood**)

not to surrender; to bear (the force of)

People differ in their ability to **withstand** cold weather.

Unable to **withstand** the force of the hurricane, the tree broke in half.

The fortress **withstood** many attacks without falling to the enemy.

Gitobu Imanyara, editor of *Nairobi Law Monthly,* has *withstood* much persecution as publisher of a magazine that speaks freely about Kenyan politics. At times, the magazine has been banned. Mr. Imanyara has been physically attacked and has served time in prison. For his bravery, Mr. Imanyara has received many awards from international organizations.

Exercises

Part 2

■ Matching Words and Definitions

Check your understanding of useful words by matching each word in the left-hand column with a definition from the right-hand column. Use each choice only once.

1. chronological _____

2. withstand _____

a. top

b. use of a positive word in place of a negative one

3. procrastinate _____

4. euphemism _____

5. cultivate _____

6. adulation _____

7. mammoth _____

8. pinnacle _____

9. accelerate _____

10. copious _____

c. to delay

d. to speed up

e. without interruption

f. very large

g. not to surrender

h. plentiful

i. extreme admiration

j. making less severe

k. in order of time

l. to grow deliberately

■ *Words in Context*

Complete each sentence with the word that fits best. Use each choice only once.

a. accelerate
b. adulation
c. chronological
d. copious

e. cultivate
f. euphemism
g. mammoth
h. mitigating

i. pinnacle
j. procrastinate
k. successive
l. withstand

1. The _____ blue whale is one hundred feet long and weighs 400,000 pounds.

2. The boy's apology had a(n) _____ effect on his mother's anger.

3. Edmund Hillary and Tenzing Norkay were the first people to reach

the _____ of Mount Everest.

4. I always _____ when there is something I don't want to do.

5. A calendar lists dates in _____ order.

6. Unable to _____ the lack of rain, the crops died.

7. The man wished to _____ the friendship of the famous artist.

8. The English teacher used the _____ "not quite acceptable" to describe the failing paper.

9. Seattle has had light rain for four _____ days.

10. Because food was in _____ supply at the picnic, we ate well.

■ *Using Related Words*

Complete each sentence by using a word from the group of related words above it. You may need to capitalize a word when you put it into a sentence. Use each choice only once.

1. mitigated, mitigating

   Since Nairobi, Kenya, is only 80 miles from the equator, we would

   expect it to be hot. However, the heat is _____ _____ by Nairobi's high altitude and cloudy weather. These two

   _____ _____ circumstances ensure that Nairobi is usually cool.

2. acceleration, accelerated

   The growth of world population has _____ dramatically in the past one hundred years. Expressed in billions, world population was 1.2 in 1900, 1.6 in 1950, and is expected to be 6 in 2000 and 8.5 in 2024. Scientists hope that this

   _____ will not cause food shortages and environmental problems.

3. adulation, adulatory

   In 1927, Charles Lindberg made the first solo flight across the Atlantic Ocean. He received the _____ of thousands

   of people. Their _____ comments praised his courage and skill. His plane, *The Spirit of St. Louis,* is now on display at the Smithsonian Institution in Washington, D.C.

4. cultivate, cultivation, cultivated, cultivating

   Many people are now _____ rare flowers and

fruits as a hobby. One of my friends is a member of a society ded-

icated to the _____ of rare apples, such as the Melrose and the Cornish Gilliflower. In this society, people can

_____ one another's acquaintance and share

a common interest. My friend is also a _____ person who enjoys listening to classical music, visiting museums, and reading.

■ *Reading the Headlines*

This exercise presents five headlines that might appear in newspapers. Read each headline and then answer the questions that follow. (Remember that small words, such as *is, are, a,* and *the,* are often left out of newspaper headlines.)

SCIENTIST CULTIVATES MAMMOTH ROSE

1. Did the rose grow accidentally? _____

2. Is the rose large? _____

COPIOUS AMOUNTS OF RAIN ACCELERATE PLANT GROWTH

3. Has there been a lot of rain? _____

4. Have plants been growing faster? _____

AT PINNACLE OF CAREER, HEROINE RECEIVES ADULATION OF CROWD

5. Is the heroine at the beginning of her career? _____

6. Does the crowd act positively toward the heroine? _____

COOL WEATHER FINALLY MITIGATES THREE SUCCESSIVE WEEKS OF HEAT

7. Has the weather become less severe? _____

8. Have hot days followed each other? _____

UNABLE TO WITHSTAND FAMILY'S PROCRASTINATION IN CLEANING HOUSE, GRANDFATHER SELLS HOME

9. Does the family clean house promptly? _____

10. Does the grandfather find things hard to bear? _____

Chapter Exercises

■ *Practicing Strategies: Context Clues of Opposition*

In each of the following sentences, a difficult word is italicized. Using context clues of opposition, make an intelligent guess about the meaning of the word as it is used in the sentence. Your instructor may ask you to look up each word in your dictionary after you have finished the exercise.

1. The *nebulous* clouds did not have a clear outline.

    Nebulous means _____ .

2. Although she was usually *garrulous,* Anne was quiet at the party.

    Garrulous means _____ .

3. The *pusillanimous* warrior lacked courage.

    Pusillanimous means _____ .

4. Barbara is *reticent* about revealing her background, despite the fact that she talks freely about other things.

    Reticent means _____ .

5. This *diminutive* type of hummingbird hardly ever grows over three inches long.

    Diminutive means _____ .

6. Although she was sick, Melody managed to *discharge* her duties.

    Discharge means _____ .

7. She thought she would be *recompensed,* but she was never paid.

    Recompensed means _____ .

8. He *feigned* ignorance, although he knew about all of their plans.

Feigned means _____ .

9. Since we were at an equal point on the pay scale, there was no *disparity* between my salary and hers.

Disparity means _____ .

10. Suddenly called upon to talk publicly, Jesse Jackson gave a brilliant *extempore* speech.

Extempore means _____ .

■ *Writing with Your Words*

This exercise will give you practice in writing effective sentences that use the vocabulary words. Each sentence is started for you. Complete it with an interesting phrase that also indicates the meaning of the italicized word.

1. The *zealous* student _____

_____ .

2. You might *jeopardize* your job by _____

_____ .

3. It is important to be *meticulous* when _____

_____ .

4. The *chivalrous* knight _____

_____ .

5. A *cultivated* person _____

_____ .

6. It is difficult for me to *withstand* _____

_____ .

7. When I *procrastinate,* _____

_____ .

8. It is *mandatory* to _____   _____

_____ .

9. When I reach the *pinnacle* of success, I will _____ _____

_____ .

10. There is a *copious* supply of _____ _____

_____ .

Passage

Australia: From Prison to Paradise

When we think of Australia today, we think of a sunny, prosperous country visited yearly by thousands of tourists. But for generations, the very name Australia brought fear to the hearts of the English people, because Australia was founded to serve as a prison for England.

In the late 1700s, England was a country of contrasts. Gentlemen lived on rich estates with beautiful gardens. Yet in the city of London, poor families crowded together into single rooms near the dark, evil-smelling factories where they worked. In the early days of industrialization, children as young as six held jobs. **(1)** Young girls ruined their eyesight by doing **meticulous** sewing in dim light. Boys grew up with backs bent from years of carrying coal.

Yet those who worked were relatively fortunate, for thousands had no jobs. Without government help, the unemployed were simply left to starve. **(2)** The crime rate **augmented,** as more poor families were forced to steal in order to stay alive.

The rich of England knew little about the fate of the poor. **Complacent** in their own situations and unaware of the depth of this poverty, many simply believed that there was a "criminal class." To try to control it, the government passed laws of extreme harshness. Hanging was made **mandatory** for stealing property worth 40 shillings, burning a pile of straw, or cutting down an ornamental bush. Public executions were considered "educational." **(3)** Despite the fact that the smallest offense could

jeopardize one's life, desperate poverty caused the crime rate to **accelerate.**

Finally, sickening of the sight of death for small offenses, **(4)** the government began to **mitigate** the harsh punishments. It was decided that if "royal mercy" were granted, the death sentence could be replaced by sending prisoners out of the country to do forced labor. However, no one could decide where to send criminals, so within a few years, prisons became stuffed with convicts awaiting transportation. **(5)** Government officials could **procrastinate** no longer; they had to send the prisoners somewhere.

The **mammoth** island of Australia seemed a wise choice. The British had claimed rights to it and needed to support this claim with settlement. Prisoners could do the hard labor needed to establish farms, and those who wished to escape would simply drown. Best of all, the "criminal element" would be 8,000 miles from England.

Who were the "criminals" transported to Australia in 1787? They included Thomas Chaddick, who ate twelve cucumber plants, and William Francis, who stole a book. Eleven-year-old James Grace took ribbons and a pair of stockings; Elizabeth Beckford, seventy years old, stole some cheese.

For these crimes, each was sentenced to years of hard labor in an unknown land. **(6)** Many prisoners believed that exile would be **perpetual,** and they would never see England again. Parting from their families was difficult to **withstand.** One man wrote to his wife, "I don't mind where I go nor what I suffer, if I have your company to cheer my almost broken heart." Yet he sailed off alone, in chains.

In the first years of Australia's English settlement, many prisoners died. **(7)** The land proved difficult to **cultivate.** For three **successive** years, supply ships from England failed to come, forcing the population into near starvation. One Australian remembered living on a diet of boiled seaweed and whale blubber.

Nature, too, was unwelcoming and unfamiliar. **(8)** People tried to build ships from Australia's **copious** supply of pines, but the trees had brittle, useless bark. Winter and summer were reversed in the southern hemisphere. Unfamiliar kangaroos and parakeets replaced cows and horses. The ground had aloe plants, but grew no grass.

Convicts were forced to work for bosses who might refuse them food or sentence them to whippings. **(9)** Humane governors received criticism, rather than **accolades,** from the English government. Doctors who treated the poor might earn the **adulation** of convicts, but they received little pay.

Yet, convicts built the country. One freed convict, Samuel Terry, became the largest landowner in Australia. Simeon Lord became an important manufacturer; James Underwood's firm constructed ships. Mary Haydock, transported at age thirteen, built a chain of warehouses and

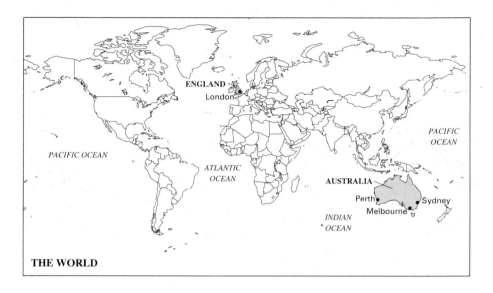

THE WORLD

Australia is now a prosperous country with a low crime rate.

boats. As the "criminal class" became a **powerful** force in Australia's success, it became more respectable. **(10)** Soon the **euphemism** "government man" was substituted for "convict." Later the term became "empire builder." Amazingly, the children of transported convicts committed almost no crimes.

Today, Australia, a prosperous country with a cosmopolitan population, continues to have one of the world's lowest crime rates. For these blessings, Australia must thank the 160,000 "criminals" who were sentenced to years of hard labor in a strange land for crimes as small as shoplifting.

■ *Exercise*

Each numbered sentence below corresponds to a sentence in the Passage. Fill in the letter of the choice that makes the sentence mean the same thing as its corresponding sentence in the Passage.

1. Young girls ruined their eyesight doing _____ sewing.
   a. difficult   b. dark   c. horrible   d. careful

2. Crime _____ .
   a. hurt   b. grew   c. stopped   d. paid

3. The smallest offense could _____ one's life.
   a. risk   b. save   c. improve   d. weaken

4. The government began to _____ the harsh punishments.
   a. soften   b. change   c. increase   d. consider

5. Government officials could _____ no longer.
   a. help   b. stay   c. finish   d. delay

6. Many prisoners believed that exile would be _____ .
   a. difficult   b. permanent   c. poor   d. ridiculous

7. The land proved difficult to _____ .
   a. farm   b. hold   c. build   d. buy

8. People tried to build ships from Australia's _____ supply of pine trees.
   a. helpful   b. plentiful   c. healthy   d. increasing

9. Humane governors received criticism, rather than _____ .
   a. praise   b. money   c. help   d. employment

10. Soon the _____ "government man" was substituted.
   a. longer phrase   b. nices phrase   c. harder phrase   d. harshes phrase

■ Discussion Questions

1. How did "royal mercy" change a punishment?

2. From the evidence in this passage, does crime appear to stem from evil people or from economic conditions? Defend your answer.

3. Do you find parallels between the treatment of criminals as described in the passage and in today's world? Why or why not?

◀ ENGLISH IDIOMS

Rhyme and Repetition

Speakers of English create many forceful and appealing idioms by putting together two words that sound almost alike. Most of these idioms are informal and more appropriate in everyday speech than in formal conversation and writing.

To *dilly-dally* means to delay, or to take too much time. A person who cannot hold a firm opinion, or whose mind is easily changed, is called *wishy-washy*.

To *hobnob* means to associate closely with, as in "He hobnobs with the rich people in town." If you *hobnob* with the rich, you may be considered *hoity-toity*, which means that people think you're a snob. (A snob is also referred to as *stuck up*.)

Something that contains many things that don't fit together is said to be a *hodgepodge*. For example, an essay might be a *hodgepodge* of unrelated ideas. However, if the essay contained many false or silly ideas, it could be called *claptrap*.

In 1919, cartoonist Billy DeBeck created the comic strip "Barney Google," about the adventures of a man and his racehorse. On October 26, 1923, DeBeck coined the phrase *heebie-jeebies* to refer to nervousness. Since then "to have the *heebie-jeebies*" is to be nervous or upset. So popular was the term that jazz trumpeteer Louis Armstrong even made a record called "Heebie Jeebies."

REVIEW

Chapters 1-4

■ Reviewing Words in Context

Complete each sentence with the word or term that fits best.

a. ascetic	g. entreprencur	m. media
b. chronological	h. euphemism	n. obsolete
c. contend	i. gauche	o. ominous
d. cryptic	j. hypocritical	p. procrastinate
e. dogmatic	k. indulge	q. Third World
f. elicit	l. mammoth	r. zealous

1. Since we wanted the letters we received first to be in the front, we filed them in _____ order.

2. A(n) _____ word is no longer used.

3. The term *tipsy* is a(n) _____ for *drunk*.

4. The _____ parking lots at Disney World and Universal Studios in Orlando, Florida, have room for many cars.

5. An increase in crime is a(n) _____ sign for society.

6. The _____ built up a large import business.

7. Some _____ countries have high infant death rates.

8. A cut or a scratch will _____ cries from a child.

9. We couldn't understand the meaning of Danuta's _____ remark.

10. I would like to _____ myself by sleeping late and cating breakfast in bed.

11. The _____ woman talked about family values but neglected her own children.

12. Two swimmers will _____ in the championship race.

13. My clumsy attempts to impress others were so _____ that I decided to just be myself.

14. His _____ beliefs are never changed by contrary evidence.

15. The _____ denied himself all luxuries.

■ *Passage for Word Review*

Complete each blank in the Passage with the word that makes the best sense. The choices include words from the vocabulary lists along with related words. Use each choice only once.

a. adroitly	e. conservative	i. indulge
b. affluent	f. copious	j. meticulous
c. appalled	g. defer	k. mitigated
d. astute	h. elated	l. pinnacle

A Family Christmas

(This essay was written by college student José Luis Gamboa.)

Christmas is the most special time of the year to me, for my family and friends gather together in a huge celebration. My mother and aunts

cook **(1)** _____ amounts of traditional foods: tamales, enchiladas, frijoles, and rellenos for main courses, plus chópes, gorditas

de dulce, and buñuelos for dessert. I **(2)** _____ myself by eating all my favorites. We sing, dance, and watch fights on television.

This year, my joy will be **(3)** _____ with some sadness, for my two eldest sisters now live in San Jose, California, and will not be with us.

Watching my nephews on Christmas Eve reminds me of my own childhood. Boy, could I get into trouble! One year, a few days before Christmas, my parents went shopping, leaving my brother and me alone.

Unable to **(4)** _____ our wish to know what our presents would be, we decided to open just one. We chose the largest and most

beautiful package, which had been wrapped with **(5)** _____ care. We saved the paper so that the gift could be wrapped up again. We

were **(6)** _____ to find that it was the toy gas station that

we had wished for all year. We **(7)** _____ put the pieces together and spent some time admiring our work.

But when we went to put it back, we could not take it apart. We

were **(8)** _____ ! When my parents found out, something awful was sure to happen. Quickly, we stuffed the toy into a closet.

When my parents returned, they saw that a package was missing. From our strange behavior, they soon guessed what had happened. They

were **(9)** _____ enough to realize that we meant no harm, and, instead of punishing us, they merely laughed and kissed us.

This Christmas I wish for world peace. Until the problem of poverty

is solved, I hope that **(10)** _____ people will give charitably to the poor. Most of all, I remember the gift of my parents' forgiveness. Sometimes an opened present can be more meaningful than a wrapped one.

■ *Reviewing Learning Strategies*

Dictionary Skills   Complete each sentence with the answer that fits best.

1. An etymology gives the _____ of a word.
   a. pronunciation   b. meaning   c. history

2. The most complete dictionary is called a(n) _____ dictionary.
   a. unabridged   b. college   c. pocket

Context Clues   Using context clues, make an intelligent guess about the meaning of the italicized word in each sentence.

3. There was *bedlam,* or total confusion, after the riot.

   Bedlam means _____ .

4. Since the dodo bird died out centuries ago, it is no longer *extant.*

   Extant means _____ .

5. The *noxious* gas caused sickness and death.

   Noxious means _____ .

6. The *fervor* of his plea was emphasized by his wild gestures.

   Fervor means _____ .

7. The teenager *beseeched* her mother to let her go to the party; in other words, she begged her.

   Beseeched means _____ .

8. In school, the unfortunate child could not master even the *rudiments* of arithmetic.

   Rudiments means _____ .

9. As a child, Beverly Sills *evinced* so much musical talent that she gave her first performance at the age of three.

   Evinced means _____ .

10. We try to *vanquish,* or conquer, our grief.

   Vanquish means _____ .

P A R T

2

Word Elements

Part 2 of this book focuses on word elements, the parts of words that have separate meanings. For example, the parts *re* (meaning "back") and *tract* (meaning "pull") are the two elements in the word *retract* (meaning "to pull back"). If you break up an unknown word into separate elements, you can often figure out its meaning. If you then combine context clues, which you learned about in Part 1 of this book, with the word element clues you will learn in Part 2, you will have a powerful approach to understanding new words. Context clues provide hints from the sentence surrounding a word; word elements give hints within the word itself.

Prefixes, Roots, and Suffixes

There are three kinds of word elements: prefixes, roots, and suffixes. A **prefix** is a group of letters that attaches to the beginning of a word root. A **root** is the central, or main, portion of a word. A **suffix** is a group of letters that attaches to the end of a word root. An example of a word that contains all three elements is *impolitely: im-* is the prefix, *polite* is the root, and *-ly* is the suffix. Now let us look at each element separately.

Prefixes. A prefix, such as *im-*, is attached to the beginning of a word root and changes its meaning. The hyphen at the end shows that it is a prefix. In the example above, the prefix *im-* means "not." When *im-* is joined to the root word *polite,* the new word formed by the root and prefix means "not polite." Next, we can see what happens when the prefix *co-,* which means "together," is joined to two familiar word roots.

131

co- (together) + *exist* = *coexist* (to exist together)
co- (together) + *operate* = *cooperate* (to work or operate together)

In both of these examples, the prefix *co-* changes the meaning of the root word.

Roots. A root is the central portion of a word, and it carries the basic meaning. There are two types of roots: base words and combining roots. A **base word** is simply an English word that can stand alone, such as *polite* or *operate,* and may be joined to a prefix or a suffix. **Combining roots** cannot stand alone as English words; they are derived from words in other languages. For example, the combining root *ject* is derived from the Latin word *jacēre,* which means "to throw." Although the root *ject* is not an English word by itself, it can combine with many prefixes to form words. Two examples are *reject* and *eject.*

e- (a prefix meaning "out") + *ject* (a root meaning "throw") = *eject*
re- (a prefix meaning "back") + *ject* (a root meaning "throw") = *reject*

How do a prefix and a root create a word with a new meaning? Sometimes the new word's meaning is simply the sum of its root and prefix. Thus, *eject* means "to throw out." At other times the meaning of a word may be different from the combined prefix and root. *Reject* does not mean "to throw back," but rather "not to accept." These two meanings are related, since we could imagine that someone who did not accept something might throw it back. In fact, "to throw back" gives an imaginative mental picture of *reject.* Prefixes and roots often give an image of a word rather than a precise definition. This image can help you to remember the meaning of a word. The formation of several words from *ject* is illustrated on page 133.

Suffixes. A suffix, such as *-ly,* is added to the end of a root. The hyphen at the beginning shows that it is a suffix. Most suffixes change a word from one part of speech to another (see the table on pages 5 and 6). For example, *-able* changes a verb *(reach)* to an adjective *(reachable).* Suffixes may also indicate a plural or a past tense, as in boy*s* and reach*ed.* A few suffixes extend the basic meaning of a word root. The root, *psych* (mind), and the suffix *-logy* (study of) are joined to form *psychology* (the study of the mind).

Many common words contain word elements. Each of the following words consists of a prefix, a root, and a suffix: *reaction, unlikely, exchanges, reviewing,* and *invisibly.* Can you identify each element?

Using Word Elements

Word elements provide valuable clues to the meanings of unknown words, but they must be used carefully.

Some word elements have more than one spelling. For example, the root *ject* is occasionally spelled *jac.* The prefix *anti-* is also spelled *ant-* (as in *antacid* and *antagonist*). Some spelling differences make words easier to pronounce. Others reflect the history of a word element. Fortunately, spellings usually vary by only one or two letters. Once you learn to look for the common letters, you should easily be able to identify word elements.

Some word elements have more than one meaning. For example, the combining root *gen* can mean both "birth" and "type." This book gives all the common meanings of roots, prefixes, and suffixes, and some hints about when to use them. When you encounter word elements that have more than one meaning, remember to use the context clues you learned in Part 1 of this book. If you combine your knowledge of word elements with context clues, you can usually determine the most appropriate meaning.

Finally, when you see a certain combination of letters in a word, those letters may not always form a word element. For instance, the appearance of the letters *a-n-t-i* in a word does not mean that they always form the prefix *anti-.* To find out whether or not they do, you must com-

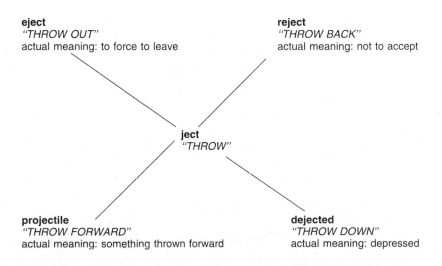

bine context clues with your knowledge of word elements. To illustrate this, *a-n-t-i* is used in two sentences below. Which sentence contains the prefix *anti-* (meaning "opposite" or "against")?

1. The *antihero* was a villain.

2. We *anticipate* you will come.

The answer is the first sentence; *antihero* ("villain") is the opposite of *hero*.

Despite these cautions, the use of word elements is an excellent way to increase your vocabulary. Prefixes, roots, and suffixes can help you unlock the meanings of thousands of difficult words. The chapters in Part 2 of this book present many different word elements. Each one is illustrated by several new words that will be valuable to you in college. If you relate these words to the word elements they contain, you will remember both more effectively.

As you work through the word elements in Part 2, keep in mind the context clues that you learned in Part 1. Together, word elements and context clues will give you very powerful strategies for learning new words on your own.

Word Elements: Prefixes

The rich cultural heritage that the ancient Greeks and Romans left to us includes many word elements that are still used in English. This chapter introduces some prefixes from ancient Greek and from Latin, the language of the ancient Romans. Learning these prefixes will help you figure out the meanings of many difficult words.

Chapter Strategy: Word Elements: Prefixes

Chapter Words:

Part 1

anti-	antidote	re-	reconcile
	antipathy		revelation
	antithesis		revert
equi-	equilibrium	sub-	subconscious
	equitable		subduc
	equivocal		subordinate

Part 2

auto-	autobiography	im-, in-	impartial
	autocratic		incongruous
	autonomous		ingenious
ex-	eccentric		interminable
	exorbitant		invariably
	exploit		
	extricate		

Did You Know?

Where Does English Come From?

The origins of language are lost in the mists of time. Archaeologists discover examples of ancient jewelry, weapons, and art, but no one knows how or why people first spoke. We do know that most of the languages of Europe, the Middle East, and India are descended from a common source. Linguists trace these languages back to a possible parent language called *Indo-European,* which would have been spoken at least five thousand years ago. The Indo-European root *mater* (mother), for example, shows up in many different languages.

Languages No Longer Spoken		*Modern Languages*	
Ancient Greek	mētēr	English	mother
Latin	mater	German	mutter
Old English	modor	Italian	madre
		Spanish	madre
		French	mère
		Polish	matka

English vocabulary descends from Indo-European through several other languages that are no longer spoken. In modern English, much of our difficult vocabulary comes from ancient Greek and Latin. (These are often called the *classical languages.*) A knowledge of the Greek and Latin word elements used in English will help you master thousands of modern English words.

Who were these Greeks and Romans from whom so much language flows? The civilization of the ancient Greeks flourished between 750 and 250 B.C. Greece was a land of small, separate city-states that created the first democracies and the first concept of citizenship. Sparta and Athens were two important city-states. The citizens of Sparta were accomplished athletes who excelled in warfare, whereas Athens was a center of art and learning. Athenians produced the first lifelike sculpture, wrote the first tragedies and comedies, and learned philosophy from Socrates and Plato. Unfortunately, the vigorous Greek civilization also had its dark side. The economic system was based on slavery, and only a small percentage of the population—free men—were full citizens. Women had few political rights. Greek history was also marred by tragic wars between city-states.

In contrast to the divided Greek city-states, the city of Rome steadily took over first the whole of Italy, then more and more countries, and finally ruled over a vast empire. From about 200 B.C. to 450 A.D., the Roman empire, which stretched from Israel to Britain, gradually brought peace to much of the known world. Roman officials introduced a highway system, a postal service, water supplies, public baths, and border patrols to

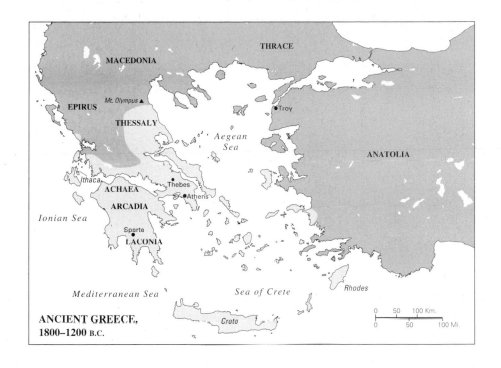

ANCIENT GREECE,
1800–1200 B.C.

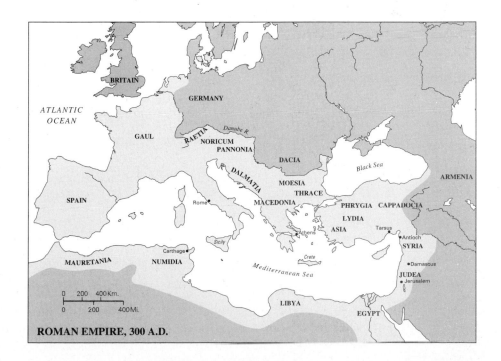

ROMAN EMPIRE, 300 A.D.

many uncivilized areas, and Latin was the official language of the empire. But, like Greece, Rome had its troubles. After the first emperor, Augustus, died, plots and murders became common in the Roman court. Several Roman emperors were poisoned or smothered. Meanwhile, officials and the army continued to rule the empire efficiently.

If you have studied the ancient Greeks and Romans, you may be able to answer these questions.

1. An epic poem, the *Iliad,* tells of a Greek war that started when Helen, the daughter of Zeus, was stolen from her husband. Helen is often

   called "Helen of _____ ."
   a. Athens   b. Sparta   c. Troy   d. Crete

2. _____ was a famous Roman leader who said, "I came, I saw, I conquered."
   a. Augustus   b. Brutus   c. Cato   d. Caesar

3. Cleopatra, queen of Egypt, did *not* have a romance with _____ .
   a. Augustus   b. Caesar   c. Anthony

(*Answers:* *1. c   2. d   3. a*)

Learning Strategy

Word Elements: Prefixes

Our heritage from the Greeks and Romans includes many word elements that are still used in English. The learning strategy in this chapter concentrates on *prefixes,* word elements added to the beginning of word roots. The seven prefixes presented in this chapter (see the following table) are very common, and learning them will help you build a large vocabulary. One dictionary lists over four hundred words that use *ex-* and more than six hundred formed from *in-* or *im-*.

Element	Meaning	Origin	Chapter Words
			Part 1
anti-, ant-	against; opposite	Greek	antidote, antipathy, antithesis
equi-, equa-	equal	Latin	equilibrium, equitable, equivocal
re-	back; again	Latin	reconcile, revelation, revert
sub-	below; under; part of	Latin	subconscious, subdue, subordinate

Part 2

auto-	self	Greek	autobiography, autocratic, autonomous
ex-, e-, ec-	out of; former	Latin	eccentric, exorbitant, exploit, extricate
im-, in-	not; in	Latin	impartial, incongruous, ingenious, interminable, invariably

Prefixes give clues to word meaning when they join with word roots. Let us look first at how prefixes can combine with roots that are base words.

re- (again) + *print* makes *reprint,* meaning "to print again."
   A popular book is usually *reprinted* several times.
sub- (below) + *normal* makes *subnormal,* meaning "below normal."
   Subnormal temperatures are colder than usual.
auto- (self) + *suggestion* makes *autosuggestion,* meaning "a suggestion made to yourself."
   Some people use *autosuggestion* when they try to diet.

See if you can use prefixes to determine the meaning of the following words. Write in the word and its meaning.

equi- (equal) + *distant* makes ___equidistant___ , meaning

___equal same distance___

anti- (against) + *crime* makes ___anti crime___ , meaning

___being against___ the crime.

in- (not) + *active* makes ___inactive___ , meaning

___not working___ .

Now let's look at how prefixes join with combining roots (roots that cannot stand alone as English words). The Latin root *scrib* or *script* ("write") combines with some prefixes in our list to make English words whose meanings are the combined meanings of the prefix and root.

in- (in) + *scrib* makes *inscribe,* "to write in."
   People often *inscribe* their names in books.
sub- (under) + *script* makes *subscript,* "written under."
   A *subscript* is a tiny number or letter written beneath a line, such as the 2 in H_2O, the chemical symbol for water. Subscripts are used mainly in math and science.

At other times, the meaning of a word is rather different from the combined meanings of a prefix and combining root. Still, word elements will give you valuable clues to the meaning of the word. The Latin root *vert* (to turn) combines with three prefixes that you will study in this chapter to make three different English words, but the idea of "turn" appears in all of them.

re- (back) + *vert* (turn) makes *revert,* or "turn back."
> When people *revert* to an old habit, they start to do it again. Perhaps you know someone who *reverted* to smoking cigarettes after having quit.

in- (in) + *vert* (turn) makes *invert,* or "turn in."
> *Invert* means to turn inside out or upside down, or to change in order. If you *invert* a pocket, you turn it inside out.

sub- (under) + *vert* (turn) makes *subvert,* or "turn under."
> *Subvert* means to make something worse by corrupting it or trying to overthrow it. Traitors seek to *subvert* their countries' governments.

As you can see, using prefixes sometimes requires a little imagination. Prefixes and roots may not give the *entire* meaning of an unknown word, but they do provide excellent hints. If you combine the use of context clues with the use of word elements, you can often figure out the precise meaning of a difficult word.

Two words formed from a prefix and a root are presented below. The meanings of the roots and prefixes are given, followed by a sentence that uses the word. Write in the meaning of each word.

revive, from *re-* (again) and *vivere* (to live)
> The plant *revived* after we gave it water.

Revive means ___to live again__.

incredulous, from *in-* (not) and *cred* (to believe)
> She was *incredulous* when she heard the fantastic story.

Incredulous means ___to not believe__.

Prefixes

Part 1

Four prefixes are presented in Part 1 of this chapter. Each prefix is described below.

anti-, ant- (against; opposite)

The two meanings of *anti-* are related and therefore easy to remember. *Antifreeze* protects a car radiator from freezing, and *antiabuse* laws help us fight child abuse. New English words continue to be formed with *anti-*, especially as people find new things to protest against.

equi-, equa- (equal)

Equi- is used in many English words. Two homes that are *equidistant* from a school are the same distance from the school. *Equivalent* sums of money have the same value. For example, one dollar is equivalent to four quarters.

re- (back; again)

Re- has two distinct meanings. It usually means "again" when it is attached to other English words (or base words). For example, when *re-* is added to the base words *wind* and *do* it forms *rewind* ("wind again") and *redo* ("do again"). However, when *re-* is added to combining roots that cannot stand alone, it often means "back." *Recede*, for instance, means "to go back" and comes from *re-* ("back") and *cēdere* ("to go").

sub- (below; under; part of)

In the word *substandard*, *sub-* means "below the standard." *Sub-* can also refer to a classification that is "part of" something else, as a *subdivision*, which is part of a division. In biology, animals from one species may be further classified into several *subspecies*.

Words to Learn

Part 1

anti

1. **antidote** (noun)   ăn′tĭ-dōt′

From Greek *anti-* (against) + *didonai* (to give) (to give a remedy against something harmful)

a substance that acts against a poison

> The doctor gave Maria an **antidote** to fight the effects of the rattlesnake bite.

something that acts against a harmful effect

> The beautiful violin playing of Chen Chong is an **antidote** to stress for people who ride on the New York subway.

NOTE: Do not confuse *antidote* with *anecdote*, which means a short story about an interesting incident.

The prefix *anti-* is widely used in medicine. Health care professionals prescribe *antibiotics* such as penicillin and neomycin to kill organisms that can cause disease. The word *antibiotic* comes from *anti-* and *bio,* meaning "life." We take an *antihistamine* to stop the sneezing and runny nose of a cold or an allergy. Antihistamine comes from *anti-* plus *histi,* the ancient Greek word element meaning "tissue," or body substance. Immunizations against smallpox, measles, polio, and tuberculosis allow us to form *antibodies* that prevent these diseases. Currently, medical researchers are trying to locate substances that will form antibodies against the deadly AIDS virus.

2. **antipathy** (noun)   ăn-tĭp′ə-thē

From Greek: *anti-* (against) + *patho* (feeling)

great hatred, opposition, or disgust

> Modern human beings feel **antipathy** toward slavery.

3. **antithesis** (noun)   ăn-tĭth′ə-sĭs (plural: **antitheses**)

From Greek: *anti-* (against) + *tithenai* (to put)

contrast; opposite

> John's rude behavior was the very **antithesis** of good manners.
>
> A quietly elegant designer shop, intended for only rich customers, is the **antithesis** of a cheap clothing store.

▶ *Related Word*
   antithetical (adjective)   (ăn′tə-thĕt′ĭ-kəl)   Censorship is *antithetical* to freedom of the press.

equi-

4. **equilibrium** (noun)   ē′kwə-lĭb′rē-əm

From Latin: *equi-* (equal) + *libra* (balance)

balance between forces; stability

> The reaction was in **equilibrium,** since an equal number of molecules were changing from ice to water and from water to ice.
>
> The tightrope walker almost lost his **equilibrium.**
>
> His **equilibrium** vanished when he lost his temper.

▶ *Common Phrase*
   in equilibrium

NOTE: The concept of balance can be used in several ways, including evenness of temperament.

The astrological sign of Libra comes directly from the Latin root *libra*, meaning "balance." Libras are born between September 23 and October 23. They are said to have calm, even natures and a sense of justice. The symbol for Libra is a balanced scale, which also relates to the meaning of *equilibrium*.

---

5. **equitable** (adjective)   ĕk'wə-tə-bəl

From Latin: *equi* (equal)

fair; just

> The **equitable** professor graded all students by the same standard.

> Police should treat people of all origins, ages, and incomes in an **equitable** manner.

NOTE: In *equitable*, the *equi* word element is used as a root.

Many early rock stars were not given *equitable* financial rewards. In the early 1950s, New York's Morrisania High School echoed with the sound of "Doo Wop," vocal music with complex harmonies and nonsense syllables (such as "sh-boom"). Famous songs included "Pretty Little Angel Eyes," "Who Put the Bomp," and "Nag." Unfortunately, the young singers often were unaware of copyright laws and were easily cheated. In 1994, Doo Wop singers released a compact disc titled *Voices: A Legendary Morrisania Review*. This time they hope for *equitable* artistic and financial rewards.

---

6. **equivocal** (adjective)   ĭ-kwĭv'ə-kəl

From Latin: *equi-* (equal) + *vox* (voice) (When something is equivocal, it seems as if two equally strong voices are sending different messages.)

having two or more meanings or interpretations

> Since test results of the new drug were **equivocal,** the company was not able to release it for sale.

doubtful

> Although people pay high prices for her paintings, her position as a great artist is **equivocal.**

NOTE: Equivocal statements are often meant to mislead and deceive people.

▶ *Related Words*
   equivocate (verb) (ĭ-kwĭv′ə-kāt′) Don't *equivocate;* answer directly.

   equivocation (noun) The President's *equivocation* on foreign policy issues showed he had not yet made up his mind.

re-

7. **reconcile** (verb) rĕk′ən-sīl′

From Latin: *re-* (back) and *concilare* to bring together (to bring back together)

To bring to peace, agreement, or understanding

> Democrats and Republicans worked hard to **reconcile** their differences on environmental policy.

> I try to **reconcile** my bank statement and checking account every month.

> After her husband died, Lan had to **reconcile** herself to life without him.

▶ *Related Word*
   reconciliation (noun) After a period of separation, the married couple decided to try a *reconciliation.*

According to Lakota Sioux tribal legend, the birth of a white buffalo brings *reconciliation* among nations. A story is told that a beautiful woman once appeared to rescue Indians from starvation. As she left, promising to return, she turned into a white buffalo. In 1994, a rare white buffalo was born in Wisconsin. Named "Miracle," it has captured the imagination of many who hope for world peace.

---

8. **revelation** (noun) rĕv′ə-lā′shən

From Latin: *re-* (back) + *vēlāre* (to veil) This makes *revēlāre,* "to draw back the veil." (When a veil is drawn back, something shocking may be discovered.)

dramatic disclosure; shocking news

> Citizens were shocked by the **revelation** that the trusted diplomat had spied on his own country.

NOTE: Revelation can have a positive religious meaning. The prophet Mohammed, founder of the Islamic religion, passed on many *revelations* to his followers.

▶ *Related Word*
> **reveal** (verb) (rĭ-vēl′) The newspaper reporter *revealed* the public corruption.

9. **revert** (verb)   rĭ-vûrt′

From Latin: *re-* (back) + *vert* (turn)

to return to a former practice or condition

> Unfortunately, the man **reverted** to using drugs soon after he left the treatment program.

> Whenever his brother was around, my boyfriend **reverted** to childish behavior.

> After 100 years of British rule, the city of Hong Kong will **revert** to Chinese control in 1997.

▶ *Common Phrase*
revert to

sub-

10. **subconscious** (adjective, noun)   sŭb′kŏn′shəs

From Latin: *sub-* (under) + *conscius* (aware of)

not aware (or conscious) in the mind (adjective)

> Colors can have **subconscious** meanings; red often suggests excitement, and blue suggests peace.

> Advertisers try to appeal to our **subconscious** desires.

the part of the mind that is beneath awareness (noun)

> When the psychiatrist Sigmund Freud explored the **subconscious,** he found that some dreams were disguised wishes.

NOTE: The *unconscious* (not conscious) is that part of the mind which can *never* become conscious. The word *unconscious* also describes a sleeping person or someone in a coma. The *subconscious* can be made conscious, but only with great effort.

11. **subdue** (verb)   səb-do͞o′

    From Latin: *sub-* (under) + *dūcere* (to lead) (Someone who is sub-dued is led, or placed, under the control of another.)

    to conquer or bring under control

    > The forest patrol **subdued** the wild bear that invaded our camp-site.

    > Alexander the Great (356–323 B.C.) **subdued** lands now occupied by Greece, Iran, Turkey, Afghanistan, and Egypt.

    to make less intense or noticeable

    > We **subdued** our voices to avoid waking the child.

    ▶ *Related Word*
    subdued (adjective)   My mother wears *subdued* colors, such as black and gray.

12. **subordinate** (adjective, noun)   sə-bôr′də-nĭt;
    (verb)   sə-bôr′də-nāt

    From Latin: *sub-* (under) + *ōrdīnāre* (to arrange in order)

    less important; of lower rank (adjective)

    > Regina holds a **subordinate** position to the president of the company.

    a person of lower rank or importance (noun)

    > A **subordinate** delivered the U.S. President's message to the press.

    to place in a lower or less important position (verb)

    > I try to **subordinate** my personal wishes to the needs of the rest of my family.

    ▶ *Common Phrases*
    subordinate to (adjective)

    a subordinate of (noun)

    NOTE: The pronunciation of the verb *subordinate* differs from the adjective and noun forms.

    ▶ *Related Word*
    subordination (noun)   No one should accept *subordination* to the rule of another.

Exercises

Part 1

■ *Definitions*

Match each word in the left-hand column with a definition from the right-hand column. Use each choice only once.

1. revert _____ g
2. antipathy _____ f
3. subdue _____ a
4. equivocal _____ i
5. reconcile _____ c
6. subconscious _____ l
7. equilibrium _____ b
8. equitable _____ h
9. revelation _____ k
10. antidote _____ e

a. conquer
b. balance
c. bring to peace
d. opposite
e. something that acts against a poison
f. hatred
g. return to a former practice
h. fair
i. doubtful
j. less important in rank
k. shocking news
l. beneath awareness

■ *Meanings*

Match each prefix to its meaning. Use each choice only once.

1. anti-, ant- _____ b
2. equi-, equa- _____ a
3. re- _____ d
4. sub- _____ c

a. equal
b. against
c. under, below, part of
d. again, back

■ *Words in Context*

Complete each sentence with the word that fits best. Use each choice only once.

a. antidote	e. equitable	i. revert
b. antipathy	f. equivocal	j. subconscious
c. antithesis	g. reconcile	k. subdue
d. equilibrium	h. revelation	l. subordinate

1. The loud rock music was the _____ of the quiet classical piece.

2. When I am on vacation, I _____ to my old habit of sleeping late.

3. The police were able to _____ the man who threatened us with a gun.

4. The _____ decision enabled everyone to feel that justice had been done.

5. Because the housewife kept her _____, she was able to deal calmly with three crying children and a broken window.

6. People are not aware of _____ desires.

7. Slater's compliment was _____ , and we were afraid that it was actually an insult.

8. The convicted criminal had to _____ himself to life in prison.

9. The company president, Ms. Lopez, was so busy that her

   _____ had to handle many details for her.

10. The man took a(n) _____ to cure his lead poisoning.

■ *Using Related Words*

Complete each sentence by using a word from the group of related words above it. You may need to capitalize a word when you put it into a sentence. Use each choice only once.

1. reconcile, reconciliation

    Although it could never be easy to _____ oneself to slavery, some slaves in ancient Rome had high status. After Rome conquered Greece, educated Greeks were enslaved to serve as tutors, teachers, and advisers to Roman masters. Of course, we

    do not know if their _____ to slave status was ever complete.

2. subordinate, subordination

    After achieving much political success, the great Julius Caesar set

    out to _____ Gaul (now France and Belgium) to

    the Romans. He achieved this _____ and returned home a hero. Six years later, he was assassinated.

3. revelation, revealed

    While Augustus, nephew of Caesar, was in Illyria, a letter from his

    mother brought the shocking _____ that Caesar had been murdered. His mother warned Augustus to flee. Instead,

    his decision _____ his character: he immediately went to Rome. This courage later helped him become Rome's first emperor.

4. antithesis, antithetical

    The city of Rome was destroyed in a series of barbarian invasions.

    With their lack of culture, the invaders were _____ to the highly civilized Romans. The destructive violence of the

    attacks was the _____ of the principles on which the Roman Empire stood. After many invasions, the last Roman emperor was forced to resign in A.D. 467.

5. equivocating, equivocal

    My feelings toward studying Latin were _____ .
    I knew that Latin would help me become a cultured person and improve my English vocabulary. However, I feared that it would

not be as useful as Spanish. After _____ for a few weeks, I decided to take courses in both Latin and Spanish.

■ *Reading the Headlines*

This exercise presents five headlines that might appear in newspapers. Read each headline and then answer the questions that follow. (Remember that small words, such as *is, are, a,* and *the,* are often left out of newspaper headlines.)

SUBCONSCIOUS FORCES CAUSE MAN TO REVERT TO CHILDLIKE BEHAVIOR

1. Is the man aware of the forces? _____

2. Has the man behaved like a child before? _____

ANTIPATHY PREVENTS RECONCILIATION BETWEEN FATHER AND SON

3. Do the father and son like each other? _____

4. Did the father and son make peace? _____

BOSS STRIVES TO SUBDUE NEGATIVE FEELINGS TOWARD SUBORDINATE

5. Is the boss trying to control his feelings? _____

6. Is the other person of higher rank than the boss? _____

SHOCKING REVELATION SHOWS PRESIDENT TO BE ANTITHESIS OF HERO

7. Has something been made public? _____

8. Is the president a hero? _____

AFTER EQUITABLE DIVORCE AGREEMENT, LIVES SETTLE INTO EQUILIBRIUM

9. Is the divorce agreement unfair? _____

10. Are the lives now calm? _____

Prefixes

Part 2

The following three prefixes are introduced in Part 2.

auto- (self)
> This prefix comes from the Greek word for "self." The word *automobile* comes from *auto-* and *mobile,* meaning "moving." When the automobile was invented, it was named for the amazing sight of something moving all by itself.

ex-, e-, ec- (out of; former)
> When *ex-* is combined with base words, it usually means "former." The words *ex-wife* (former wife) and *ex-president* (former president) show *ex-* used in this sense. The hyphens in these words give a hint that the "former" meaning is being used. When *ex-* is used with combining roots, it usually means "out of," as in *exhale* (to breathe out). The words introduced in this lesson join *ex-* to combining roots, so *ex-* means "out of" in all these words. However, you should remember that *ex-* can also mean "former."

im-, in- (not; in)
> This prefix is spelled in two different ways, and either spelling may have two different meanings. The most common meaning of *im-* and *in-* is "not," as in the words *impure* (not pure) and *indecent* (not decent). *Im-* and *in-* can also mean "in," as in *inhale* (to breathe in) and *import* (to carry into a country). The prefix is spelled *ir-* or *il-* before roots that begin with *r* or *l,* such as in *irregular* and *illogical.* The *il-* and *ir-* spellings always mean "not."

Words to Learn

Part 2

auto-

13. **autobiography** (noun)   ô′tō-bī-ŏg′rə-fē

    From Greek: *auto-* (self) + *bio* (life) + *graph* (to write)

    account of a person's life written by himself or herself

    > Country music star Glen Campbell's **autobiography** is entitled *Rhinestone Cowboy.*

▶ *Related Word*

autobiographical (adjective)   The novel was *autobiographical.*

14. **autocratic** (adjective)   ô′tə-krăt′ək

From Greek: *auto-* (self) + *krates* (ruling)

having absolute power; domineering

> After fifty years of **autocratic** Russian rule, Lithuania became independent.

> **Autocratic** landowners refused to give any power to farmers.

> The **autocratic** CEO ran the company without any input from employees.

▶ *Related Words*

autocrat (noun; person)   ô′tə-krăt′   The *autocrat* Peter the Great ruled Russia from 1682 to 1725.

autocracy (noun)   ô-tŏk′rə-sē   The *autocracy* was under the complete control of the ruler.

15. **autonomous** (adjective)   ô-tŏn′ə-məs

From Greek: *auto-* (self) + *nomos* (law)

self-governing; independent

> The Vatican is an **autonomous** area within the country of Italy.

> People usually need to be self-supporting before they can truly be **autonomous.**

▶ *Related Word*

autonomy (noun)   Slaves have no *autonomy.*

ex-

16. **eccentric** (adjective)   ĕk-sĕn′trĭk

From Greek: *ek-* (out) + *kentron* (center)

odd; different from normal or usual

> The **eccentric** man attached strings to large bugs and walked them like dogs.

▶ *Related Word*

eccentricity (noun)   (ĕk′sĕn-trĭs′ə-tē)   One of Albert Einstein's *eccentricities* was going without socks in cold weather.

17. **exorbitant** (adjective)   ĭg-zôr′bə-tənt

From Latin: *ex-* (out) + *orbita* (path)

expensive; unreasonable; exceeding proper limits

> Although no one bought the paintings of Vincent Van Gogh during his lifetime, they now sell for **exorbitant** prices.

> Management refused to meet the baseball player's **exorbitant** contract demands.

18. **exploit** (verb)   ĭk-sploit′; (noun)   ĕks′ploit′

From Latin: *ex-* (out) + *plicāre* (to fold), making *explicāre* (to unfold) (When we *exploit* something, we "fold it out" and make it work for us.)

to take advantage of; to use (verb)

> In the 1920s, child movie stars were often **exploited** by managers who enriched themselves, but left little for the youngsters.

> Alaska **exploited** its rich oil and natural gas reserves without harming the environment.

great adventure; great deed (noun)

> Homer's *Odyssey* relates the **exploits** of the Greek hero Odysseus as he returns home from the Trojan War.

NOTE: 1) *Exploit,* when used as a verb, often suggests taking unfair advantage (as in the exploitation of women or minorities). However, it can mean simply "to take advantage of" or "to use wisely." 2) Notice the difference in pronunciation stress between *ex-ploit′* (verb) and *ex′ploit* (noun).

▶ *Related Word*
   exploitation (noun)   (ĕks′ploi-tā′shən)   The cruel *exploitation* of workers finally led to a strike.

19. **extricate** (verb)   ĕk′strĭ-kāt′

From Latin: *ex-* (out) + *tricae* (difficulties), making *extricāre* (to disentangle, to free)

to free from difficulty; to disentangle

> Paramedics **extricated** the injured couple from the wrecked car.

> Roy **extricated** himself from an embarrassing situation by leaving the room.

▶ *Common Phrase*
to extricate (oneself) from

Harry Houdini (1874–1926) was a world-famous escape artist. Houdini *extricated* himself from many seemingly escape-proof devices, including ten pairs of handcuffs, jail cells, nailed crates, and an airtight tank filled with water. Once, tied into a straitjacket and hung upside-down from the top of a tall building, he extricated himself within minutes.

---

im-, in-

20. **impartial** (adjective)   ĭm-pär′shəl

From Latin: *im-* (not) + *pars* (part)

fair; just; not biased

It is important for a basketball referee to be **impartial.**

An **impartial** taster judged the "Best Ribs in New Orleans" contest.

The peacekeepers were **impartial** towards both countries involved in the war.

▶ *Common Phrase*
impartial towards

▶ *Related Word*
impartiality (noun) (ĭm′pär-shē-al′ə-tē)   It is difficult to judge a good friend with *impartiality*.

21. **incongruous** (adjective)   ĭn-kŏng′grōō-əs

From Latin: *in-* (not) + *congruere* (to agree)

out of place; not consistent or in harmony

The modern furniture looked **incongruous** in the ancient castle.

Violence seemed **incongruous** in the peaceful village.

▶ *Related Word*
incongruity (noun)   Her formal gown was an *incongruity* in the crowd of people dressed in jeans.

22. **ingenious** (adjective)   ĭn-jēn′yəs

From Latin: *in-* (in) + *gen* (born), making *ingenium* (inborn talent)

clever; inventive

Scientists are perfecting an **ingenious** plastic wrap that will produce electric power from sunlight.

The **ingenious** slogan "snap, crackle, pop" has sold many boxes of Rice Krispies.

▶ *Related Word*

ingenuity (noun) (ĭn′jə-nōo′ə-tē) Computer programmers are known for their *ingenuity*.

Benjamin Franklin, a Philadelphian who lived in the 1700s, produced many *ingenious* inventions, including the lightning rod, bifocals (glasses with two visual corrections), and the Franklin stove (which stood in the middle of a room, heating all parts evenly). Franklin also developed some valuable public services, such as the public library and the volunteer fire department.

---

23. **interminable** (adjective) ĭn-tûr′mə-nə-bəl

From Latin: *in-* (not) + *terminus* (end, boundary)

endless; too long

The lecture seemed **interminable,** but we were afraid to get up and leave.

NOTE: 1. *Interminable* has a negative connotation. 2. This word often describes something that seems endless rather than actually is endless.

24. **invariably** (adverb) ĭn-vâr′ē-ə-blē

From Latin: *in-* (not) + *variabilis* (changeable)

consistently; always

Superman and Batman **invariably** win their fights against evil.

Exercises

Part 2

■ *Definitions*

Match each word in the left-hand column with a definition from the right-hand column. Use each choice only once.

1. extricate _____g_____   a. holding all power

2. invariably _____k_____   b. endless; too long

3. autonomous _____   c. the story of one's own life

4. autobiography _____c_____   d. odd

5. eccentric _____d_____   e. clever

6. impartial _____h_____   3 f. to take advantage of

7. exorbitant _____j_____   g. to free from difficulty

8. incongruous _____l_____   h. not biased

9. autocratic _____a_____   i. self-ruling

10. interminable _____b_____   j. very expensive

                                  k. always; consistently

                                  l. out of place; not in harmony

■ Meanings

Match each prefix to its meaning. Use each choice only once.

1. auto- _____a_____   a. self

2. ex-, e-, ec- _____c_____   b. in; not

3. im-, in- _____b_____   c. out; former

■ Words in Context

Complete each sentence with the word that fits best. Use each choice only once.

a. autobiography   e. exorbitant   i. incongruous
b. autocratic   f. exploit   j. ingenious
c. autonomous   g. extricate   k. interminable
d. eccentric   h. impartial   l. invariably

1. In his _____ , Lee Iacocca revealed the secrets of his success.

2. In a(n) _____ plan to prevent water shortages, Alaska's plentiful water may be shipped in huge bags to dry areas.

3. We find it _____ when very rich people shop at discount stores.

4. The _____ ruler suddenly announced that everyone had to pay a new tax.

5. As a(n) _____ person, I make all my own decisions.

6. Most people feel that $100,000 is a(n) _____ price to pay for a car.

7. The _____ lady kept ninety-nine cats in her home.

8. People _____ close their eyes when they sneeze, since it is not possible to keep them open.

9. It is important not to _____ migrant workers by making them work long hours for very low pay.

10. The time I spent waiting to find out if I got the job seemed

    _____ .

■ *Using Related Words*

Complete each sentence by using a word from the group of related words above it. You may need to capitalize a word when you put it into a sentence. Use each choice only once.

1. exploitation, exploited

   Aesop, the famous Greek fable teller, lived about 500 B.C. In one of his fables, a couple had a goose that laid one golden egg each day.

   When the couple _____ their good fortune wisely, they grew wealthier. However, one day they decided to get all the gold. They killed the goose, only to find that there was no gold in-

   side it. Thus, when their wise _____ turned to greediness, they lost everything. From this fable comes the phrase "to kill the goose that lays the golden egg."

2. impartial, impartiality

> Socrates, whose teachings have inspired many people, was among the most famous citizens of Athens. Unfortunately, he criticized the city leaders, and in 399 B.C., he was brought to trial for corrupting youth. Emotions were so strong that it was difficult to
>
> be _____ in the debate. Socrates was condemned to die by drinking poison hemlock. Although the city elders thought
>
> they had acted with _____, others disagreed. Among Socrates' most famous pupils was the philosopher Plato, author of *The Republic*.

3. autonomy, autonomous

> In 490 B.C., Darius, king of the enormous Persian empire, decided
>
> to conquer the city-state of Athens and end its _____ . Against all odds, Athens defeated the Persian army on the Plain of
>
> Marathon and remained _____. Pheidippides ran 26 miles to deliver news of the victory to Athens. Since then, a race of 26 miles, or any long, difficult contest, has been called a "marathon."

4. ingenious, ingenuity

> Euclid, who lived in Alexandra at about 500 B.C., was a mathemati-
>
> cian of great _____ . His _____ system of teaching geometry through proofs is still used in classrooms today.

5. extricated, extricate

> Homer's *Iliad* tells the story of the Trojan War. After several years of fighting, the Greeks had not conquered the Trojans. Finally, the
>
> Greeks used a trick to _____ themselves from their difficulties. Greek soldiers hid inside a large wooden horse just outside the gates of Troy. Assuming the horse was a gift, the Trojans brought it inside. When night fell, the Greeks
>
> _____ themselves from the horse, attacked, and conquered Troy.

■ *True or False?*

Each of the following statements contains at least one word from this section. Read each statement and then indicate whether you think it is probably true or probably false.

_____   1. An autobiography gives a personal point of view.

_____   2. An impartial person would be likely to settle an argument in a fair manner.

_____   3. One thousand dollars is an exorbitant price to pay for a house.

_____   4. An autocrat allows other people to be autonomous.

_____   5. Eccentric actions are often incongruous with normal behavior.

_____   6. An interesting, well-acted play would seem interminable.

_____   7. Talking with friends can be described as an exploit.

_____   8. Ingenious inventions are clever.

_____   9. We would want to extricate ourselves from a good situation.

_____   10. Rain is invariably wet.

Chapter Exercises

■ *Practicing Strategies: New Words from Word Elements*

See how your knowledge of prefixes can help you understand new words. Complete each sentence with the word that seems to fit best. Use each choice only once.

a. antiwar	e. equipoise	i. reenter
b. antibacterial	f. impression	j. refill
c. autoinoculation	g. invalid	k. subliminal
d. equator	h. illogical	l. subcontractors

1. After exploring the Moon, the spacecraft will _____ the Earth's atmosphere.

2. You cannot drive on a(n) _____ license.

3. The _____ movement worked for peace.

4. The process in which chemicals from your own body are injected back into you to fight disease is called _____ .

5. Several _____ may work under a contractor.

6. The _____ divides the Earth equally into the Northern and Southern hemispheres.

7. When two forces are poised equally against each other, they are in a state of _____ .

8. After I drank all of my coffee, the waiter offered to _____ my cup.

9. Something _____ is beneath the limits of your hearing or vision.

10. A(n) _____ is made when something is pressed into soft cement.

■ *Practicing Strategies: Combining Context Clues and Word Elements*

Combining the strategies of context clues and word elements is a good way to figure out unknown words. In the following sentences, each italicized word contains a word element that you have studied in this chapter. Using the meaning of the prefix and the context of the sentence, make an intelligent guess about the meaning of the italicized word. Your instructor may ask you to check the meaning in your dictionary after you have finished.

1. At the time of an *equinox*, there are twelve hours of daylight per twenty-four-hour day.

    Equinox means _____

    _____ .

2. Since our computer is *infallible,* the mistake must be due to human error.

Infallible means _____ .

3. The *subcellar* was the first room to flood during the storm.

Subcellar means _____ .

4. Using the *autofocus* feature of the camera, even an amateur can take a clear picture.

Autofocus means _____ .

5. The criminal was *extradited* from England and sent to the United States.

Extradited means _____ .

■ *Practicing Strategies: Using the Dictionary*

Read the following definition and then answer the questions below it.

> **bloom**[1] (bloom) *n.* **1.** The flower of a plant. **2a.** The condition of being in flower. **b.** A condition or time of vigor and beauty; prime: *"the radiant bloom of Greek genius"* (Edith Hamilton). **3.** A fresh, rosy complexion: *"She was short, plump, and fair, with a fine bloom"* (Jane Austen). **4.a.** A waxy or powdery coating sometimes occurring on the surface of plant parts, such as the fruits of certain plums. **b.** A similar coating, as on newly minted coins. **c.** *Chem.* See **efflorescence** 3a. **5.** Glare that is caused by a shiny object reflecting too much light into a television camera. **6.** A colored area on the surface of water caused by planktonic growth. —*v.* **bloomed, bloom•ing, blooms.** —*intr.* **1a.** To bear a flower or flowers. **b.** To support plant life in abundance. **2.** To shine; glow. **3.** To grow or flourish with youth and vigor. **4.** To appear or expand suddenly. —*tr.* **1.** To cause to flourish. **2.** *Obsolete.* To cause to flower. [ME *blom* < ON *blōm.* See **bhel-**[3*].] —**bloom′y** *adj.*

1. Which common word in the dictionary key contains a vowel pronounced like the *oo* in bloom? _____

2. Give the number and part of speech of the definition in which a quote is used from author Edith Hamilton to define *bloom.* _____

3. Give the number and part of speech of the definition most often used in chemistry. _____

4. Give the number and part of speech of the definition that best fits this sentence: "Her face had a rosy bloom." _____

5. In which language did *bloom* appear just before it entered modern English? _____

■ *Companion Words*

Complete each sentence with the word that fits best. Choose your answers from the words below. You may use each word more than once.

Choices: in, to, toward, of, from

1. The party was an antidote _____ her depression.

2. We felt antipathy _____ our enemy.

3. War is the antithesis _____ peace.

4. Please don't revert _____ childish behavior.

5. The revelations _____ dishonesty among city politicians shocked us.

6. We extricated ourselves _____ the problem.

7. The vice president is subordinate _____ the president.

8. The vice president is a subordinate _____ the president.

9. Please maintain an impartial attitude _____ both sides.

10. We enjoyed hearing about the exploits _____ Dr. Living-stone.

■ *Writing with Your Words*

This exercise will give you practice in writing effective sentences that use the vocabulary words. Each sentence is started for you. Complete it with an interesting phrase that also indicates the meaning of the italicized word.

1. An *autocratic* ruler might _____

   _____ .

2. It would be *incongruous* to see _____

   _____ .

3. I hope I never have to *reconcile* myself to _____

   _____ .

4. A man would be considered *eccentric* if _____

   _____ .

5. I *invariably* have difficulty _____

   _____ .

6. An *antidote* to envy is _____

   _____ .

7. The *exploits* of the adventurer included _____

   _____ .

8. The word needs an *ingenious* solution to the problem of _____

   _____ .

9. Since the wait seemed *interminable,* we _____

   _____ .

10. The *exorbitant* price of the car _____

   _____ .

Antiquity and early Middle Ages: Nobles in formal costume often wore the same loose robes, regardless of their gender.

Passage

Clothes and Society

What do clothes say about society? A look at the history of clothing reveals much about how our culture has changed, but it also shows that some of today's most modern fashions are echoes of the past. Ponytails and earrings for men seem to symbolize a new freedom of dress, so it may come as a **revelation** that men wore long hair and jewelry centuries ago.

The origins of today's fashion date back two thousand years, to the Romans. In that **autocratic** society, fashion was regulated by law, and clothes displayed one's social class in visual form. A rich Roman wore a tunic, or loose-fitting shirt, covered with a toga, or cloak. The color, style, and draping instantly defined the wearer, enabling people to distinguish a chief officer from his **subordinates.** Victorious generals, for example, wore purple togas with gold embroidery. Rules for dress were so complicated that rich people often had special slaves whose chief duty was to arrange their masters' clothes.

Formal clothing continued to be loosely shaped until about 1200 A.D.

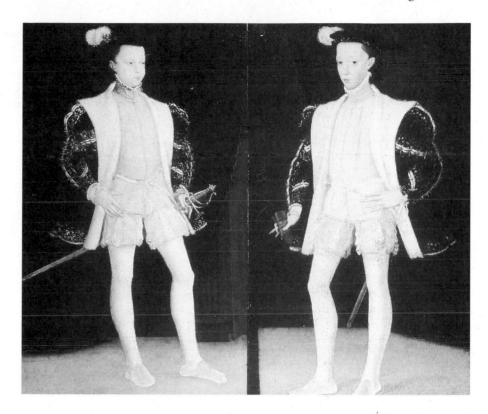

About 1200 A.D.: Body-fitting clothing for men developed from linen armor.

Nobles in formal costumes often wore the same loose robes, regardless of their sex. In portraits of the time, men can often be distinguished from women only by their headdress and facial features.

However, about 1200 A.D., men and women started to dress very differently from each other. The invention of plate armor, metal plates that were fitted over a fighter's body, started a revolution in men's fashion. Plate armor required clothes under it to protect the wearer, and these clothes, called "linen armor," had to fit the shape of the body. Once linen armor was developed, men started to wear it as clothing, even without plate. Thus, men wore perfectly fitting short coats and, below their waists, tights fitted to the shape of their legs. **(1)** In a style that would seem **eccentric** today, the two legs of the tights were often different colors. **(2)** This close-fitting clothing for men was the **antithesis** of the modest long skirts and headdresses that women continued to wear.

An occasional shocking woman adopted the lifestyle of a man. One example was Joan of Arc (1412–1431), whose daring **exploits** on the field of battle saved her country. She **subdued** the English invaders and restored the throne to the rightful French king. **(3)** Joan was an independent woman whose efforts at **autonomy** included wearing fashionable, form-fitting men's clothing on and off the battlefield. Her wish to be a man,

Married couples of the late 1700s and 1800s often looked incongruous.

although perhaps **subconscious,** shocked the people of her time. In fact, her clothing was one factor that caused her to be condemned and then burned at the stake.

The fashion of form-fitting clothing for men and loose, covered clothing for women continued for several hundred more years. **(4)** These two different styles were not **equitable** to the sexes, for while men could move easily, women had to drag long, heavy skirts.

Fashions also continued to reveal the social station of their wearers through elaborate jewelry, headpieces, and embroidery. In fact, fashionable people had to **reconcile** themselves to considerable discomfort. In the early 1500s, Henry VIII wore huge sleeves and a heavy gold chain. Later in that century, his daughter Elizabeth I had a stiff, white ruff at her neck and clothes embroidered with gold.

In the French court of Queen Marie Antoinette (who ruled from 1774 to 1793), a woman's formal wig sometimes towered more than a foot above her head. These headpieces often held miniature displays of fashionable

In the twentieth century, women have adopted their own versions of the man's suit.

topics, such as the American Revolution. **(5)** Because of the weight of these wigs, some women found it hard to maintain their **equilibrium** and had to spend much time sitting. **(6)** Marie Antoinette's elaborate clothing and jewelry aroused the **antipathy** of the French people. In fact, her **exorbitant** expenditures were one cause of the French Revolution.

Perhaps as an **antidote** to all this discomfort, in about 1800 a new costume appeared: the first modern man's suit. Suddenly, men abandoned their jewelry and showy clothing and began to wear something that looked like a uniform. Early suits had an overcoat (today's jacket), a waistcoat (today's vest), and a shirt. They also featured pants down to the knees and hose beneath. Gradually, these developed into the loose-fitting pants worn today. This new clothing was relatively **subdued,** and it gave men a rather standardized appearance.

(7) Earlier clothing had **invariably** defined a man's social status; however, the invention of the suit made it difficult to tell a rich man from a poor man by just looking at them. This change in clothing reflected a change in the way society viewed men. Modern man became defined not by his looks, but by what he did.

However, women's clothing continued to be large, decorated, and uncomfortable. **(8)** In fact, portraits of married couples in the 1800s often look **incongruous.** Dressed in huge, decorated skirts, ribbons, and jewelry, the wife takes up twice as much space as her plainly dressed husband. **(9)** To the **impartial** observer, the woman looks like a decorated object and the man seems to be a person of action.

Another important change has taken place in modern times, as women's clothing has become more comfortable. In the twentieth century, women have adopted their own version of the man's suit. Women now wear pantsuits, trousers, and shorts. **(10)** At the same time, many men are abandoning the uniformity of the suit and **reverting** to the more expressive, decorated fashions of several centuries ago.

Without a doubt, trends will continue to change. Future fashions may once again reflect the clothing and jewelry of the past.

■ *Exercise*

Each numbered sentence below corresponds to a sentence in the Passage. Fill in the letter of the choice that makes the sentence mean the same thing as its corresponding sentence in the Passage.

1. The style would seem _____ today.
   a. pleasing   b. strange   c. fashionable   d. comfortable

2. This close-fitting clothing was the _____ of modest skirts.
   a. other part   b. best   c. comfort   d. opposite

3. Joan of Arc's efforts at _____ included her clothing.
   a. comfort   b. pride   c. movement   d. freedom

4. These two different styles were not _____ to the sexes in terms of freedom.
   a. fair   b. good   c. helpful   d. fashionable

5. Some women found it hard to maintain their _____ .
   a. comfort   b. clothing   c. jewelry   d. balance

6. Marie Antoinette's clothing and jewelry aroused the _____ of the French people.
   a. fear   b. poverty   c. hatred   d. pride

7. Earlier clothing _____ defined a man's social status.
   a. properly   b. efficiently   c. clearly   d. always

8. In fact, married couples often looked _____ .
   a. uncomfortable   b. not rich   c. not in harmony   d. not at peace

9. To the _____ observer, the wife looks like a decorated object.
   a. fearless   b. intelligent   c. fair-minded   d. clothes-minded

10. Many men are abandoning the suit and _____ to more expressive and decorated clothing.
   a. going forward   b. going away   c. going out   d. going back

■ Discussion Questions

1. Why was Joan of Arc's clothing unusual?

2. How did men's suits change the messages that clothes gave about their social positions?

3. Identify a change in dressing customs that has taken place during the past twenty years.

ENGLISH IDIOMS

Beginnings, Ends, and Time

Since this chapter deals with prefixes, elements that start words, our idioms will deal with beginnings, ends, and time. To *start from scratch* means to start from the beginning. However, to *start up with someone* means to argue with that person.

To *wind up* something means to end it, as in "winding up my assignment." People *at the end of their rope* or *at the end of their tether* are desperate and do not know what to do.

If a woman *takes her time*, she does things slowly, at her own rate. If she *has time on her hands*, she has time to spare, or extra time. If she has *the time of her life*, she has a *good time*, or is enjoying herself very much.

When something is done that is long overdue, we say, "It's *high time*" for it to be done. When something is no longer in fashion or up-to-date, we call it *behind the times*.

Until the invention of quartz controls, most clocks and watches were driven by small wheels with notches, or *nicks*, in them. You may actually have some clocks with these ticking gears. The nicks catch on a wheel and move as frequently as every second. Therefore, to be *in the nick of time* means to be on time to the second, or nearly late. A person who catches a train *in the nick of time* almost misses it.

CHAPTER

Word Elements: People and Names

Many words in English are derived from descriptions of people and names. Characters from classical myths, as well as the names of famous people, have been a rich source of words. The first part of this chapter introduces four word roots that relate to people. The second part adds two prefixes that were taken from names of characters in Greek mythology and then introduces some additional words formed from names.

Chapter Strategy: Word Elements About People

Chapter Words:

Part 1

anthrop	anthropological	nom	nominal
	misanthrope		pseudonym
	philanthropist		renowned
gen	congenital	viv	viable
	genesis		vital
	genocide		vivacious

Part 2

pan-	pandemonium	Name Words	boycott
	panorama		chauvinism
psych-	psyche		gargantuan
	psychosomatic		martial
			maverick
			odyssey
			quixotic
			spartan

Did You Know?

Which Words Come from Names?

Many English words are taken from names in classical mythology. The Greeks and Romans had a well-developed and colorful mythology, whose legends reflected the violence and passion of life in a time when natural forces and disease could not be controlled.

According to myth, Jupiter, king of the gods, ruled thunder—a fearful force to ancient people. His many exploits included dethroning his father and turning himself into a swan in order to seduce a young girl. He loved to play nasty jokes on others. The word *jovial,* meaning "merry," was taken from Jove, another name for Jupiter.

Mercury, often shown in paintings with wings on his feet, was the speedy messenger of the gods. The metal *mercury,* used in thermometers, is a quickly moving liquid at room temperature. A quick-tempered person is often called *mercurial.*

Venus, or Aphrodite, was the goddess of love. An *aphrodisiac* is a drug or food that is said to increase sexual desire.

Two English words derive from the Titans, giants who ruled the earth before Jupiter's thunderbolts conquered them. Something of enormous size and power is called *titanic.* Since one Titan, Atlas, was condemned to support the world on his shoulder, a book containing maps is now called an *atlas.*

Modern characters have also been the source of English words. In the 1920s, to amuse himself during lonely hours, struggling artist Walt Disney drew a comic-strip mouse called Mortimer. The mouse, renamed Mickey, later became the hero of many cartoons. Something that is silly or easy might now be called *Mickey Mouse,* as in a "Mickey Mouse job."

Words are also based on the names of real people. The Earl of Sandwich (1718–1792) loved to gamble so much that he refused to leave the game, even to eat. Instead he had meat brought to him between two pieces of bread, thus creating the *sandwich. Braille,* the system of raised dots that allows blind people to read, was first published in 1829 by Louis Braille, who had lost his vision in childhood. U.S. Union Civil War general Ambrose Burnside, a fashion leader, allowed his hair to grow down the side of his face, inventing a style we still call *sideburns.*

Some words come from names of organizations. The coffee drink *cappucino* comes from the Italian order of Capuchin, a group of Roman Catholic monks. The idea for the *frisbee* came from the easy-to-catch pie tins manufactured by the Frisbie company in Bridgeport, Connecticut.

Places also have donated their names. The word *dollar* comes from *taler,* short for *Joachimstal,* the city in Bohemia where it was first used. The *tuxedo,* a type of men's formal wear, comes from Tuxedo Park in New

York State. Scotch liquor comes from Scotland. The *peach* was the Latin word for Persia (now Iran), where this fruit originated.

Even names of some imaginary places have been used. In about 1500, a Spanish novelist described a beautiful, imaginary island inhabited by strong women. When exploring the Americas, one Spaniard used the novelist's word to name a real place of great natural beauty, at first thought to be an island. The name, *California*, is still used today.

In this chapter, you will be learning several words derived from names and places. Perhaps one day a word will be named after you!

Learning Strategy

Word Elements About People

This first part of the chapter discusses word roots and how they function in words. Four specific roots dealing with people are used as examples. The second part continues with prefixes and presents two prefixes taken from names.

Element	Meaning	Origin	Function	Chapter Words
				Part 1
anthrop	human	Greek	root	anthropological, misanthrope, philanthropist
gen	birth; type	Latin; Greek	root	congenital, genesis, genocide
nom, nym	name	Latin; Greek	root	nominal, pseudonym, renowned
vit, viv	life	Latin	root	viable, vital, vivacious
				Part 2
pan-	all	Greek	prefix	panorama, pandemonium
psych-	mind; soul	Greek	prefix	psyche, psychosomatic

A root is the word element that carries the most meaning. Although prefixes and suffixes may alter the meaning of a root, they never carry as much meaning as the root itself.

There are two kinds of roots—base words and combining roots. Base words can stand alone as English words. They may or may not have prefixes and suffixes attached to them. *Work* is an example of a base word.

Combining roots cannot stand alone as English words. They require a prefix, a suffix, or at least a change in spelling in order to form a word. Most of the roots you will study in this book are combining roots that come from ancient Greek and Latin. Although they were words in these ancient languages, they appear in modern English only as root word elements.

The root *anthrop* (human) is an example of a combining root. It can form a word when it is attached to a prefix (*misanthrope*) or a suffix (*anthropological*).

Nom or *nym,* meaning "name," is another example of a combining root. This root has more than one spelling because it comes from both Latin and Greek. It forms over thirty English words. Slight changes in spelling give us the words *name* and *noun;* adding a suffix gives us *nominate;* adding different prefixes gives us *antonym* and *synonym.*

Each of the words formed from the root *nom* or *nym* carries a meaning related to "name." Sometimes the meaning is directly related to "name"; at other times the word root gives a hint about a word's meaning rather than supplying a direct meaning. The word *name* has the same meaning as the root *nom* or *nym;* the word and the root are directly related. Other words have an indirect relationship to *nom* and *nym:*

A *noun* is a word that names something.
To *nominate* is to name somebody to a position, or to name somebody as a candidate in an election.
A *synonym* means the same thing as another word; two synonyms "name" the same thing. (*Syn* means "same.")
An *antonym* is a word opposite in meaning to another word; two antonyms "name" opposite things. (As you learned in Chapter 5, *ant-* means "opposite.")

Word Roots

Part 1

The four roots presented in Part 1 of this chapter all deal with people and their lives.

anthrop (human)
The root *anthrop* comes from the Greek word for "human," *anthropos.* Perhaps you have taken a course in *anthropology,* the study of human life.
gen (birth; type)
Because it forms overs fifty English words, *gen* is an extremely useful root. *Gen* has two meanings: "birth" and "type." The ancients felt that these meanings were related because when someone was born, he or she was a certain "type" of person. *Gen* means "birth" in the word *gene,*

which refers to the hereditary information in each cell of a living plant or animal. We are all "born with" our genes. Another word, *generation*, refers to people born during the same time period.

Gen means "type" in the word *gender,* which tells what type of person you are, male or female. Perhaps you buy *generic* foods at the grocery. These have no brand names and are of a "general type." The use of context clues will help you to determine whether *gen* means "birth" or "type" when you see it in a word.

nom, nym (name)

This root word comes from both Latin and Greek. *Nomen* is Latin for "name," and the word originally appeared in Greek as *onoma*.

vit, viv (life)

In Latin, *vita* means "life." *Vit* forms such words as *vitamin,* a chemical necessary for human life. Manufacturers have used this root to make brand names, such as the hair product Vitalis, which is supposed to add life to your hair.

Words to Learn

Part 1

anthrop

1. **anthropological** (adjective)   ăn′thrə-pə-lŏj′ĭ-kəl

referring to the study of human beings

> In a landmark **anthropological** study, Margaret Mead studied the social structure of tribes on the island of Samoa.

▶ *Related Words*

anthropologist (noun)   Judy MacDonald, an *anthropologist,* studies southeast Asian society in the United States.

anthropology (noun)   In the physical *anthropology* course, students examined fossils of early humans.

The field of *anthropology* studies the physical and social characteristics of human beings. Physical *anthropology* gives insight into human origins. Through cultural studies, we see how fundamental human needs for food, reproduction, and companionship are met. *Anthropologists* sometimes research exotic cultures, such as those of primitive tribes, by living with them and learning their language. They can also study more familiar environments, such as shopping malls, hospitals, and factories.

---

2. **misanthrope** (noun)   mĭs′ən-thrōp′

From Greek: *misein* (to hate) + *anthrop* (human)

a person who hates or distrusts other people

> The **misanthrope** viewed people as basically greedy.

▶ *Related Words*
misanthropic (adjective)   (mĭs′ən-thrŏp′ĭk)   *Misanthropic* people can make cruel remarks to others.

misanthropy (noun)   (mĭs-ăn′thrə-pē)   The boss showed his *misanthropy* by refusing to allow his workers any holidays.

Two famous literary characters exemplify *misanthropy*. Ebenezer Scrooge, created by Charles Dickens in the classic novel *A Christmas Carol*, mistreats his employees and wishes ill to everybody. He tries to make everyone miserable at Christmas time. Scrooge has become famous for his classic expression, "Bah, Humbug!" A more modern *misanthrope*, the Grinch, actually steals Christmas. The Grinch was created by the famous children's author Theodore Geisel, better known as Dr. Seuss.

---

3. **philanthropist** (noun)   fĭ-lăn′thrə-pĭst

From Greek: *philos* (loving) + *anthrop* (human)

one who wishes to help humanity; a person who makes large gifts to charity

> One **philanthropist,** David Rockefeller, has donated a million dollars to Manhattan's National Museum of American Indians.

▶ *Related Words*
philanthropic (adjective)   (fĭl′ən-thrŏp′ĭk)   The hospital named the new building in honor of the person who made the *philanthropic* gift.

philanthropy (noun)   Mexican workers who make money in the United States often demonstrate *philanthropy* by donating money to improve their home towns.

gen

4. **congenital** (adjective)   kən-jĕn′ə-təl

From Latin: *com-* (together; with) + *gen* (birth) (If something is *congenital,* you are born with it.)

existing at birth

> Surgery corrected the infant's **congenital** heart defect.

> According to recent studies, fingerprint patterns can often reveal **congenital** health problems.

naturally being a certain way; habitual

> He was a **congenital** liar who could not tell the truth, no matter how much pressure was put on him.

5. **genesis** (noun)   jĕn′ə-sĭs

From Greek: *gen* (birth) (*Genesis* meant "birth" or "origin" in ancient Greek.)

origin; beginning

> The **genesis** of writing is found in Sumerian figures of approximately 3500 B.C.

> Many scientists think that the **genesis** of our universe was an enormous explosion called the "big bang."

Genesis, the first book of the Bible, tells the story of a great flood that only Noah, his family, and two of each type of animal survived. Many other religions and cultures have tales of a large flood. In southern Mesopotamia (now largely Iraq), references to a flood are recorded on a stone tablet (dated at 2100 B.C.) and in the Babylonian Epic of Gilgamesh (about 700 B.C.). Other references are found in India, Burma, Australia, and among native American Indian tribes. Was there ever a great flood? In 1929, Sir Leonard Woolley, after exploring lower Mesopotamia, concluded that a widespread area had been badly flooded in about 3000 B.C.

NOTE: Sega Genesis is a computer system that starts, or originates, many popular video games.

6. **genocide** (noun)   jĕn′ə-sīd′

From Greek: *gen* (type) + Latin: *-cidium* (killing) (*Genos* meant "race" in ancient Greek, so *genocide* means "the killing of an entire race.")

the planned murder of an entire group

The **genocide** of Armenians during World War I resulted in over a million deaths.

The most horrible recent example of *genocide* occurred from 1939 to 1945, when the leader of Nazi Germany, Adolf Hitler, planned the destruction of all of Europe's Jews. This dreadful plan, often called the Holocaust, resulted in the deaths of over six million people. Another six million civilians were murdered in countries occupied by the Nazis because of their ethnic origins, beliefs, or resistance to Nazi oppression.

---

nom; nym

7. **nominal** (adjective)   nŏm′ə-nəl

From Latin: *nom* (name)

in name only

> Although Queen Elizabeth is the **nominal** ruler of England, the prime minister actually holds most of the power.

a very small amount

> The accountant did the charity's financial work for the **nominal** sum of $20 per year.

8. **pseudonym** (noun)   so͞o′də-nĭm′

From Greek: *pseudes* (false) + *nym* (name)

assumed name; pen name

> Stephen King has published successful novels under the **pseudonym** of Richard Bachman.

NOTE: The word *pseudonym* often refers to authors or artists. In contrast, *alias*, which usually refers to names assumed by criminals, has a negative connotation.

▶ *Common Phrase*
under the pseudonym of

Many celebrities have adopted *pseudonyms*. Can you match the real names and pseudonyms of the following?

1. Rodney Dangerfield
2. Chuck Norris
3. Sting

a. Pal
b. Jacob Cohen
c. Stanley Kirk Burrell

4. Lassie   d. Carlos Ray

5. Hammer   e. Gordon Sumner

(*Answers:* 1. b, 2. d, 3. e, 4. a, 5. c)

9. **renowned** (adjective) rĭ-nound′

famous; well-regarded

From Latin: *re-* (again) + *nom* (to name) (A person who is "named repeatedly" becomes famous.)

> **Renowned** Spanish opera star Placido Domingo has raised money for many worthy causes.
>
> Jamaica is **renowned** for its beautiful beaches and pleasant climate.

► *Related Word*
   renown (noun)   Jonas Salk won **renown** for developing a vaccine to prevent polio.

vit; viv

10. **viable** (adjective) vī′ə-bəl

From Latin: *vit* (life), becoming French *vie* (life)

capable of living; capable of success; workable

> Mosquito eggs remain **viable** for four years, awaiting enough rain to hatch.
>
> A second career has become a **viable** alternative to retirement.

11. **vital** (adjective) vī′təl

From Latin: *vit* (life)

referring to life

> The doctor measured her pulse, blood pressure, and other **vital** signs.

necessary; essential

> Endurance is **vital** to a champion swimmer.

lively; full of life; busy

> Seattle's **vital** downtown area attracts many tourists.

▶ *Common Phrase*
vital to

▶ *Related Word*
vitality (noun) (vī-tăl′ə-tē) The plumber's *vitality* enabled him to work long hours. (*Vitality* means "life energy.")

12. **vivacious** (adjective)   vĭ-vā′shəs

From Latin: *viv* (to live) (*Vivax* meant "lively.")

lively; full of spirit

> The girl's **vivacious** temperament and sense of fun made her popular at school.

▶ *Related Word*
vivacity (noun) (vĭ-văs′ə-tē) The *vivacity* of actress Jada Pinkett has enriched her roles in *A Different World* and *Menace II Society*.

Exercises

Part 1

■ Definitions

Complete each sentence in the left-hand column by choosing a word or phrase from the right-hand column. Use each choice only once.

1. A renowned person is ___d___ .	a. the murder of an entire group
	b. charitable
	c. a false name
2. Anthropology means ___i___ .	d. famous
3. Genesis is ___e___ .	e. a beginning
	f. a person who distrusts others
4. Something vital to a person is ___h___ .	g. workable
	h. lively

5. A viable idea is ___g___ .

6. A philanthropist is ___b___ .

7. A congenital condition

is ___j___ .

8. Genocide is ___a___ .

9. A pseudonym is ___c___ .

10. A person in nominal control

is ___i___ .

i. not really in power

j. present at birth

k. necessary

l. study of human beings

■ Meanings

Match each word element to its meaning. Use each choice only once.

1. nom, nym ___d___

2. vit, viv ___a___

3. gen ___c___

4. anthrop ___b___

a. life

b. human

c. birth; type

d. name

■ Words in Context

Complete each sentence with the word that fits best. Use each choice only once.

a. anthropological
b. misanthrope
c. philanthropist
d. congenital

e. genesis
f. genocide
g. nominal
h. pseudonym

i. renowned
j. viable
k. vital
l. vivacious

1. The _____ of agriculture dates back ten thousand years.

2. Some people are born with hemophilia, a(n) _____ condition that slows the ability of their blood to clot.

3. The _____ scientist Madame Curie gained fame for her experiments with uranium.

4. The company's president was only the _____ head of the company, since the vice president made all the decisions.

5. Theodore Geisel used the _____ Dr. Seuss for many of his books.

6. The _____ donated money to build a new student center.

7. The evil creatures from Mars planned the _____ of the entire human race.

8. Only a(n) _____ would turn away from this scene of human happiness.

9. The heart is a(n) _____ organ to the human body.

10. The small chick was not _____ , so it soon died.

■ *Using Related Words*

Complete each sentence by using a word from the group of related words above it. You may need to capitalize a word when you put it into a sentence. Use each choice only once.

1. anthropological, anthropologist

The _____ Colin Turnbull made an

_____ study of several African societies. He found that Pygmies lived in gentle harmony with nature, in a society with little violence. As hunters who depended on the forest, they came to respect the balance of natural life.

2. vivacious, vivacity

According to one of Aesop's fables, as a _____ girl walked to town with milk on her head, she thought of how the milk would make cream to buy eggs. The eggs would make chickens, and she could sell the chickens for a gown, which would attract a

rich husband. As she fantasized, her _____ over-
came her. She tossed her head and spilled the milk. From this story
comes the proverb "Don't count your chickens before they've
hatched."

3. misanthrope, misanthropic

In the ancient Greek classic the *Odyssey*, hero Odysseus has to

choose between two _____ monsters, Scylla, a
six-headed horror that eats people for lunch, and Charybdis, a
whirlpool that sucks in ships. Deciding that the less dangerous

_____ is Scylla, he loses only six men, rather than
his entire crew.

4. vital, vitality

In Greek mythology, the efforts of the hero Achilles were

_____ to the success of the Greeks over
Troy. At his birth, Achilles' mother, a goddess, wanted to make her
son immortal, so she dipped him in the River Styx to preserve his

_____ . Unfortunately, she held him by his heel,
which the protective water failed to touch. As battle raged in Troy,
an arrow struck Achilles in his heel, killing him. A point of weak-
ness that can be easily harmed is now called an "Achilles heel."

5. renown, renowned

When the legendary hero Odysseus went to fight in the Trojan war,

he entrusted the education of his son to the _____
tutor Mentor. In today's sports and business, a coach or adviser

of great _____ is often called a "mentor."

■ Say It Again

Each sentence in the following exercise contains two or three vocabulary
words. Read the sentence and then decide which of the three sentences
listed after it has nearly the same meaning.

_____   1. The renowned philanthropist had a congenital hearing problem.

    a. The lively donor developed a hearing problem.

    b. The energetic student was born with a hearing problem.

    c. The famous donor was born with a hearing problem.

_____   2. The genesis of genocide is in misanthropy.

    a. The end of the hatred of people is in ill will toward them.

    b. The beginning of the murder of people is in hatred of them.

    c. The aim of the bad feeling toward people is murder.

_____   3. It was vital that the spy take a pseudonym.

    a. It was inborn that the man took his name.

    b. It was important that the man take another name.

    c. It was a beginning when the spy took another name.

_____   4. The anthropologist was vivacious.

    a. The specialist in the study of humans was lively.

    b. The specialist in the study of humans was important.

    c. The specialist in the study of names was lively.

Prefixes and Name Words

Part 2

Part 2 of this chapter deals with words taken from names. The two prefixes presented also occur as names in Greek mythology. Four words using these prefixes and eight words taken directly from names are introduced.

pan- (all)

The prefix *pan-* is the Greek word for "all." It appears in two names in Greek mythology. Pan was the god of woods, fields, and shepherds. He had the lower body of a goat and the upper body of a man. He got his name "because he delighted all," wrote Homer. Pandora (*pan-*, all, + *dora*, gifts) was the first woman. The gods sent her to Earth and gave her a box that she was told not to open. When curiosity got the better of her, she disobeyed, and out flew all the world's troubles. Only Hope remained shut up in the box. (Like Eve in the Bible, Pandora was a woman blamed for causing all the world's problems.) The prefix *pan-* is used in such words as *pan-American*, which refers to all of America: North, South, and Central.

psych-; psycho- (mind; soul)

The Greek word *psyche* originally meant "breath" and thus means the soul or the spirit of a person. It is personified in Greek mythology as Psyche, a beautiful mortal, who was loved by Eros (or Cupid), the god of love. He visited her every night but told her never to look at him. One night, overcome by curiosity, Psyche held a lamp up to Eros as he slept. A drop of oil dripped on his shoulder, waking him, and he fled. Psyche searched frantically for Eros and performed many difficult tasks to win the favor of the gods. As a reward, the gods made her immortal and allowed her to marry Eros. In this story, Psyche, with her beauty and dedication, symbolizes the soul. When she is made immortal, Psyche shows how the human soul finally goes to heaven. In modern words, *psych-* usually means "mind" rather than "soul." *Psychobiology* is the study of the biology of the mind. In some words, *psych* functions as a root. Perhaps you have taken a class in *psychology,* the study of the mind.

Words to Learn

Part 2

pan-

13. **pandemonium** (noun)   păn′də-mō′nē-əm

   From Greek: *pan-* (all) + *daimōn* (demon)

   chaos, wild disorder, and noise

   > **Pandemonium** broke loose when 300,000 people fled Rwanda in one week.

   In John Milton's poem *Paradise Lost*, published in 1667, *Pandaemonium* was the principal city of Hell, where "all the demons" lived.

14. **panorama** (noun)   păn′ə-răm′-ə

From Greek: *pan-* (all) + *horan* (to see)

a clear view over a wide area

> The view from a hilltop in Carmel, California was a breathtaking **panorama** of the Pacific Ocean.

a wide-ranging survey

> In her first lecture, the professor presented a **panorama** of the Middle Ages.

▶ *Related Word*
> **panoramic** (adjective)   The office window displayed a *panoramic* view of the Denver skyline.

NOTE: Panorama can refer either to a physical view of something or a "view" in one's mind, as in a wide-ranging presentation of a subject.

psych-

15. **psyche** (noun)   sī′kē

From Greek: *psych-* (soul)

mind; soul; mental state

> Mozart's beautiful music gives no clue to his troubled **psyche.**

> Psychologists believe that the human **psyche** is governed by primitive needs for food and love.

16. **psychosomatic** (adjective)   sī′kō-sō-măt′ĭk

From Greek: *psych-* (mind; soul) + *soma* (body)

referring to physical disorders that are caused by the mind

> Parents can develop **psychosomatic** stomach problems from the stress of raising teenagers.

Name Words

17. **boycott** (verb, noun)   boi′kŏt′

to refuse to use or buy something as an act of protest (verb)

> The official golf tournament decided to **boycott** country clubs that did not admit minorities.

the act of boycotting (noun)

> A **boycott** of grapes helped migrant workers to unionize.

The Irish potato famine of the mid 1800s had made farmers so poor that a law was passed in 1881 to reduce rents. Captain Charles C. Boycott, a cruel English land agent, angered the Irish people by insisting on the old payments, thus forcing many farmers out of business. In response, the Irish Land League *boycotted* him by refusing to deal with him in any way.

---

18. **chauvinism** (noun)   shō′vən-ĭz′əm

prejudiced devotion to a group or country

> Jim's **chauvinism** was so strong that any bad word about his native country would anger him.

> Men of the primitive Yanomamo tribe are so **chauvinistic** that they feel women are too clumsy to make pottery.

▶ *Related Words*
   chauvinist (noun)   Michael angered us because he was a male *chauvinist*.

   chauvinistic (adjective)   The city of Sacramento helped to eliminate *chauvinistic* labels by renaming a "manhole" as a "maintenance hole."

NOTE: The commonly used term *male chauvinism* refers to the view that men are superior to women, and a *male chauvinist* shows by his words and behavior that he shares this view.

Nicholas Chauvin was a legendary lieutenant in the French army who was extremely devoted to his general, Napoleon Bonaparte. Even after Napoleon's defeat, Chauvin continued in his blind loyalty. Such excessive devotion is now called *chauvinism*.

---

19. **gargantuan** (adjective)   gär-găn′chōō-ən

huge; immense

> Steve's **gargantuan** breakfast consisted of a three-pound steak and a dozen eggs.

> Tyrannosaurus Rex was a **gargantuan** dinosaur.

Gargantua appears in *Gargantua and Pantagruel*, a book by the French author François Rabelais, published in 1532–62. Gargantua was an enormous giant with an appetite to match. At one point, he ate five people in a salad! He arranged his hair with a comb nine hundred feet long. Right after his birth, he cried out, "Drink, drink!" The book may be a satire (something that makes fun) of Francis I, the French king. Rabelais led a colorful life, which is reflected in the vitality of his book's hero.

20. **martial** (adjective)   mär′shəl

referring to war or soldiers

> Dressed in armor and carrying a sword, the knight had a splendid **martial** appearance.

> Marina learned to defend herself in her tae-kwon-do **martial** arts class.

▶ *Common Phrase*
martial law   The dictator imposed *martial law*. (Martial law is rule by military authorities imposed on a civilian population.)

Mars was the Roman god of war, after whom the month of March is named. His name is also honored as the name of a planet, Mars, which appears to be faintly red, suggesting the color of blood. Each of the names of planets in our solar system is named for a Greek or Roman god. Closest to the sun is *Mercury*, the quickly rotating planet named for the messenger god. *Venus*, named for the god of love, is followed by *Earth* and *Mars*. *Jupiter* is named for the king of the gods. *Saturn* is Jupiter's father, and *Uranus* is his grandfather. *Neptune* is ruler of the sea. Finally, *Pluto*, the planet farthest from the sun, honors the gloomy god of the underworld, the region of the dead.

21. **maverick** (noun)   măv′ər-ĭk

an independent-minded person who does not conform or adhere to rules

> Ross Perot is a **maverick** who opposed both Democrats and Republicans in the 1992 U.S. Presidential election.

In the 1800s, cattlemen began branding their calves to indicate ownership. Samuel Maverick, a Texan rancher of independent spirit, refused to follow this custom. This annoyed the other ranchers, who called all unbranded cattle *mavericks*. Maverick led a colorful life, fighting duels, spending time in prison, and serving in the Texas legislature.

---

22. **odyssey** (noun) ŏd′ĭ-sē

a long and adventurous journey

> People have made **odysseys** to the United States in over-crowded, dangerous boats.

> During his spiritual **odyssey,** Bob sought guidance from religious leaders and philosophers.

The *Odyssey,* a classic ancient Greek poem, details the journey of Odysseus (also known as Ulysses) home from the Trojan wars. His adventures include a shipwreck, a visit to the underworld, the irresistible songs of the dangerous sirens, and a choice between meeting one of two monsters, Scylla and Charybdis (mentioned earlier in this chapter). Since then, an intense physical or spiritual journey has been called an *odyssey* in honor of this epic poem by Homer.

---

23. **quixotic** (adjective) kwĭk-sŏt′ĭk

noble, but not practical; having unreachable ideals

> We admired the mayor's **quixotic** behavior in defending an unpopular cause that he knew was right.

Miguel de Cervantes published his classic novel *Don Quixote* in 1605. In the book, an old man, Don Quixote, decides to become a wandering knight and does noble but strange deeds that no one quite understands. For example, he duels with a windmill that he thinks is a giant. He mistakes an inn for a castle and a peasant girl for a noble lady. His squire (helper), Sancho Panza, sees how ridiculous all of this is, but remains loyal to his master.

Although *Don Quixote* was originally written in Spanish, many of its famous phrases are used in modern-day English. These include "in a pickle," "too much of a good thing," "a wink of sleep," "a stone's throw," "smell a rat," "honesty is the best policy," "turn over a new leaf," and "faint heart never won a fair lady."

24. **spartan** (adjective)   spär′tn

lacking in comfort; requiring self-discipline

His **spartan** routine included walking ten miles each day.

The professional football players were annoyed when they had to stay at a **spartan** college dorm rather than at a luxurious hotel.

Exercises

Part 2

■ *Definitions*

Complete each sentence in the left-hand column by choosing a word or phrase from the right-hand column. Use each choice only once.

1. Chauvinism is __c__ .

2. Gargantuan is __k__ .

3. A maverick is __f__ .

4. A psyche is __l__ .

5. Psychosomatic illness has __b__ .

6. An odyssey is __j__ .

7. Pandemonium is __d__ .

8. To boycott is __a__ .

9. A quixotic person is __h__ .

10. A spartan life is _____ .

a. not to buy or use

b. a mental cause

c. prejudiced devotion

d. confusion

e. without comforts

f. an independently minded person

g. warlike

h. idealistic

i. a wide view

j. a journey

k. huge

l. a mind or mental state

■ *Meanings*

Match each word element to its meaning. Use each choice only once.

1. pan- __b__

2. psych- __a__

a. mind; soul

b. all

■ *Words in Context*

Complete each sentence with the word that fits best. Use each choice only once.

a. panorama   e. boycott   i. maverick
b. pandemonium   f. chauvinism   j. odyssey
c. psyche   g. gargantuan   k. quixotic
d. psychosomatic   h. martial   l. spartan

1. The ____g____ monster held three ships in one hand.

2. The soldier was tried by the army in a ____h____ court.

3. In Lu's _____ across the 8,000 miles of Russia, she traveled through eleven time zones.

4. The _____ man defended his idealistic position.

5. People decided to _____ e _____ the store until it lowered its unfair prices.

6. The book presented a(n) _____ of major world religions.

7. Lan's _____ headaches disappeared when she got a good job.

8. The riot caused _____ in the city.

9. The political _____ refused to follow the policies of his party.

10. Scott had trouble adjusting to the ____ _____ existence in the lumber camp because he was uncomfortable.

■ *Using Related Words*

Complete each sentence by using a word or phrase from the group of related words or phrases above it. You may need to capitalize a word when you put it into a sentence. Use each choice only once.

1. panorama, panoramic

   Looking down from the top of the Grand Canyon, one can see a

   _____ panorama of rock and river below. The

   _____ panoramic view is an example of the wonderful sights of Colorado, Arizona, and Nevada.

2. psyche, psychosomatic, psychosomatically

   Does the _____ govern the body? Studies have found that people who experience tragedy tend to become ill. Are

   these illnesses _____ caused? If so, discussing

the _____ roots of the illness may help the sufferer.

3. chauvinism, chauvinists, chauvinistic

Football aficionados are often _____ toward their home teams. One's opinion on whether the 49ers or the Giants is a better football team often depends on whether one lives in San Francisco or New York. _____ from San Francisco will choose the 49ers, and the _____ of New Yorkers will make them root for the Giants.

4. martial, martial law

In some nations, a group of soldiers will seize power and declare _____ . However, many such governments have returned to civil rule. People are often afraid of the unlimited powers of a _____ government.

■ *Say It Again*

Each sentence below contains two or three vocabulary words. Read the sentence and then decide which of the three sentences listed after it has nearly the same meaning.

____   1. From the top of the gargantuan mountain, the panorama included our spartan hotel.

   a. From the top of the small mountain, the view included our luxurious hotel.

   b. From the top of the large mountain, the view included our uncomfortable hotel.

   c. From the journey on the large mountain, the view included our large hotel.

____   2. The quixotic maverick decided to boycott all restaurants that did not recycle their waste.

   a. The large idealist decided to do a study of recycling.

    b. The idealistic nonconformist decided not to eat at restaurants that did not recycle.

    c. The sick conformist decided to make a mess at all restaurants that did not recycle.

_____   3. Chauvinistic feelings seem to be part of the psyche of a patriot.

    a. Idealistic feelings seem to be part of the journey toward being a patriot.

    b. Nonconformist feelings seem to be part of the illness of a patriot.

    c. Prejudiced feelings seem to be part of the mental state of a patriot.

_____   4. The martial exercises ended in pandemonium.

    a. The warlike exercises ended in disorder.

    b. The psychological exercises ended in a spiritual journey.

    c. The long exercises ended in mental illness.

Chapter Exercises

■ Practicing Strategies: New Words from Word Elements

See how your knowledge of roots and prefixes can help you understand new words. Complete each sentence with the word that seems to fit best. Use each choice only once. You may need to capitalize some words.

a. anthrogenesis	e. nomenclature	i. psychopath
b. genealogy	f. pan-American	j. rename
c. generation	g. pandemic	k. revive
d. homogenize	h. psychodrama	l. vivid

1. In _____ , acting is used to solve problems of the mind.

2. _____ is the study of the origin of human beings.

3. The word _____ refers to all of America.

4. When referring to plants and animals, scholars often use scientific

   _____ .

5. Since -*logy* means "study of," _____ is the study of your heredity, or the family into which you were born.

6. A worldwide epidemic of a disease is _____ .

7. The root *path* can mean "sick," so a person with a sick mind is a(n)

   _____ .

8. The prefix *homo-* means "same," so to _____ milk is to make it the same type, or mixture, throughout.

9. When people faint and then awaken, they are said to _____ , or "live again."

10. A picture may be so _____ that it appears to be living.

■ *Practicing Strategies: Combining Context Clues and Word Elements*

Combining the strategies of context clues and word elements is a good way to figure out unknown words. In the following sentences, each italicized word contains a word element that you have studied in this chapter. Using the meaning of the word element and the context of the sentence, make an intelligent guess about the meaning of the italicized word. Your instructor may ask you to check the meaning in your dictionary after you have finished.

1. The scientists were observing the behavior of the tigers in the *vivarium*.

   Vivarium means _____

   _____ .

2. It is a *misnomer* to call only citizens of the United States "Americans," for America consists of North, Central, and South America.

   Misnomer means _____ .

3. A *psychosis* is a serious illness.

Psychosis means _____ .

4. Conditions of poverty can *engender* criminal behavior.

Engender means _____ .

5. It would be difficult to find a *panacea* for all the problems of humanity.

Panacea means _____ .

■ *Companion Words*

Complete each sentence with the word that fits best. Choose your answers from the words below. You may use each word more than once.

Choices: of, for, to

1. Roberta Streeter performs under the pseudonym _____ Bobbie Gentry.

2. Vitamins are vital _____ health.

3. Mother Teresa is renowned _____ her work with the poor.

4. The boycott _____ automatic weapons greatly reduced sales.

5. Ilya rented his apartment for the nominal sum _____ $30.

6. The genesis _____ the steam engine dates back to the Greeks.

■ *Writing with Your Words*

This exercise will give you practice in writing effective sentences that use the vocabulary words. Each sentence is started for you. Complete it with an interesting phrase that also indicates the meaning of the italicized word.

1. On our *odyssey,* we _____

_____ .

2. A *gargantuan* workload might include _____

_____ .

3. It is *vital* that _____

_____ .

4. A *vivacious* teenager _____

_____ .

5. Your plan is not *viable,* so _____

_____ .

6. *Spartan* living conditions _____

_____ .

7. *Pandemonium* broke loose when _____

_____ .

8. The *nominal* ruler _____

_____ .

9. A *pseudonym* I would like to use _____

_____ .

10. The *quixotic* man _____

_____ .

Passage

The Greek Myth of Winter

In modern times, science has explained the causes of storms, floods, earthquakes, and disease, but ancient people were awed by these mysterious events. Perhaps to gain a sense of control, they created tales about the world around them. **(1)** Since humans are **congenitally** self-centered, it was natural for ancient people to assume that the forces driving nature were just like themselves. Stories were told of gods who ate, loved, and hated just as we do, but on a larger scale. **(2)** Because these gods had

gargantuan powers, their smallest wish could mean disaster or good fortune for all the Earth. A **misanthropic** god might send deadly storms; a **philanthropic** one might share the secrets of fire and food.

(3) One ancient Greek tale of humanlike gods deals with the **genesis** of winter. **(4)** The legend blames it on a common problem of the human **psyche,** a mother-in-law's jealousy of her daughter's husband.

According to the ancient Greeks, the Earth was once a warm, green paradise where the goddess Demeter provided summer throughout the year. **(5)** But one day, Persephone, Demeter's beautiful and **vivacious** daughter, wandered away from her friends to explore a flowered field. Unfortunately, Hades, the god of the underworld, was visiting the Earth and enjoying a **panoramic** view of the very same place. With one look at Persephone, Hades instantly fell in love. Unable to control himself, he carried her off to the underworld and made her his bride.

(6) Pandemonium broke loose when word of Hades' crime reached the other gods. Demeter frantically tried to get her daughter back, begging Zeus, king of the gods, to order her return. **(7)** But although Zeus was **renowned** for his power, **(8)** Hades, a **maverick** who resisted all control, refused to return Persephone.

In her desperation, Demeter forgot to provide the Earth with the warmth and sunshine **vital** to growing crops, and the world was plunged into winter. Plants began to die one by one, and when no **viable** crops were left, humans faced starvation. **(9)** Through her personal sadness, Demeter was causing the **genocide** of the human race. Zeus appealed to Hades, who finally agreed to let Persephone return home, as long as she had not eaten anything.

What had Persephone been doing while Demeter was trying to release her? **(10)** Sitting unhappily in the underworld, she had led a **spartan** existence, refusing all the luxuries that Hades offered. She had eaten no food—except for seven pomegranate seeds. Alas! Persephone had eaten only a **nominal** amount, but she had eaten. Hades did not have to let her go.

Zeus and Demeter quickly thought of another arrangement. For nine months of the year, Persephone would live with her mother, and for three months she would live with Hades. Just as Persephone's life was divided, Demeter decreed that for nine months the earth would have warm weather, and for three months it would have winter. Although this arrangement was not perfect, it was a relief from endless winter.

And that is how, according to the ancient Greeks, winter began.

■ *Exercise*

Each numbered sentence below corresponds to a sentence in the Passage. Fill in the letter of the choice that makes the sentence mean the same thing as its corresponding sentence in the Passage.

1. Humans are _____ self-centered.
   a. naturally   b. usually   c. fortunately   d. horribly

2. These gods had _____ powers.
   a. evil   b. mysterious   c. great   d. wonderful

3. One ancient Greek tale deals with the _____ of winter.
   a. hunger   b. coldness   c. problems   d. beginning

4. The legend blames it on a common problem of the human _____ .
   a. family   b. psychology   c. terror   d. loneliness

5. Persephone was Demeter's beautiful and _____ daughter.
   a. innocent   b. careless   c. young   d. lively

6. _____ broke loose when word of Hades' crime reached the other gods.
   a. Punishment   b. Disorder   c. Revenge   d. Sadness

7. Zeus was _____ for his power.
   a. happy   b. jealous   c. famous   d. crazy

8. Hades was a(n) _____ who resisted all control.
   a. independent individual   b. strong individual
   c. clever individual   d. romantic individual

9. Demeter was causing the _____ of the human race.
   a. death   b. suffering   c. sadness   d. hunger

10. She had led a(n) _____ existence.
    a. sad   b. uncomfortable   c. married   d. lonely

■ Discussion Questions

1. What reasons explain why the Greeks thought of their gods as being like humans, but on a larger scale?

2. Was Zeus's power limited? Explain your answer.

3. Describe a human situation that would bring forth the same types of emotions that Demeter felt.

◀ **ENGLISH IDIOMS**

Body Words

Since this chapter concerns people and their names, the idioms presented here all deal with the human body. Many such idioms use the concept of cold. For example, to *give people the cold shoulder* means to ignore them. When people get *cold feet*, they become nervous, and just before they plan to do something, they may refuse to do it, or *back out*. When a man becomes nervous, something *freezes his blood, makes his blood run cold*, or *makes his hair stand on end*. When people are made to wait, they *cool their heels*.

People who put forth an opinion that is completely wrong, or not supported by evidence, *don't have a leg to stand on*. If you listen to another person, you *lend an ear*. If, on the other hand, you do not listen carefully, information goes *in one ear and out the other*.

To *raise eyebrows* is to shock people. When a person is embarrassed or shamed by a failure, that person *loses face*.

Long ago in China, the emperor was considered a god. To mention his body or health in any way was forbidden, since it implied that he was human. People who made this mistake had their feet pulled upward and forced into their mouths, remaining in this position for several hours. Today, to *put your foot in your mouth* means to say something that should not be said.

This man "puts his foot in his mouth."

This man "lends an ear."

7

Word Elements: Movement

Many word elements originally referred to physical movement. Each of the six roots and two prefixes in this chapter describes actions such as pulling and turning. These word elements combine with others to form many widely used English words.

Chapter Strategy: Word Elements: Movement

Chapter Words:

Part 1

duct	abduction	*stat*	stature
	conducive		status quo
	deduction		staunch
ject	dejected	*ten*	abstain
	eject		tenable
	jettison		tenacious

Part 2

tract	distraught	*circum-*	circumscribe
	extract		circumspect
	retract		circumvent
vert	adversary	*trans-*	transcend
	inadvertently		transformation
	perverse		transitory

Did You Know?

How Did Inventions Get Their Names?

The last three hundred years have been a time of great progress in the fields of invention and discovery. If we were put back on Earth in 1700, we would hardly recognize the way of life. Travel, food, and medicine were vastly different from what we experience today.

People traveled on foot or used horses, on unpaved roads with deep ruts. A twenty-mile trip from an English country village to London took all day. Today the same trip takes less than half an hour by automobile or subway.

Because there were no stoves or refrigerators, food was prepared differently in the 1700s. People cooked over open fires and just hoped that the temperature would be suitable. Meat could not be kept by cooling or freezing. It was either eaten immediately or preserved as sausage or salted meat. In Europe and America, pepper and other spices were very valuable, for they were used to keep meat from spoiling. Nevertheless, people sometimes had to eat rotten meat.

Medical science in the 1700s was primitive. There were few methods of disease prevention and control. In fact, fewer than half of all children survived to adulthood. Operations were often carried out by barbers, who were unclean and had few healing techniques. Doctors treated sick patients by applying leeches to suck the "bad blood" from them. Medical historians now think that such "bleeding" caused George Washington's death.

Society has made great advances since those times. Today, science and technology have greatly improved our travel, diet, and health. Automobiles, trains, and airplanes provide rapid transportation. We use freezers and refrigerators to preserve our food and stoves to cook it with precision. Many diseases have been controlled, and the average life expectancy has almost doubled.

The astonishing number of inventions in the last three hundred years has both improved the quality of life and brought many new words into English as each new device received a name. Often, scientists and inventors have composed these names from ancient Greek and Latin word elements. This tradition started in 1611 when a Greek poet suggested a name for Galileo's new invention, using two Greek word elements, *tele-* (far) and *-scope* (look). The invention is called the *telescope.*

Modern inventors continue to create names from ancient Greek and Latin word elements. This makes a knowledge of classical word elements more useful than ever.

The following inventions and discoveries have made your life easier.

Each contains at least one classical prefix, root, or suffix. You will be studying some of these elements in this book.

Invention	Classical Word Elements	Approximate Date of Invention
microscope	*micro-* (small) + *-scope* (look)	1665
antiseptic	*anti-* (against) + *sepsis* (rotten)	1745
photography	*photo-* (light) + *-graph* (written)	1780
anesthetic	*an-* (without) + *aisthēsis* (feeling)	1850
bicycle	*bi-* (two) + *kuklos* (wheel)	1862
phonograph	*phono-* (sound) + *-graph* (written)	1875
telephone	*tele-* (far) + *-phone* (sound)	1880
automobile	*auto-* (self) + *movēre* (to move)	1885
refrigerator	*re-* (again) + *frigus* (cold)	1890
television	*tele-* (far) + *visus* (sight)	1925
computer	*com-* (together) + *-putāre* (to reckon)	1940
microwave	*micro-* (small) + *wave*	1963

Learning Strategy

Word Elements: Movement

Each of the word elements in this chapter describes a type of movement, such as leading *(duct)*, pulling *(tract)*, and turning *(vert)*. A large number of words are formed from classical word elements that refer to movement. Every one of these elements forms at least fifty English words, so learning them will help you increase your vocabulary word power.

Element	Meaning	Origin	Function	Chapter Words
				Part 1
duc, duct	lead	Latin	root	abduction, conducive, deduction
ject	throw	Latin	root	dejected, eject, jettison
stans, stat	standing; placed	Latin; Greek	root	stature, status quo, staunch
tain, ten	hold	Latin	root	abstain, tenable, tenacious
				Part 2
tract	pull	Latin	root	distraught, extract, retract

vers, vert	turn	Latin	root	adversary, inadvertently, perverse
circum-	around	Latin	prefix	circumscribe, circumspect, circumvent
trans-	across	Latin	prefix	transcend, transformation, transitory

Words formed from movement word elements often have interesting histories. Many started out describing physical movement but over the years gained abstract, nonphysical meanings. Although these words may no longer describe movement itself, the elements in them will still give you hints about their meanings.

The word element *ject* (throw) illustrates how word elements and meanings relate. Two *ject* words in this chapter consist of a prefix and a root. If you think about the meanings of the word elements below, you will get an imaginative physical picture of each word's meaning.

The word elements *de-* (down) and *ject* (throw) make *deject,* or "throw down." The word *dejected* actually means depressed, or how we feel when our mood is "thrown down."

The word elements *e-* (out of) and *ject* (throw) make *eject,* or "throw out of." When a candy bar is *ejected* from a vending machine, it is "thrown out."

Circumstance is another word in which the elements give us a mental picture. It combines two word elements presented in this chapter, the prefix *circum-* and the root *stans. Circumstances* are things that are "standing" *(stans)* "around" *(circum-)* an event; in other words, they surround it. Circumstances that might "stand around" and keep you from studying are noise in the library or a friend who wants to talk!

Word Roots

Part 1

The four word roots of movement presented in Part 1 are discussed below.

duc, duct (lead)

This root appears in many different words. The *ducts* in a building lead air and water to different rooms. A *conductor* leads an orchestra so that all the players stay together. (*Con-* means "together.") European noblemen are called *dukes* because long ago their ancestors led troops into battle.

ject (throw)

This root appears as *jet,* a stream of water or air thrown into space. *Ject* can also represent the idea of throwing rather than the physical action itself. Although the word elements of *reject* actually mean "to throw back," the word itself has the related but nonphysical meaning of "not to accept."

stans, stat (standing; placed)

This root indicates a lack of movement, as in *statue. Stans, stat* can also refer to standing in an imaginative, nonphysical way. For example, one's *status* is one's "standing" or "placement" in society.

tain, ten (hold)

This root can mean "hold" in a physical sense; a pan *contains,* or holds, baked beans. This word root can also mean "hold" in a nonphysical sense. For example, a *tenet* is a belief that somebody "holds."

Words to Learn

Part 1

duc, duct

1. **abduction** (noun)   ăb-dŭk′shən

   From Latin: *ab-* (away) + *duct* (lead)

   kidnapping

   > The **abduction** of children is a serious problem in the United States.

   ▶ *Related Word*
   abduct (verb)   The terrorists tried to *abduct* the diplomat.

2. **conducive** (adjective)   kən-do͞o′sĭv

   From Latin: *con-* (together) + *duc* (lead)

   contributing to; leading to

   > The informal atmosphere of the Student Lounge was **conducive** to making new friends.

   > Candlelight and soft music are **conducive** to romance.

   ▶ *Common Phrase*
   conducive to

3. **deduction** (noun)   dĭ-dŭk′shən

From Latin: *de-* (away) + *duct* (lead)

something subtracted from a total

> The monthly **deduction** in Pat's paycheck covered her health insurance.

a conclusion drawn from evidence

> After I got sick each time I ate chocolate, I drew the **deduction** that this food was causing my illness.

▶ *Related Words*
deductive (adjective)   The mathematician's well-developed *deductive* skills enabled her to solve difficult problems.

deduce (verb)   (dĭ-do͞os′)   The detective was able to *deduce* the criminal's identity.

Sherlock Holmes, a fictional English detective created by Sir Arthur Conan Doyle, is a master of *deductive* reasoning. Holmes amazes his companions by drawing brilliant conclusions from the smallest bits of evidence. The famous, but fictional, Holmes was based on a real-life Scottish doctor, Joe Bell, who was an expert in diagnosing disease from little evidence.

---

ject

4. **dejected** (adjective)   dĭ-jĕkt′əd

From Latin: *de-* (down) + *ject* (throw)

depressed; downcast

> Albert was **dejected** after he failed the exam for his driver's license.

▶ *Related Word*
dejection (noun)   After their team lost the Super Bowl, the fans were in a state of *dejection*.

5. **eject** (verb)   ĭ-jĕkt′

From Latin: *ex-* (out) + *ject* (throw)

to force to leave; to expel

> The usher **ejected** the noisy person from the theater.

We put in fifty-five cents, pushed the button, and watched the machine **eject** a bag of potato chips.

▶ *Related Word*

ejection (noun)   Seconds before the plane crashed, an automatic *ejection* device saved the pilot.

6. **jettison** (verb)   jĕt′-ĭ-sĕn

From Latin: *ject* (throw)

To throw out forcefully; to throw overboard

The lifeboat was able to hold two more sailors after we **jettisoned** the extra supplies.

The television network **jettisoned** the unpopular talk show.

NOTE: Jettison can also apply to nonphysical things, as in to "jettison an unworkable plan."

stans, stat

7. **stature**   stăch′ər

level of achievement and honor

Winston Churchill achieved great **stature** as the prime minister of Great Britain during World War II.

Brazilian Milton Nascimento is a singer of great **stature.**

physical height

Despite his short **stature,** Tyrone "Mugsy" Bogues's remarkable athletic ability enables him to play professional basketball.

8. **status quo** (noun)   stā′təs kwō′

From Latin: *stat* (standing, placed) + *quo* (in which), making "the condition in which"

the existing conditions; present state of things

The young idealist challenged old-fashioned politicians to change the **status quo.**

9. **staunch** (adjective)   stônch

From Latin: *stans* (standing), through the French word *estanche* (watertight, firm) (Something *staunch* stands firm and strong.)

faithful; firmly supporting

Athlete Jackie Joyner-Kersee is a **staunch** supporter of her home town, East St. Louis, Illinois.

healthy; strong

My **staunch** constitution can withstand cold easily.

▶ *Related Word*
staunchness (noun)   The *staunchness* of a friend's support helped me during my difficult divorce.

tain, ten

10. **abstain** (verb)   ăb-stān′

From Latin: *abs-* (away) + *tain* (hold) ("To hold away from" is not to do something.)

not to do something by choice

My mother **abstains** from smoking whenever she visits my grandmother.

not to vote

Seven people voted yes, seven voted no, and seven **abstained.**

▶ *Common Phrase*
abstain from

▶ *Related Words*
abstinence (noun)   (ăb′stə-nəns)   Members of Alcoholics Anonymous practice *abstinence* from all alcoholic beverages. (*Abstinence* usually refers to self-denial.)

abstention (noun)   (ăb-stən′shən)   China's *abstention* allowed the resolution to pass in the United Nations. (*Abstention* usually refers to voting.)

11. **tenable** (adjective)   tən′ə-bəl

From Latin: *ten* (hold)

capable of being defended; logical

Although germ theory was once laughed at, it is now considered a **tenable** explanation of how diseases spread.

The army general chose a **tenable** position for his troops to defend.

▶ *Related Words*
tenability (noun)   Trung convinced others that his argument had *tenability.*

untenable (adjective)   The theory that the world is flat is now considered *untenable*. (Untenable is the opposite of tenable.)

When the great Italian scientist Galileo (1564–1642) proposed that the Earth rotated around the sun, many thought that his theory was *untenable*. It seemed ridiculous that the Earth, with its heavy mass, could move around the sun, which appeared so small in the sky. Most people believed the Earth was the center of the universe. However, as more evidence accumulated, it became clear that Galileo's theory had great *tenability*. Today, it is accepted as scientific fact.

---

12. **tenacious** (adjective)   tə-nā′shəs

From Latin: *ten* (hold)

firmly holding; gripping; retaining

> The ship's captain kept a **tenacious** grasp on the wheel throughout the storm.

> The law enforcement official's **tenacious** investigation revealed the identity of the murderer.

▶ *Related Words*

> **tenaciousness** (noun)   Winston Churchill's *tenaciousness* in believing that Nazi Germany was a threat helped prepare England for World War II.

> **tenacity** (noun)   (tə-năs′ə-tē)   The *tenacity* of the police played a large part in solving the crime.

The *tenacious* Aung San family has fought for political freedom in Myanmar (formerly Burma) for many years. The father, General Aung San, was a famous independence leader. Daughter Aung San Suu Kui, under house arrest since 1989, has been repeatedly attacked by the country's news media. Although the military leaders would like her to leave the country, she *tenaciously* refuses, preferring to serve as a symbol of freedom. In 1991, she won the Nobel Prize for Peace.

Exercises

Part 1

■ *Definitions*

Match each word in the left-hand column with a definition from the right-hand column. Use each choice only once.

1. stature ___l___   a. something thrown forward
2. deduction ___g___   b. kidnapping
3. staunch _____   c. gripping
4. tenable ___f___   d. contributing to
5. conducive ___d___   e. depressed
6. status quo ___i___   f. logical
7. dejected ___e___   g. something subtracted
8. abduction ___b___   h. to throw overboard
9. jettison ___h___   i. the present state of things
10. tenacious _____   j. faithful
                                      k. not to do
                                      l. level of achievement

■ Meanings

Match each word root to its meaning. Use each choice only once.

1. duc, duct ___b___   a. hold
2. tain, ten ___a___   b. lead
3. ject ___c___   c. throw
4. stans, stat ___d___   d. standing; placed

■ Words in Context

Complete each sentence with the word that fits best. Use each choice only once.

a. abduction   e. ejection   i. staunch
b. conducive   f. jettison   j. abstain
c. deduction   g. stature   k. tenable
d. dejected   h. status quo   l. tenacity

1. The kidnappers were captured and convicted for the _____ .

2. The wise minister had great _____ in her community.

3. To avoid a fire, the crew of the airplane had to _____ its fuel.

4. Because of his _____ , my uncle never gives up on a crossword puzzle until he has filled in every word.

5. Defense of the city was no longer _____ , so the army surrendered.

6. Lack of sleep is not _____ to feeling energetic.

7. It is safest to _____ abstain _____ from alcohol before driving.

8. If all money were divided equally among people, there would be quite

   a change in the _____ .

9. The woman became _____ when she realized she could not possibly support her children.

10. The man took a(n) _____ for business expenses on his income taxes.

■ *Using Related Words*

Complete each sentence by using a word from the group of related words above it. You may need to capitalize a word when you put it into a sentence. Use each choice only once.

1. tenable, untenable

   During the Middle Ages, people believed that attitudes and general health were controlled by four types of "humors": choleric (angry), melancholic (sad), sanguine (happy), and phlegmatic (easygoing).

   Scientific evidence has shown that this theory is _____ . However, the theory that mental states can affect physical health

   is considered _____ by today's physicians.

2. staunch, staunchness

Hitler's strong German army easily overran most of Europe in

World War II (1939–1945). But it met _____ resistance in Russia. Although the Germans blockaded Leningrad for
1,000 days, starving much of the population, the people refused

to surrender. The _____ of their resistance gave
Hitler his first major setback.

3. abstain, abstentions, abstinence

Nonsmoking areas have been hotly debated in our town. Some peo-

ple feel that everyone should _____ from smoking
in public buildings. However, it is difficult for many smokers to

practice _____ throughout their working hours.
When our town council met to debate this issue, several representa-

tives were undecided, so there were many _____
among the votes.

4. deductive, deduce, deduction

Dorothy Sayers, one of England's leading detective writers, created
the aristocratic Lord Peter Wimsey. Lord Peter's rather silly man-

ner hides a _____ mind of great brilliance. In
The Nine Tailors, for example, a man is found dead in the bell
tower of a church. There are few clues to help Lord Peter

_____ the identity of the murderer. Yet he is able

to make the correct _____ about the man's death.

5. ejection, eject

Should guards have the right to _____ from a
public gathering people who are making nasty comments? On the

one hand, their _____ helps keep meetings or-
derly. On the other hand, such people may only be exercising the
right to speak their minds.

■ *True or False?*

Each of the following statements contains one or more words from this section. Read each sentence carefully and then indicate whether you think it is probably true or probably false.

_____   1. Deductions increase amounts.

_____   2. Abstention from liquids would make you thirsty.

_____   3. Dejection is a positive feeling.

_____   4. A world-famous scientist is a person of great stature.

_____   5. A rocket that ejects a missile throws off the missile.

_____   6. Tenable opinions are ridiculous.

_____   7. People with tenacious opinions are likely to change them.

_____   8. A staunch friend would help people abduct you.

_____   9. Preserving the status quo is conducive to change.

_____   10. When company officials jettisoned the unprofitable division, they decided to keep it.

Words to Learn

Part 2

Part 2 continues with more word elements that show movement: first, two additional roots, *tract* (pull) and *vert* (turn); and then two prefixes, *circum-* (around) and *trans-* (across).

tract (pull)

Tractor, a machine the pulls plows and other equipment through the earth, is an example of a common word formed from this root. Like many movement roots, *tract* is used in words that no longer carry the physical meaning of *pull.* For example, when we *distract* someone's attention, we "pull it away" in a mental rather than in a physical sense.

vers, vert (turn)

Vert can mean "turn" in a direct sense. When we *invert* a cup, we turn it upside down. The root can also hint at a nonphysical meaning of *turn*. When we *advertise,* we "turn attention toward" a product.

circum- (around)

Circum- is a prefix with the movement meaning of "around." The distance around a circle is called its *circumference.* Like other movement word elements, *circum-* can indicate the idea, rather than the physical action, of "around." For example, a library book that *circulates* "goes around" and is used by many different people.

Circus is the Latin word for "circle." A circus was originally a large circular area surrounded by seats used for viewing shows. Roman emperors were said to stay in power by giving the people "bread and circuses"—that is, food and entertainment. In modern English, a "three-ring circus" is a commonly used expression. This originally meant a very large circus, but it has come to mean any event that causes a great deal of excitement.

---

trans- (across)

Transcontinental jets cross a continent—say, from New York to Los Angeles. The prefix *trans-* can also suggest the idea of "across" rather than physical movement. When we *translate* something, it goes "across" languages, or from one language to another.

Words to Learn

Part 2

tract

13. **distraught** (adjective)   dĭs-trôt′

From Latin: *dis-* (apart) + *tract* (pull) (*Tract* changed to *traught* in Middle English.)

crazy with worry

> **Distraught** over his troubled marriage, the man broke down in tears.

> Wayne was **distraught** when he realized that the bank holding his life savings had gone out of business.

NOTE: Distracted, which comes from the same word elements as *distraught,* has a less extreme meaning. It can be used simply for "confused" or "not attentive."

14. **extract** (verb)   ĭk-străkt′; (noun) ĕk′străkt

From Latin: *ex-* (out) + *tract* (pull)

to pull out; to draw out (verb)

> It was difficult to **extract** the main ideas from the confusing lecture.

> Scientists **extracted** a large amount of information from the pictures of Mars.

something that is drawn out (noun)

> An **extract** of the aloe plant is used for treating burns and cuts.

▶ *Related Word*
  extraction (noun)   *Extraction* of oil from shale is expensive. I am of Polish *extraction*. (Here, *extraction* means ancestry.)

Vanilla *extract,* a popular flavoring for baked goods, is drawn from the pods of orchids. The Aztecs of Mexico used it for centuries to flavor their *xocolatl* (chocolate) drinks. The Spaniard Hernando Cortés drank it at the court of the Aztec ruler Montezuma and brought it to Europe, where it soon became popular. The extract is widely used as an ingredient in perfume. In fact, in an effort to make gasoline more pleasant, the French are now adding the odor of vanilla.

---

15. **retract** (verb)   rĭ-trăkt′

From Latin: *re-* (back) + *tract* (pull)

to withdraw a promise or statement; to pull something back

> The newspaper **retracted** its false statements about the political candidate.

> When we **retracted** the outside awnings, sunlight streamed into the windows.

▶ *Related Word*
  retraction (noun)   The President issued a *retraction* of his statement.

vert

16. **adversary** (noun)   ăd′vər-sĕr′ē; plural: adversaries

From Latin: *ad-* (toward) + *vert* (turn) (When we "turn toward" an enemy or adversary, we prepare to fight.)

opponent; foe

> After a hard-fought tennis match, the two **adversaries** shook hands.

> In the Civil War, former slaves proved to be brave **adversaries** of the Confederate Army.

▶ *Related Word*
  adversarial (adjective)   Enemies have *adversarial* relationships.

NOTE: Adversary connotes a stubborn and determined foe.

What contests were these adversaries engaged in?

1. George Bush and Bill Clinton
2. Julius Caesar and Pompey
3. Joe Louis and Max Schmeling (1938)
4. Rita Repulsa and Kimberly, Jason, Aisha, Tommy, Billy, Trina, Zack

(*Answers:* 1. The 1992 U.S. presidential race 2. Control of the ancient Roman republic 3. The heavyweight boxing world championship 4. Continuing fights of evil against good on *Mighty Morphin Power Rangers* TV show.

---

17. **inadvertently** (adverb)   in′əd-vûr′tənt-lē

From Latin: *in-* (not) + *ad-* (toward) + *vert* (turn) (When you are "not turned toward" something, events often happen inadvertently, or accidentally.)

unintentionally; by accident

> Tom **inadvertently** locked his keys in the car.

> Fishing nets meant for tuna may **inadvertently** catch dolphins.

▶ *Related Word*
  inadvertent (adjective)   The *inadvertent* activation of the car's air bag caused the driver to lose control.

18. **perverse** (adjective)   pər-vûrs′

From Latin: *per-* (completely) + *vert* (turn) (A perverse person is "completely turned away" from what is natural.)

contrary; determined not to do what is expected or right

My **perverse** mother-in-law ordered us to cook her favorite meal and then refused to eat it.

In a **perverse** trend, cheap, used clothing became fashionable among wealthy people.

▶ *Related Words*

perverseness (noun)   Because of the child's *perverseness*, he refused to wear a coat in the freezing weather.

perversity (noun)   The old man's *perversity* caused him to will his money to a stranger instead of to his relatives.

circum-

19. **circumscribe** (verb)   sûr′kəm-skrīb′

From Latin: *circum-* (around) + *scrib* (to write)

to limit; to restrict; to enclose

The Constitution of the United States **circumscribes** the authority of the President so that he or she does not have absolute power.

The European cities of Paris and London were originally **circumscribed** by a protecting wall.

20. **circumspect** (adjective)   sûr′kəm-spĕkt′

From Latin: *circum-* (around) + *spec* (to look) (To be circumspect is "to look around" or be careful.)

cautious; careful; considering results of actions

Since scandal has ruined many careers, public figures should be **circumspect** in their personal lives.

▶ *Related Word*

circumspection (noun)   The senator's *circumspection* kept her from accepting any gifts.

21. **circumvent** (verb)   sûr′kəm-vĕnt′

From Latin: *circum-* (around) + *venīre* (to come)

to avoid; to outwit

Students can **circumvent** long lines by using the telephone to register.

We **circumvented** the need to shop for presents by ordering them from catalogues.

▶ *Related Word*
circumvention (noun)   *Circumvention* of child support payments has become more difficult in recent years.

trans-

22. **transcend** (verb)   trăn-sĕnd′

From Latin: *trans-* (across) + *scandere* (to climb) (When we transcend something, we "climb across" limits and overcome them.)

to overcome; to go above limits

Marcy **transcended** a background of poverty to graduate from college and get a good job.

Grief **transcended** hatred as people from the two fighting nations mourned together for their dead.

Many mysteries of the universe **transcend** our understanding.

Many brave people have *transcended* physical disabilities. In Minneapolis, Darcy Pohland, paralyzed since 1983, became the first full-time television newscaster to work from a wheelchair. Accomplished amateur astronomer William Becker, a Chicagoan, lost his eyesight at 16, but blindness has not prevented him from interpreting information about stars and serving as president of his local astronomy society.

---

23. **transformation** (noun)   trăns′fər-mā′shən

From Latin: *trans-* (across) + *forma* (shape), making *transformāre* (to change shape)

a complete change

We were amazed by the sudden **transformation** of the awkward girl into a beautiful woman.

The second-graders were amazed when they saw the **transformation** of the caterpillar into a butterfly.

▶ *Related Word*
transform (verb)   (trăns-fôrm′)   The start of the semester *transformed* the video-game addict into a hard-working student.

24. **transitory** (adjective)   trăn'sə-tôr'ē

From Latin: *trans-* (across) + *īre* (to go), making *transīre* ("to go across" or to pass through quickly)

short-lived; existing briefly; passing

> People hope their sorrows will be **transitory.**

> The child's **transitory** wish to own a dog left her parents with the responsibility of caring for it.

Exercises

Part 2

■ *Definitions*

Match each word in the left-hand column with a definition from the right-hand column. Use each choice only once.

1. distraught _____

2. circumvent _____

3. retract _____

4. extract _____

5. transcend _____

6. perverse _____

7. transitory _____

8. inadvertently _____

9. circumscribe _____

10. adversary _____

a. something taken out

b. to overcome

c. to withdraw

d. opponent

e. to avoid

f. complete change

g. cautious

h. crazy with worry

i. accidentally

j. short-lived

k. to limit

l. determined not to do what is expected

■ *Meanings*

Match each word element to its meaning. Use each choice only once.

1. trans- ___d___

2. vers, vert ___c___

3. circum- ___a___

4. tract ___b___

a. around

b. pull

c. turn

d. across

■ *Words in Context*

Complete each sentence with the word that fits best. Use each choice only once.

a. distraught
b. extract
c. retract
d. adversary

e. inadvertently
f. perverse
g. circumscribe
h. circumspect

i. circumvent
j. transcend
k. transformation
l. transitory

1. The doctor was able to _____ the man's diseased appendix from his body.

2. A turtle can _____ its head into its shell.

3. Leshan tried to _____ the traffic jam by taking a side street.

4. I was _____ after I realized that the diamond earrings my friend had loaned me were missing.

5. People saw a _____ of the area as farms were replaced by city streets.

6. The child's sadness was _____ , and he soon was smiling again.

7. My _____ uncle complained constantly about his illnesses yet refused to call a doctor.

8. The government agency was _____ in dealing with foreign firms and checked them carefully.

9. The country's president wanted to _____ the power of the military leaders, who were trying to seize control.

10. I _____ tripped when I got out of the car.

■ *Using Related Words*

Complete each sentence by using a word from the group of related words above it. You may need to capitalize a word when you put it into a sentence. Use each choice only once.

1. adversaries, adversarial

The Geneva Conventions, which have been recognized throughout the world, are guidelines for making war less brutal. According to

them, _____ may not destroy each other's hospitals and must treat prisoners in a humane manner. These guide-

lines for _____ nations were developed by the Red Cross.

2. inadvertent, inadvertently

In 1928, while Sir Alexander Fleming was researching bacteria, he went on vacation. During his absence, a test-tube lid

_____ slipped off, and his sample was killed by an unknown mold. Fleming returned and was just about to throw the sample out when he realized that the mold might be able to

kill harmful bacteria. In this _____ manner, he discovered the great antibiotic, penicillin.

3. transformed, transformations

The city of Santa Fe has undergone several _____ since it was founded in 1610 to serve as a capital of Spain in the New World. In 1912 it became part of the United States and the capital of the state of New Mexico. Recently its carefully protected ancient ruins and fine cultural institutions have

_____ it into an attractive cultural and tourist center.

4. extract, extraction

   Commercial plants _____ oxygen, hydrogen, and argon from the air. These gases have many industrial uses.

   The _____ and separation of these elements is a highly technical process.

5. circumspect, circumspection

   Banking is a profession that requires great _____ . Since bankers handle other people's money, they must be

   _____ in avoiding even the appearance of irregularity in their own business or personal dealings.

■ *True or False?*

Each of the following statements contains one or more words from this section. Read each sentence carefully and then indicate whether you think it is probably true or probably false.

____   1. A distraught person is calm.

____   2. People hope that bad weather will be transitory.

____   3. A perverse person is agreeable.

____   4. Perfume is made from the extracts of flowers.

____   5. A marriage often has to transcend small difficulties.

____   6. A circumspect person would have undergone a great transformation if she suddenly started to be careless.

____   7. You might circumvent a long wait at the bank by using a cash machine.

____   8. Your adversary would be happy if your authority were circumscribed.

____   9. Most people inadvertently forget things from time to time.

____   10. A person retracts a statement if he is pleased with it.

Chapter Exercises

■ *Practicing Strategies: New Words from Word Elements*

See how your knowledge of prefixes and roots can help you understand new words. Complete each sentence with the word that seems to fit best. Use each choice only once.

a. aqueducts
b. attract
c. circuitous
d. conduct

e. detain
f. injection
g. stately
h. statement

i. tenor
j. traction
k. transatlantic
l. vertigo

1. A _____ person stands in a dignified, formal manner.

2. When we get a(n) _____ , something is "thrown in" to our bodies.

3. A _____ path goes in a roundabout way.

4. *Ad-* or *at-* can mean "toward," so to _____ is to draw someone toward you.

5. The _____ voice was named because these singers held the melody in a song with many different parts.

6. When the police _____ someone, they hold that person in jail.

7. *Aqua* means "water"; the ancient Romans built _____ to lead water to their cities.

8. When your leg is broken, _____ , or a pulling motion, may help the bones mend properly.

9. You suffer from _____ when you get dizzy and things around you seem to turn.

10. The _____ cable carries phone calls across the Atlantic Ocean.

■ *Practicing Strategies: Combining Context Clues and Word Elements*

Combining the strategies of context clues and word elements is a good way to figure out unknown words. In the following sentences, each italicized word contains a word element that you have studied in this chapter. Using the meaning of the word element and the context of the sentence, make an intelligent guess about the meaning of the italicized word. Your instructor may ask you to check the meaning in your dictionary when you have finished.

1. In a mysterious ceremony, people were *inducted* into the secret society.

    Inducted means _____ .

2. In a terrible *subversion* of justice, the man's innocent words were twisted to seem evil.

    Subversion means _____ .

3. The headlight of the car *projected* onto the road.

    Projected means _____ .

4. For hundreds of years, alchemists sought methods to *transmute* iron and copper into gold.

    Transmute means _____ .

5. In 1522, the ships of Magellan became the first to *circumnavigate* the world.

    Circumnavigate means _____ .

6. The company offered many *inducements* to attract qualified computer operators.

    Inducements means _____

    _____ .

■ *Practicing Strategies: Using the Dictionary*

Read the following definition and then answer the questions below it.

quick (kwĭk) *adj.* **quick•er, quick•est.   1.** Moving or functioning rapidly and energetically; speedy. **2.** Learning, thinking, or understanding with speed and dexterity; bright: *a quick* *mind.* **3.a.** Perceiving or responding with speed and sensitivity; keen. **b.** Reacting immediately and sharply: *a quick temper.* **4.a.** Occurring or achieved in a relatively brief period of time: *a quick promotion.* **b.** Done or occurring immediately: *a quick inspection.* See Syns at **fast**[1]. **5.** Tending to react hastily: *quick to find fault.* **6.** *Archaic.* **a.** Alive. **b.** Pregnant. —*n.* **1.** Sensitive or raw exposed flesh, as under the fingernails. **2.** The most personal and sensitive aspect of the emotions. **3.** The living: *the quick and the dead.* **4.** The vital core; the essence: *the quick of the matter.* —*adv.* Quickly; promptly. [ME, alive, lively, quick < OE *cwicu*, alive. See **gʷei-***.] —**quick′ly** *adv.* —**quick′ness** *n.*

1. In which language was *quick* first recorded? _____

2. Give the number and the part of speech of the definition that is no

   longer used. _____

3. Give the adverb that is closely related to *quick.* _____

4. List the parts of speech that *quick* functions as. _____

5. Give the number and part of speech that best fits this sentence: "His

   quick intelligence enabled him to solve the problem." _____

■ Companion Words

Complete each sentence with the word that fits best. Choose your answers from the words below. You may use each word more than once.

Choices: in, of, to, draw, from

1. The queen is circumspect _____ her personal life.

2. We have witnessed a transformation _____ aircraft from small propeller planes to large modern jets.

3. The NAACP is a staunch defender _____ the rights of African Americans.

4. The extraction of information _____ the large data base involved many months of work.

5. Freedom is conducive _____ creativity.

6. The chemistry students will _____ a deduction from the results of the experiment.

7. Abduction _____ children is a horrible crime.

8. Circumvention _____ long waits is pleasant.

9. The professor issued a retraction _____ his statement when he realized it was based on faulty evidence.

10. I must abstain _____ eating for 24 hours before my surgery.

■ *Writing with Your Words*

This exercise will give you practice in writing effective sentences that use the vocabulary words. Each sentence is started for you. Complete it with an interesting phrase that also indicates the meaning of the italicized word.

1. I would like to *circumscribe* the power of _____

_____ .

2. One difficulty I would like to *transcend* is _____

_____ .

3. The *tenacious* detective _____

_____ .

4. The *circumspect* woman _____

_____ .

5. People should *abstain* from _____

_____ .

6. I *inadvertently* _____

_____ .

7. The jury drew the *deduction* that the man was guilty of the robbery when _____

_____ .

8. People often try to *circumvent* lines for ticket sales by _____

_____ .

9. My *adversary* _____

_____ .

10. The three-year-old felt *dejected* because _____

_____ .

Passage

What Body Language Tells Us

The posture of your body, where you place your arms, and how you walk may reveal more to others than the words you are speaking. Many people do not realize how effectively body language communicates.

A first-grade teacher stands by the door, smiling and greeting the children with friendly words. **(1)** If her arms are crossed, however, she is **inadvertently** communicating another message. Crossed arms can indicate negative feelings, and the children will probably see her as a foe rather than a friend.

In a nearby high school, a student sits in math class, his body straight, his hands folded, fixing a **tenacious** stare on the teacher. Is he paying attention? No! His lack of movement indicates that his thoughts are far away (perhaps on his girlfriend). If the student were interested in the lesson, he would move and react. **(2)** Only an inexperienced teacher would draw the **deduction** that a student who remains perfectly still is thinking about math.

In contrast to the math student's rigid posture, tilting one's head indicates friendliness and interest. A student who tilts her head and sits on the edge of her chair is paying attention to a lecture. People often bend their heads or bodies forward slightly to show interest in members of the opposite sex. Enlarged pupils in one's eyes also indicate this interest.

Smiling is a body language behavior with a hidden message. Most

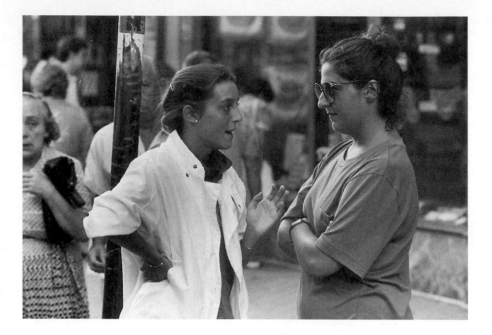

Body language sends out powerful messages.

people believe that smiling indicates happiness. **(3)** But scientists observing animals have found that another conclusion may be more **tenable:** smiling indicates apology, or the wish to avoid an attack. A gorilla often smiles when showing stronger animals that it doesn't want to fight. Similarly, a person who has accidentally hit a stranger with an elbow **(4)** will give a **transitory** smile that requests the injured person not to become angry.

Hands communicate much body language. **(5)** An open-handed gesture is **conducive** to friendliness. Perhaps this is the origin of the handshake, in which people open their hands to each other.

However, arms folded on the chest indicate defensiveness. **(6)** Baseball fans have seen this behavior many times when an umpire makes a call that a team manager wants him to **retract. (7)** As the manager approaches, the formerly neutral umpire undergoes a **transformation** into an **adversary** simply by folding his arms. **Abstaining** from movement, he listens to the manager's arguments. Finally, the umpire shows his rejection just by turning his back. The **dejected** manager walks back to the dugout, shrugging his shoulders.

Walking styles can also communicate messages. **(8)** We all have seen the controlled and measured walk of a person trying to appear dignified and **circumspect.** People who are **distraught** often walk with their heads down and their hands clasped behind their backs. The person with energy and will power moves rapidly, hands swinging freely from side to side. **(9)** Those who walk with their hands in their pockets may be **perverse** and critical of others. **(10)** People who look toward the ground may be trying to **circumvent** the glances of others.

Body language sends out powerful messages. The next time you shake hands, tilt your head, or fold your arms, think about what you are wordlessly telling others.

■ *Exercise*

Each numbered sentence below corresponds to a sentence in the Passage. Fill in the letter of the choice that makes the sentence mean the same thing as its corresponding sentence in the Passage.

1. If her arms are crossed, however, she is _____ communicating another message.
   a. hopefully   b. accidentally   c. strongly   d. probably

2. Only an experienced teacher would draw the _____ that a student who remains still is thinking about math.
   a. conclusion   b. picture   c. hope   d. question

3. Another conclusion may be more _____ .
   a. logical   b. negative   c. desirable   d. ridiculous

4. A person will give a _____ smile that requests the injured person not to start a fight.
   a. happy   b. false   c. brief   d. friendly

5. An open-handed gesture is _____ to friendliness.
   a. opposed   b. leading   c. hopeless   d. given

6. An umpire makes a call that a team manager wants him to _____ .
   a. take back   b. be firm about   c. discuss intelligently
   d. delay slightly

7. As the manager approaches, the formerly neutral umpire undergoes

   a(n) _____ .
   a. reform   b. illness   c. inspection   d. change

8. We have all seen the controlled and measured walk of a person trying

   to appear dignified and _____ .
   a. unfriendly   b. worried   c. busy   d. cautious

9. Those who walk with their hands in their pockets may be _____ and critical of others.
   a. contrary   b. unhappy   c. observant   d. lonely

10. People who look toward the ground may be trying to _____ the glances of others.
    a. capture b. greet c. avoid d. notice

■ *Discussion Questions*

1. According to the passage, what is the "hidden message" of smiling?

2. Identify two situations in which the position of a person's arms or hands indicates an attitude.

3. Suggest three ways in which dogs communicate by using body language.

◀ ENGLISH IDIOMS

Movement

Since this chapter concerns word elements of movement, the idioms introduced here all deal with action. Some idioms relate to negative actions. When people are *axed,* they are fired or lose their jobs. If a worker does something wrong, her boss may *call her on the carpet,* scold her, or *bawl her out.* If her boss makes her feel bad, she would be *cut down to size.*

To *draw the line* means to set a limit. For example, you might help a friend to study, but *draw the line* at writing his paper for him. A professor who *covers a lot of ground* in a lecture gives much information. (Similarly, a traveler might *cover a lot of ground* by going a long distance.)

If people go to a theater to see a mystery and they are kept in suspense until the last minute, the mystery is called a *cliffhanger.* If audience members enjoy the performance, clapping and cheering loudly, they would be said to *bring the house down.*

In the hill tribes of northern India, it was the custom to bend over backwards while doing a yoga exercise that symbolized submission to God. *To bend over backwards* now means to do everything possible to please or accommodate another person. A professor might *bend over backwards* to help a student who is having difficulty in a course.

Word Elements:
Together and Apart

People come together in classes, clubs, concerts, parties, and sports events. Yet disagreements and disputes can also force them apart. This chapter concentrates on word elements meaning "together" and "apart," presenting three prefixes and two roots. The chapter also introduces several words that came into English from other languages, showing how languages come together. As English speakers came into contact with people speaking different languages, English borrowed foreign words.

Chapter Strategy: Word Elements: Together and Apart

Chapter Words:

Part 1

co-, com-, con-	coherent	dis-	discord
	collaborate		disparity
	communal		disreputable
	compatible	sym-, syn-	syndrome
	concur		synopsis
	contemporary		synthesis

Part 2

greg	congregate	*Borrowed Words*	bravado
	gregarious		charisma
	segregate		cliché
sperse	disperse		cuisine
	intersperse		nadir
	sparse		zenith

Did You Know?

What Are Two Sources of English?

Modern English has roots in two languages, Old French and Old English. Old French was a Romance language; that is, it descended from Latin, which was spoken by the Romans. Old French was an ancestor of the French spoken today. Old English, spoken in England from about the beginning of the eighth century to the middle of the twelfth century, was a Germanic language, similar in many ways to the German used today. The two languages first came into contact in 1066.

In 1066, William the Conqueror crossed the English Channel from northwestern France, conquered England, and made himself king. He replaced the English nobility with his fellow Norman countrymen, who spoke a version of Old French. For many years, then, the ruling class of England spoke Old French, and the rest of the people continued to speak Old English.

Gradually the two languages merged into Middle English, which was spoken until about the fifteenth century, when it became what we know as Modern English. But to this day, many rare, fancy English words (like the ones you find in vocabulary books) tend to be of Old French origin. The common words of English are usually from Old English.

What does this mean to you? Perhaps you speak or have studied Spanish, Italian, French, or Portuguese. If so, you may realize that these languages are related to the Old French that William the Conqueror brought to England. They are all Romance languages. If you speak a Romance language, you can easily learn many difficult English words. All you need to do is to think of a *cognate*, a word that sounds the same and has the same meaning, from a Romance language. As an example, *furious* is an English word descended from Old French. The Spanish cognate is *furioso*.

Modern English is full of pairs of words that have the same or similar meanings. In these cases, one word is often derived from Old French and the other from Old English. Several of these word pairs are listed below. Notice that the words descended from Old French are often longer and less common.

Old English (Germanic Origin)	*Old French (Romance Origin)*
eat	devour
talk	converse
give	donate
earth	terrain
top	pinnacle
late	tardy

During the 1400s and the 1500s, interest in the ancient Greeks and Romans resulted in another great expansion in English vocabulary. Writers sometimes coined new words from ancient Greek and Latin ones. In this way, words such as *compatible, congenital,* and *conspicuous* (all found in this book) entered the English language. The great English playwright, Shakespeare, was the first to use the words *misanthrope* and *frugal.*

Finally, English has borrowed words from many other languages, including Arabic, Hindi, Urdu, Italian, German, and Spanish. If you know another language, you'll probably recognize many words that are similar in English. In this chapter you will study several words that English has borrowed. These words are a spoken and written record of the explorations that brought English speakers together with people of other cultures and languages.

Learning Strategy

Word Elements: Together and Apart

Part 1 of this chapter presents three common prefixes that refer to being together or apart: *com-* and *syn-* mean "together"; *dis-* means "apart." These prefixes are very useful, since each one is used to form more than one hundred English words.

Part 2 presents two roots that are related to the idea of together and apart, *greg* (flock, herd) and *sperse* (scatter).

Element	Meaning	Origin	Function	Chapter Words
				Part 1
co-, col-, com-, con-, cor-	together	Latin	prefix	coherent, collaborate, communal, compatible, concur, contemporary
dis-	apart; not	Latin; Greek	prefix	discord, disparity, disreputable
sym-, sy-	together; same	Greek	prefix	syndrome, synopsis, synthesis
				Part 2
greg	flock	Latin	root	congregate, gregarious, segregate
sperse	scatter	Latin	root	disperse, intersperse, sparse

Prefixes

Part 1

The three prefixes presented in Part 1 are discussed in more detail below.

co-, col-, com-, con-, cor- (together)
  This prefix is used in several hundred English words. Its five spelling variations help us pronounce it more easily when it is attached to various roots, as in these examples: *coworker, collect, communicate, contact,* and *correspond.* Each of these words carries some sense of "together." For example, when people *communicate,* they come together through speech or writing. When two electrical wires establish *contact,* they come together by touching. A *coworker* is someone who works together with another worker. The word *companion* is formed from *com-* (together) and the Latin word *panis* (bread). Originally, a companion was a person with whom one shared bread or other food.
dis- (apart; not)
  Dis- means "apart" in some words. For example, students often *dissect* (cut apart) frogs in biology classes. A noisy student may *disrupt* (break apart into confusion) a class. *Dis-* can also mean "not." The word *distrust,* formed from the prefix *dis-* and the base word *trust,* means "not to trust." A person in *disgrace* is not in the "grace," or favor, of others. In a new slang usage, "dis" appears as a verb meaning *to show disrespect for* as in "She dissed me."
sym-, syn- (together; same)
  The two meanings of *syn-* and *sym-* are related, making them easy to remember. For example, *sympathy* is composed from *sym-* (same) and the root *path* (feeling). *Synagogue,* a place where Jewish people meet to worship, is composed from *syn-* (together) and *agein* (to lead).

Words to Learn

Part 1

co-, com-, con-

1. **coherent** (adjective)   kō-hîr′ənt

   From *co-* (together) + *haērere* (to cling or stick)

   logical; consistent; clearly reasoned

The Canadian government worked out a **coherent** policy for admitting refugees.

The **coherent** lecture was easy for students to understand.

▶ *Related Words*

    coherence (noun)   Lacking any *coherence,* the student's paper was simply a disorganized collection of sentences.

    cohere (verb)   In the cold weather, ice *cohered* to the surface of the road. (*Cohere* means "to stick.")

    incoherent (adjective)   The alcoholic's senseless talk was *incoherent.* (*Incoherent* is the opposite of *coherent.*)

2. **collaborate** (verb)   kə-lăb′ə-rat′

From Latin: *col-* (together) + *labōrāre* (to work)

to work together

    J. D. Watson and F. H. C. Crick **collaborated** to find the structure of DNA, which carries the genetic information of all living organisms.

    Andrew Lloyd Webber and David Cullen **collaborated** on the music for *Phantom of the Opera.*

▶ *Related Word*

    collaboration (noun)   Working in *collaboration,* Jose, Phillip, and Suzuki produced an award-winning science project.

NOTE: The word *collaborator* can have the negative meaning of "one who aids an enemy occupying one's country."

3. **communal** (adjective)   kə-myo͞on′əl

From Latin: *com-* (together) (*Communis* meant "shared," "public.")

referring to a community or to joint ownership

    During summer camp, eight children slept in a **communal** bedroom.

    People in Swiss towns once baked bread in **communal** ovens.

    The swimming pool was **communal** property, so everyone in the neighborhood shared the cost of repairs.

▶ *Related Word*

    commune (noun)   (kŏm′yo͞on′)   A *commune* is a place where people live as a group, sharing their incomes.

4. **compatible** (adjective)   kəm-păt′ə-bəl

From Latin: *com-* (together) + *path* (feeling)

harmonious; living in harmony

> A messy person and a neat person would not make **compatible** roommates.

> My new printer was not **compatible** with my old computer.

▶ *Common Phrase*
compatible with

▶ *Related Word*
compatibility (noun)   *Compatibility* is an important factor in a happy marriage.

5. **concur** (verb)   kən-kûr′

From Latin: *con-* (together) + *currere* (to run)

to agree

> The court of appeals **concurred** with the decision of the district court.

> My wife and my mother **concurred** on the suit I should wear to the interview.

to happen at the same time

> The times that the two of us left the house **concurred** exactly.

▶ *Common Phrase*
concur with

▶ *Related Words*
concurrence (noun)   There is general *concurrence* that recycling helps our environment.

concurrent (adjective)   The criminal was serving two *concurrent* jail sentences.

6. **contemporary** (noun, adjective)   kən-tĕm′pə-rĕr′ē   plural: contemporaries

From Latin: *com-* (together) + *tempus* (time)

a person living at the same time as another person (noun)

> Thomas Jefferson was a **contemporary** of Alexander Hamilton.

> Great artists are often not appreciated by their **contemporaries.**

existing at the same time (adjective)

The expansion of railroads and the migration to the West were **contemporary** developments in U.S. history.

current; modern (adjective)

According to **contemporary** beliefs, it is healthy for mothers to breast-feed their babies.

▶ *Related Word*
contemporaneous (adjective)   (kən-tĕm′pə-rā′nē-əs)   The two Balkan civil wars were *contemporaneous*

dis-

7. **discord** (noun)   dĭs′kŏrd′

From Latin: *dis-* (apart) + *cor* (heart, mind)

strife; lack of agreement

According to experts, money is the most common cause of **discord** in marriage.

▶ *Related Word*
discordant (adjective)   (dĭs-kôr′dənt)   The horns of the cars stuck in traffic made *discordant* sounds.

A Greek legend tells the story of the apple of *discord*. The goddess Discord had not been invited to a wedding at which all the other gods were to be present. Enraged, she arrived at the party and threw onto the table a golden apple intended "for the most beautiful." Three goddesses, Juno, Minerva, and Venus, all claimed it. Paris, prince of Troy, was asked to settle the dispute. He chose Venus. As a reward, Venus promised him the world's most beautiful woman, Helen, who was, unfortunately, married to the Greek king Menelaus. When Paris abducted her, a Greek army went to Troy to get her back. This military expedition resulted in the Trojan War, the subject of Homer's *Iliad*.

---

8. **disparity** (noun)   dĭs-păr′ə-tē

From Latin: *dis-* (not) + *par* (equal)

inequality; difference

According to economists, income **disparity** in the United States has increased in the last twenty years.

There was a **disparity** between the number of miles our car actually had traveled and the number shown on the odometer.

Research indicates that a college degree increases income. The 1990 census found considerable *disparity* in the earning power of college graduates and nongraduates. On average, the difference amounted to $600,000 over a working life, or about $15,000 each year. An advanced degree (such as an M.A. or Ph.D.) can increase earning power by as much as two million dollars over a lifetime.

▶ *Related Word*

disparate (adjective)   (dĭs′pər-ĭt)   The *disparate* demands of the two supervisors caused problems for the workers.

9. **disreputable** (adjective)   dĭs-rĕp′yə-tə-bəl

From Latin: *dis-* (not) + *re-* (again) + *putāre* (to think) (Literally, *disreputable* means "not worth a second thought.")

not respectable; having a bad reputation

The student's appearance was so **disreputable** that we thought he was a beggar.

The **disreputable** tavern owner allowed people to sell drugs in his bar.

▶ *Related Word*

disrepute (noun)   (dĭs′rĭ-py$\overline{oo}$t′)   The chemist who had reported false results was held in *disrepute*.

sym-, syn-

10. **syndrome** (noun)   sĭn′drōm′

From Greek: *syn-* (together) + *dramein* (to run)

a group of symptoms that indicates a disease or disorder

After head injuries, football players can develop post-concussion **syndrome,** which affects speech and balance.

In the late 1800s, the U.S. economy suffered from a **syndrome** of alternating growth and sudden declines.

Medical and educational specialists have defined several *syndromes* that affect childhood learning, including conduct disorders and attention deficit disorders. For reasons not fully understood, boys are more likely to suffer from these. Some researchers believe that because boys are more active, they are seen as having more behavior problems. However, scientists have also shown that, even before birth, the brains of boys are more likely to be injured than those of girls.

11. **synopsis** (noun)   sĭ-nŏp′sĭs   plural: synopses

From Greek: *syn-* (together) + *opsis* (view) (In a synopsis, something is viewed "all together.")

a short summary

> The **synopsis** of the book told the plot in a few short paragraphs.

12. **synthesis** (noun)   sĭn′thə sĭs   plural: syntheses

From Greek: *syn-* (together) + *tithenai* (to put)

something made from combined parts

> The music of Brazilian composer Hector Villa-Lobos is a **synthesis** of folk melodies and classical forms.

▶ *Related Words*

synthesize (verb)   The new city hall *synthesized* classical Greek architecture and modern styles.

synthetic (adjective)   (sĭn-thĕt′ĭk)   Nylon and polyester are examples of *synthetic* materials made from petroleum.

synthetically (adverb)   *Synthetically* produced vitamins are not always as good as natural products.

NOTE: Synthetic and *synthetically* refer to products produced chemically, or by other artificial means, rather than those of natural origin.

Most people sprinkle something on their food that is a *synthesis* of two poisons: sodium and chloride. If either were swallowed alone, it would be deadly. But, when *synthesized* into a chemical compound, the result is the common seasoning known as table salt.

Exercises

Part 1

■ Definitions

Match each word in the left-hand column with a definition from the right-hand column. Use each choice only once.

1. contemporary _____   a. strife; lack of agreement

2. syndrome _____   b. something made from com-
                                    bined parts
3. compatible _____
                                 c. symptoms that make up a
4. discord _____   disease

5. synthesis _____   d. logical; consistent

6. coherent _____   e. current; modern

7. communal _____   f. inequality

8. disreputable _____   g. jointly owned

9. disparity _____   h. harmonious

10. synopsis _____   i. summary

                                 j. to work together

                                 k. to agree

                                 l. not respectable

■ *Meanings*

Match each prefix to its meaning. Use each choice only once.

1. syn- _____   a. apart; not

2. dis- _____   b. together; same

3. con- _____   c. together

■ *Words in Context*

Complete each sentence with the word that fits best. Use each choice only once.

a. coherent   e. concur   i. disreputable
b. collaborate   f. contemporary   j. syndrome
c. communal   g. discordant   k. synopsis
d. compatible   h. disparity   l. synthesis

1. The tennis court was _____ property, and everyone in the neighborhood owned a share in it.

2. The artist's work was a _____ of many different styles.

3. People felt that the _____ shopkeeper cheated his customers.

4. Since we are the same age, Alice is my _____ .

5. I was annoyed by the _____ noise from five radios playing different music.

6. The _____ children often played together.

7. Reading a _____ of the plot helped us understand what happens in Shakespeare's *Macbeth*.

8. Many people _____ with the decision to limit nuclear arms.

9. People often suffer from a withdrawal _____ when they stop taking drugs.

10. There is a great _____ of power between a master and a slave.

■ *Using Related Words*

Complete each sentence by using a word from the group of related words above it. You may need to capitalize a word when you put it into a sentence. Use each choice only once.

1. compatibility, compatible

When blood is donated, both giver and receiver must have

_____ blood types. There are four blood types: A, B, AB, and O. People with type O can donate to people with any other blood type. People with AB blood may receive blood from people with any other blood type. Otherwise, blood types must be

matched for _____ .

2. synthetic, synthesized

A German chemical company has _____ noxon,

242 Chapter 8 Word Elements: Together and Apart

a chemical that can turn ozone, a dangerous pollutant, into harm-

less oxygen. This _____ agent will help to de-
crease air pollution.

3. collaboration, collaborated

Several Peruvian women have _____ to form a
radio station that presents programs on women's health and wel-

fare. A _____ has also been formed between
women's groups in Mexico and in Boston. Latinas (Latin American
women) are leading the world in this type of networking.

4. contemporaries, contemporaneous, contemporary

Wolfgang Amadeus Mozart, who lived from 1756 to 1791, was

a _____ of the Austrian emperor Franz Joseph.
Mozart was a child prodigy who performed throughout Europe at
the age of six. However, as an adult, he had many problems.

His _____ often ignored his best music.

_____ reports tell us that he lost the sponsorship
of royalty. He died in poverty when he was thirty-six years old, but
his great music lives on today.

■ Say It Again

Each sentence below contains two or three vocabulary words. Read the
sentence and then decide which of the three sentences listed after it has
nearly the same meaning.

____   1. Economists concurred that growing income disparity would
increase social discord.

a. Economists agreed that working together on income
would increase social feelings of togetherness.

b. Economists felt that bad distribution of income would increase social strife.

c. Economists agreed that growing differences in income
would increase social strife.

Copyright © Houghton Mifflin Company. All rights reserved.

    ——   2. The collaborative synopsis lacked any coherence.

        a. Several students wrote a summary that lacked sense.

        b. Several students agreed that the summary lacked sense.

        c. There was a disagreement among students about the sense of the summary.

    ——   3. Contemporary doctors have identified many syndromes that affect the elderly.

        a. Old-fashioned doctors have identified several areas of disagreement about the elderly.

        b. Modern doctors have identified many diseases that affect the elderly.

        c. Modern doctors have identified community-style arrangements that affect the health of the elderly.

    ——   4. Because they were not compatible, the two women ended their communal living arrangements.

        a. They didn't get along, so the two women stopped living together.

        b. They didn't have the same incomes, so the two women stopped living together.

        c. They didn't work together, so the two women felt they couldn't live together.

Word Roots

Part 2

Part 2 presents two word roots that are concerned with coming together and moving apart, but do not carry these meanings directly. These roots are *greg* and *sperse*.

    This part also presents some words that were borrowed from other languages when English speakers came together with people who spoke these languages.

greg (flock; herd)

    Greg once referred to a flock of sheep or a herd of cattle. By extension, *greg* has come to be used as a word element meaning the action of coming, or "flocking," together. For example, one word you will learn, *gregarious,* describes people who like to be with other people.

sperse (scatter)

When we scatter things, we move them apart. Thus, the root *sperse* is concerned with being apart. *Disperse,* one of the words in this lesson, means "to scatter widely."

Words to Learn

Part 2

greg

13. **congregate** (verb)   kŏng′grə-gāt′

    From Latin: *con-* (together) + *greg* (flock, herd)

    to meet; to assemble

    > Both houses of Congress **congregated** to hear the President's State of the Union address.

    > Children **congregated** in the schoolyard during recess.

    ▶ *Related Word*
    congregation (noun)   The *congregation* listened intently to the minister's sermon.

    Congregation is a religious word, meaning the members of a religious organization, such as a church or synagogue. Many other religious words have interesting origins.

    Catholic, from the meaning "universal"   When spelled with a small *c, catholic* still means "universal," rather than the religion.
    Protestant, from *protest*   In the early 1500s, Martin Luther and his followers protested against certain Catholic practices. They formed a new set of "protesting" religions.
    Jewish, from the Hebrew word *Judah,* the ancient Jewish Kingdom
    Muslim, from the Arabic word *aslama,* meaning "he surrendered," referring to people who are obedient to God's will
    Hindu, from the Persian word for India, *Hind*

14. **gregarious** (adjective)   grĭ-gâr′ē-əs

From Latin: *greg* (flock; herd)

sociable; fond of company

> Since Thelma was **gregarious,** she loved to talk to clients while she styled their hair.

▶ *Related Word*
gregariousness (noun)   Because of his *gregariousness,* George hated to work at home alone.

15. **segregate** (verb)   sĕg′rə-gāt′

From Latin: *sē-* (apart) + *greg* (flock; herd) (*Sēgregāre* meant "to separate from the flock.")

to separate

> In some religious traditions, men are **segregated** from women during prayer services.

▶ *Related Word*
segregation (noun)   The *segregation* of children and adults seemed strange to us.

Baseball was once a *segregated* sport that prohibited Blacks from playing on major league teams. In response, Blacks formed their own teams. Perhaps the best known, the Kansas City Monarchs, regularly won the Black World Series. Such legendary players as Satchel Paige, Josh Gibson, Buck Leonard, Monte Irvin, and James "Cool Papa" Bell also played in Latin American countries. In fact, the Dominican Republic dictator Trujillo actually imported the Monarchs for one game—and won a championship. In 1947, *segregation* ended in the major leagues, and ever since, Blacks have been outstanding major league players.

---

sperse

16. **disperse** (verb)   dĭs-pûrs′

From Latin: *dis-* (apart) + *sperse* (scatter)

to scatter; to distribute widely

> Refinishing furniture outdoors allows harmful chemical fumes to **disperse** into the open air.

The crowd **dispersed** after the movie ended.

▶ *Related Word*
dispersion (noun)   The students observed the *dispersion* of light through a prism.

17. **intersperse** (verb)   ĭn'tər-spûrs'

From Latin: *inter-* (between) + *sperse* (scatter)

to scatter here and there; to distribute among other things

At the political rally, speeches were **interspersed** with video-taped presentations about the candidate's life.

The paved highway was **interspersed** with stretches of dirt road.

▶ *Common Phrase*
intersperse with

▶ *Related Word*
interspersion (noun)   The *interspersion* of jokes made the speech amusing.

18. **sparse** (adjective)   spärs

From Latin: *sperse* (scatter)

thinly scattered or distributed; meager

Rain is so **sparse** in western Nebraska that ruts of wagon wheels made over a hundred years ago can still be seen.

Gorillas are now **sparse** in Africa; however, at one time they existed in large numbers.

▶ *Related Word*
sparsity (noun)   There is a *sparsity* of trees on high mountain tops.

Borrowed Words

19. **bravado** (noun)   brə-vä'dō

From Spanish

false bravery; showy display of courage

In a show of **bravado,** the teenager challenged the famous gun-slinger to a shootout.

20. **charisma** (noun)   kə-rĭz′mə

From Greek

quality of leadership that attracts other people

> Lech Walesa's **charisma** made him a symbol of freedom in Poland.

▶ *Related Word*

charismatic (adjective) (kăr′ĭz-măt′ĭk) Church attendance increased dramatically under the *charismatic* leadership of the new minister.

Although the special quality of *charisma* is hard to define, history records many charismatic leaders. Soldier and statesman Simon Bolivar (1783–1830) led the people of six Latin American countries to freedom from Spain. So powerful was his influence that the country of Bolivia was named for him.

Napoleon Bonaparte became emperor of France in 1804, eleven years after the French had beheaded King Louis XVI and declared the country a republic. It is said that Napoleon's charisma was so strong that anybody who met him would be captured by his personality. Napoleon united the French behind him and managed to conquer half of Europe before he was defeated by England and Austria in 1815.

In his powerful speeches, the modern Black leader Martin Luther King, Jr., inspired all who heard him with the justice of his great cause. King employed nonviolent peace marches to win rights for Black people in the United States.

21. **cliché** (noun)   klē-shā′

From French

an overused, trite expression

> An example of a **cliché** often used in sports is "no pain, no gain."
>
> The official's speech was full of **clichés** and promises, but it gave no plan of action.

22. **cuisine** (noun)   kwĭ-zēn′

From French

a style of food or cooking

> Puerto Rican **cuisine** features delicious pasteles, which are made of cornmeal and stuffed with meat, raisins, olives, capers, and almonds.
>
> The elegant restaurant featured French **cuisine.**

NOTE: Generally, a *cuisine* refers to food prepared by skilled cooks or chefs.

Cuisines of different regions feature various specialties. Can you match each food item with its country or group of origin?

1. curry   a. Arab
2. sushi   b. Japanese
3. crepes   c. Mexican
4. phò tai   d. French
5. fajitas   e. Vietnamese
6. hummus   f. Indian

(*Answers:*   1. f   2. b   3. d   4. e   5. c   6. a)

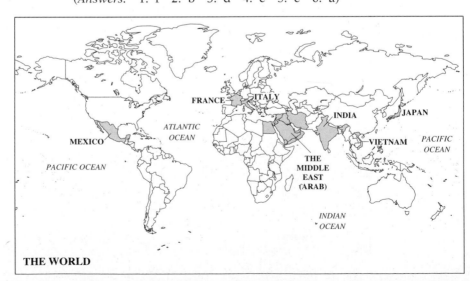

THE WORLD

23. **nadir** (noun)   nā′dər

   From Arabic: *nazīr as-samt* (the lowest point; opposite the zenith)

   the lowest point

   Human behavior reaches its **nadir** in the act of genocide.

24. **zenith** (noun)   zē′nĭth

   From Arabic: *samt ar-ra's* (the path overhead; the highest point in the heavens)

   the highest point

   Centered in present-day Iraq, the Assyrian empire was at the **zenith** of its power from 900 to 650 B.C.

Arabic astronomers have made many important contributions. As early as 800 B.C. Babylonians and Assyrians had calculated new moons and composed a seasonal calendar. The Chaldeans (about 500 B.C.) had a table of lunar eclipses and knew the cycles of five planets around the sun. The work of Abû Ma'shar (born in A.D. 787), who calculated the length of the year and catalogued the stars, was translated from Arabic into Latin. This work was one of the first books printed in Germany.

NOTE: Zenith cannot be used to refer to a physical high point, such as the top of a mountain. However, we can refer to the **pinnacle** of a mountain.

Exercises

Part 2

■ *Definitions*

Match each word in the left-hand column with a definition from the right-hand column. Use each choice only once.

1. cuisine _____   a. style of cooking

2. zenith _____   b. thinly scattered

3. sparse _____   c. to separate

                            d. overused expression

4. cliché _____

5. congregate _____

6. charisma _____

7. disperse _____

8. bravado _____

9. segregate _____

10. gregarious _____

e. to distribute among other things

f. a quality that attracts others

g. sociable

h. lowest point

i. highest point

j. showy display of bravery

k. to scatter; to distribute widely

l. to gather together

■ *Meanings*

Match each word root to its meaning. Use each choice only once.

1. sperse _____

2. greg _____

a. flock; herd

b. scatter

■ *Words in Context*

Complete each sentence with the word that fits best. Use each choice only once.

a. congregate   e. intersperse   i. cliché
b. gregarious   f. sparse   j. cuisine
c. segregate   g. bravado   k. nadir
d. disperse   h. charisma   l. zenith

1. The _____ couple went to many parties.

2. Because of his _____ , Mexican revolutionary Emiliano Zapata attracted many followers.

3. Farmers often _____ rows of corn with rows of other crops.

4. The expression "save for a rainy day" is a(n) _____ that most of us have heard many times.

5. The beginning wrestler displayed true _____ when he publicly dared the champion to a fight.

6. Health officials wanted to _____ the sick cows from the healthy ones.

7. Homeless and starving, she had reached the _____ of her fortunes.

8. People will _____ in the church to hear the address of the archbishop.

9. At the _____ of his remarkable career, Genghis Khan ruled a vast Asian empire.

10. Pakistani _____ includes many tasty vegetables and interesting spices.

■ *Using Related Words*

Complete each sentence by using a word from the group of related words above it. You may need to capitalize a word when you put it into a sentence. Use each choice only once.

1. segregated, segregation

   Because fans of different teams may fight at games, they are some-

   times _____ into different areas in a sports sta-

   dium. This _____ often results in loud cheers in one part of a park and complete silence in another.

2. dispersion, disperse

   Small, fast-moving hummingbirds _____ the pol-len that fertilizes flowers. The birds' long bills gather nectar, and as hummingbirds move, they carry it from flower to flower. In this

   way, _____ allows flowers to be fertilized. Hum-mingbirds specialize in red and orange flowers. If you wear these colors, they will be attracted to you too!

3. charisma, charismatic

With his riveting blue eyes and mysterious manner, the Russian

figure Rasputin (1872–1916) was extremely _____ .

His _____ attracted many followers, including
Queen Alexandra. Her devotion to Rasputin, deeply resented by the
Russian people, may have been a factor leading to the revolution
of 1917.

4. interspersed, interspersion

The great playwright Shakespeare often _____ a

few comic scenes into his tragic plays. This _____
allowed the audience some comic relief from the dramatic tension.

5. sparse, sparsity

In many portions of Canada, settlement is _____ .
One can go for hundreds of miles without seeing other people.

This _____ of settlement is due to the cold climate and difficult living conditions.

■ *Reading the Headlines*

This exercise presents five headlines that might appear in newspapers.
Read each one carefully and then answer the questions that follow. (Remember that little words, such as *is, are, a,* and *the,* are often left out of
headlines.)

PEOPLE CONGREGATE TO HEAR CHARISMATIC SPEAKER

1. Do the people stay apart? _____

2. Does the speaker appeal to people? _____

CLOUDS TOO DISPERSED TO FORM RAIN IN AREA WITH SPARSE CROP GROWTH

3. Are the clouds gathered together? _____

4. Are there many crops? _____

GREGARIOUS GROUP INTERSPERSES BUSINESS TALK WITH SOCIALIZING

5. Do the members of the group like to be alone? _____

6. Do the members socialize as well as talk business? _____

REBELS DISPLAY BRAVADO AT NADIR OF THEIR FORTUNES

7. Do the rebels seem courageous? _____

8. Are they enjoying good luck? _____

VIETNAMESE CUISINE CALLED ZENITH OF TASTE

9. Is food referred to? _____

10. Is it good? _____

Chapter Exercises

■ *Practicing Strategies: New Words from Word Elements*

See how your knowledge of word elements can help you understand new words. Complete each sentence with the word that seems to fit best. Use each choice only once.

a. aggregate	e. compress	i. disqualified
b. coauthor	f. conform	j. disuse
c. collide	g. disconnect	k. symmetrical
d. community	h. discourteous	l. synchronized

1. Something no longer used has fallen into _____ .

2. A person who is not qualified to compete in a race should be

   _____ .

3. A _____ writes a book together with another person.

4. *Chronos* means "time," so two things that happen at the same time

   are _____ .

5. When all of something is herded together, the total is called the

   _____ .

6. To press together is to _____ .

7. *Meter* means "measure," so a figure with two equal sides is called

   _____ .

8. Someone who is not courteous is _____ .

9. A _____ consists of many people living together.

10. When we separate parts from a connection, we _____
    them.

■ *Practicing Strategies: Combining Context Clues and Word Elements*

Combining the strategies of context clues and word elements is a good way to figure out unknown words. In the following sentences, each italicized word contains a word element that you have studied in this chapter. Using the meaning of the word element and the context of the sentence, make an intelligent guess about the meaning of the italicized word. Your instructor may ask you to check the meaning in your dictionary when you have finished.

1. Since the findings of the two scientists were completely *congruent,* they collaborated in publishing them.

   Congruent means _____ .

2. After seven active children played in the living room all day, it was in a state of *disarray*.

   Disarray means _____ .

3. In many movie musicals, stars *lip-synch* lyrics that are actually sung by other people.

   Lip-synch means _____

   _____   _____ .

4. We *dismantled* the machine into twenty-five pieces.

   Dismantled means _____   _____ .

5. At the *confluence* of the stream with the Colorado River, the color of the water revealed both sources.

   Confluence means _____ .

■ *Companion Words*

Complete each sentence with the word that fits best. Choose your answers from the words below. You may use each word more than once.

Choices: with, on, between, of, in

1. There is a disparity _____ my goals and my achievements.

2. The movie critic presented a synopsis _____ the film.

3. There is a sparsity _____ food in starving countries.

4. Two people collaborated _____ the project.

5. The style is a synthesis _____ many fashion trends.

6. In the evening, people congregate _____ the town square.

7. I like to intersperse working _____ socializing.

8. My taste in clothing is compatible _____ my sister's taste.

9. We concur _____ your decision.

10. The Beatles were contemporaries _____ my professor.

■ *Writing with Your Words*

This exercise will give you practice in writing effective sentences that use the vocabulary words. Each sentence is started for you. Complete it with an interesting phrase that also indicates the meaning of the italicized word.

1. We read the *synopsis* so that _____

_____ .

2. A *communal* kitchen _____

_____ .

3. A *charismatic* person _____

_____ .

4. A *syndrome* _____

_____ .

5. My favorite *cuisine* is _____

_____ .

6. The taste of ketchup is *compatible* with _____

_____ .

7. Most people *concur* that _____

_____ .

8. Because the plot of the movie was not *coherent,* _____

_____ .

9. You would know a person was *gregarious* if _____

_____ .

10. Students often *intersperse* periods of studying with _____

_____ .

Passage

Family Business

(1) "Like father, like son" goes the **cliché.** But this story is about three generations that are both alike and different. The Schenkman family has a grandfather, Edgar, and a father, Peter, who are classical musicians, and a son, Eric, who is a star rock guitarist and former member of the Spin Doctors.

Grandfather Edgar Schenkman played the violin and viola. He was the head of a department at the Juilliard School of Music, as well as conductor of several orchestras. **(2)** His son and grandson **concur** that his knowledge of music was "awesome." He was, as Eric says, a "heavy cat."

Edgar's son, Peter, grew up surrounded by classical music. From the time he was a small child, Edgar insisted that Peter play the violin, although Peter remembers hating the instrument. In rebellion, Peter decided to take up the cello at the age of fourteen. **(3)** With the **bravado** of a teenager, he told his father that in six months he could play better than any cellist in Edgar's orchestra. Peter proved he was right, and today he leads the cello section of the Toronto Symphony Orchestra.

(4) But music is a difficult profession and can cause strains that lead to family **discord.** After moving three times in just a few years, Peter was divorced from his wife. Eric is the son of that broken marriage.

Growing up with this heritage, Eric also became fascinated with music, but this time, it was with the rock music of his **contemporaries.** He refused to study the violin because he didn't like the squeaky sounds of the bow on the strings. Instead, he chose the electric guitar. He remembers quiet summers spent at his grandparents' country house, listening to birds sing—and wondering how to make those sounds on the guitar.

Eric finally decided to become a musician like his father and grandfather, but unlike them, he became a rock guitarist. His family reacted cautiously, for rock did not seem **compatible** with the delicate, refined sounds of classical music. **(5)** Edgar and Peter considered the electric guitar a somewhat **disreputable** instrument. As Eric said, "Rock and roll is music your parents don't like."

Although the music they make sounds different, Eric and his father, Peter, are both dedicated professionals. They start to practice before dawn, and, as night falls, they are still playing. **(6)** Eric does not fit the image of a **gregarious** rock star. Instead, he often practices alone, striving to be as fine a player on the guitar as his grandfather and father have been on the violin, viola, and cello.

Eric's first years as a musician were difficult. **(7)** He worked in ten or fifteen different bands, playing to **sparse** audiences and hoping for a record contract.

Then he **collaborated** with Chris Baron, Mark White, and Aaron Comess to form the Spin Doctors—a group that became enormously successful. The group's sound, a **synthesis** of hard rock and jazz, captured the imagination of people throughout North America. **(8)** Their hit album *A Pocket Full of Kryptonite* rocketed them to the **zenith** of the rock world. **(9)** Crowds of up to thirty thousand people **congregated** at their concerts.

After his success with the Spin Doctors, Eric formed his own group. He has since toured with such stars as Sinead O'Connor.

Although still young, Eric earns far more money than either his father or grandfather ever did. **(10)** There is a **disparity** between the incomes of rock stars and those of classical musicians. Despite their technical skill and dedication, even the best-known classical musicians do not receive the financial rewards of such **charismatic** rock performers as Mick Jagger and Madonna.

Is there a link between rock music and classical music, or will the two worlds continue to be **segregated,** with separate audiences and lifestyles? Eric's relatives admit that they still don't understand rock. Yet they appreciate the success and satisfaction it has brought him. As grandfather Edgar said, "It took two generations of classical musicians to produce one rock star."

But Eric feels that the two musical traditions form a coherent whole. To him, all music, whether classical or rock, is about emotion. He is also proud to continue his family's tradition. He says, "You rebel; then you realize you're just the same." Sometimes, as he stands on stage, he remembers the music of his grandfather or father as he expresses his own feelings through rock.

Source: "Family Business" produced by Karin Wells, Canadian Broadcasting Corporation, 1994, from the program "Sunday Morning." Used with permission.

■ *Exercise*

Each numbered sentence below corresponds to a sentence in the Passage. Fill in the letter of the choice that makes the sentence mean the same as its corresponding sentence in the Passage.

1. "Like father, like son," goes the _____ .
   a. intelligent sentence   b. sad truth   c. overused expression
   d. famous advertisement

2. His son and grandson _____ that his knowledge of music was "awesome."
   a. agree   b. think   c. state   d. know

3. With the _____ of a teenager, he told his father that he could play better than any cellist in the orchestra.
   a. sincere feelings   b. showy courage   c. bad manners
   d. hopeful bragging

4. A musical profession can cause strains that lead to family _____ .
   a. disagreement   b. poverty   c. tears   d. hopelessness

5. Eric and Peter considered the electric guitar a somewhat _____ instrument.
   a. bad sounding   b. not helpful   c. not good looking
   d. not respectable

6. Eric does not fit the image of a(n) _____ rock star.
   a. sociable   b. loud   c. intelligent   d. wealthy

7. He played to _____ audiences.
   a. loud   b. poor   c. small   d. young

8. Their hit album rocketed them to the _____ of the rock world.
   a. richest   b. happiest point   c. best   d. top

9. Crowds of up to thirty thousand people _____ at their concerts.
   a. cheered   b. danced   c. socialized   d. gathered

10. There is a _____ between the incomes of rock stars and those of classical musicians.
    a. difference   b. lot of money   c. justice   d. growth

■ *Discussion Questions*

1. In what ways does Eric feel that rock and classical music are similar?

2. How are Edgar, Peter, and Eric both alike and different?

3. Do you think it is fair to have a disparity in the incomes of classical and rock musicians? Why or why not?

◀ ENGLISH IDIOMS

Agreement and Anger

English has many idioms that express agreement, which brings us together with others, and anger, which sets us apart. People who become angry are said to *lose their heads, blow their tops,* or *lose their cool.* Such individuals *let off steam* through harsh words or actions.

Other idioms concern negative feelings that are not quite as strong as anger. *To speak one's piece* is to speak frankly, and usually with some anger, but without losing one's temper. Somebody who annoys you *rubs you the wrong way.*

People calm their anger and make peace, or *make up* with others. When people realize they have been wrong and want to regain friendship or influence, they *mend fences,* perhaps by apologizing. Similarly, when people find that they are in agreement or have interests in common, they are said to have *common ground.*

If you are angry with people, you might *read them the riot act,* or give a strong warning or scolding. The original riot act was passed in 1774 to stop protests against King George III of England. When more than a dozen people gathered, a riot act was read, ordering them to disperse. If they did not obey, they were imprisoned or shot.

REVIEW

Chapters 5–8

■ *Reviewing Words in Context*

Complete each sentence with the word or phrase that fits best. Use each choice only once.

a. abduction   g. eject   m. philanthropist
b. anthropological h. extricate   n. psychosomatic
c. autobiography   i. genocide   o. status quo
d. cliché   j. intersperse p. subdue
e. congregate   k. nadir   q. syndrome
f. disreputable   l. odyssey   r. synthesis

1. The _____ gave a large donation to the university.

2. In the 1700's Captain James Cook sailed on an adventurous

   _____ to Australia.

3. People are often advised to _____ periods of exercise with periods of rest.

4. An usher may _____ a noisy person from a theater.

5. An old _____ states that "Home is where the heart is."

6. The _____ study described several primitive cultures in Asia.

7. We were shocked by the _____ of the child, and we hoped she would be returned to her parents.

8. In the summer, many people _____ in the plaza to listen to music and drink coffee.

9. Rich and powerful people often want to preserve the

   _____ .

10. Her artistic style is a _____ of several traditions.

11. The widespread murder of the minority group was _____

12. People are often interested in reading the _____ of a sports star.

13. My _____ illness was caused by stress and tension.

14. Nobody trusted the _____ woman.

15. Abused children may suffer from "shaken baby" _____ .

■ *Passage for Word Review*

Complete each blank in the Passage with the word that makes the best sense. The choices include words from the vocabulary lists along with related words. Use each choice only once.

a. autobiography
b. compatible
c. concur
d. deduced

e. equilibrium
f. equitable
g. interminable
h. psyche

i. reconcile
j. subconscious
k. subordinate
l. vivacity

My First and Worst Job Interview

Every working person remembers the frightening experience of interviewing for a job. Before my first interview, I had a feeling there would be a disaster, and I was almost right!

Before the interview, I wondered about what the person interviewing me would be like. Would it be a man or a woman? Would he or she be a **(1)** _____ person whom I could get along with, or someone I could not like or trust?

I tried to dress in good taste for the interview. I didn't want to look too unusual, but I did want to get some attention. I thought about how to behave. I wanted to display some **(2)** _____ , but I didn't want to overshadow the person who was interviewing me. I wanted to seem willing to be a(n) **(3)** _____ to him or her, but still make it clear that I have a mind of my own.

Finally the big day arrived, and I went off for the interview. As I waited nervously in the reception room, the telephone rang. An emergency had come up!

After what seemed an **(4)** _____ wait (it was really half an hour), the boss signaled me to come into her office. The first thing she did was to ask me what had made me choose this career. I panicked! Five years of training, and I couldn't even remember why I wanted to be an engineer. I became nervous and felt like I had completely lost my

(5) _____ . Finally, I thought up a silly answer, which I'm sure wasn't satisfactory: "I like engineering."

When my interviewer saw that I was incapable of replying, she decided to talk about the company. It was well-known, and she described its excellent opportunities for advancement as well as the

(6) _____ way it treated all employees. Trying to involve me in conversation, she asked me things like "What do you think?" and

"Do you **(7)** _____ with my point of view?"

After a while, she glanced at her watch and said, "Well, it looks like we are at the end of our time. Nice talking with you, and you will hear from us."

Filled with gloom, I crawled home. My **(8)** _____

was in a terrible state. Naturally, I **(9)** _____ that I had

not been chosen for the job. I began to **(10)** _____ myself to the prospect of spending more months looking for work.

The next day, I got a call. I had gotten the job! It seems that my excellent grades in school had persuaded the supervisor to hire me. All that studying had rewarded me with a good position.

But I never want to interview for a job again!

■ *Reviewing Learning Strategies*

New words from word elements   Below are words you have not studied that are formed from classical word elements. Using your knowledge of these elements, write in the word that best completes each sentence. You may have to capitalize some words. Use each choice only once.

a. anthropogenesis   e. immobile   i. regenerates
b. coactor   f. inequity   j. sympathy
c. distaste   g. injection   k. synonym
d. ex-member   h. intractable   l. vivid

1. _____ refers to the origins of human beings.

2. When two things are not fair, or equal, there is a(n) _____ _____ .

3. If you are not moving, you are _____ .

4. When a plant grows new leaves or is "born again," after appearing

to be dead, it _____ .

5. If you do not like a particular food, you may have a(n)

_____ for it.

6. My _____ and I performed the play together.

7. A(n) _____ person is stubborn or "cannot be
pulled."

8. A person who used to belong to a club is a(n) _____ .

9. A word with the "same name," or same meaning, as another is

a(n) _____ .

10. When a nurse gives you a(n) _____ , something is
"thrown in" to your body.

Word Elements:
Numbers and Measures

In ancient Egypt, Greece, and Rome, the lives of most people were organized around farming. People needed number words to tell them *when* planting should take place, *how many* bushels of grain the soil yielded, and *how much* money they would get for their crops. From these words were developed our modern words for quantities. This chapter presents Latin and ancient Greek word elements for numbers and measurement, which will help you with the meanings of thousands of words.

Chapter Strategy: Word Elements: Numbers and Measures

Chapter Words:

Part 1

uni-	unanimity	*di-, du-*	dilemma
	unilateral		duplicity
mono-	monarchy	*tri-*	trilogy
	monopoly		trivial
bi-	bilingual	*dec-*	decade
	bipartisan		decimate

Part 2

cent-	centennial	*integer*	disintegrate
	centigrade		integrity
ambi-, amphi-	ambiguous	*magn-, mega-*	magnanimous
	ambivalence		magnitude
ann, enn	annals	*meter*	metric
	perennial		symmetrical

Did You Know?

How Were the Months of the Year Named?

Did you ever wonder how the months got their names? Many of our months are based on number word elements. It took civilization thousands of years to develop an accurate calendar. Ancient calendars were so inaccurate that people often found themselves planting crops when the calendar claimed that winter was approaching. A famous Roman, Julius Caesar, helped to reform the calendar about two thousand years ago, and we have had many other changes since then. Even now, however, we must adjust the length of our years by adding an extra day (February 29) in every fourth, or leap, year. Since the Romans enacted a major calendar reform, our months bear Latin names.

January gets its name from the god Janus, the doorkeeper of the gate of heaven and the god of doors. Since doors are used to enter, Janus represented beginnings, and the first month of the year is dedicated to him. Janus is pictured with two faces, looking back to the past year as well as forward to the new year.

February comes from Februa, the Roman festival of purification. *March* is named for Mars, the Roman god of war. *April* has an uncertain origin. It may have been from *apero*, which means "second," for at one time it was the second month of the year, or from *aperīre* (to open) since it is the month when flowers and trees open out in bloom.

May comes from the goddess of fertility, Maia. It was natural to name a spring month for the goddess who was thought to control the crops. *June* was named either for the Junius family of Roman nobles or for the goddess Juno, wife of Jupiter. *July* honors Julius Caesar, the famous Roman we have mentioned. You will read about him in the Passage for this chapter.

August is named for Augustus Caesar, the nephew of Julius Caesar and the first emperor of Rome. His actual name was Octavian, but he took the title of *Augustus* (distinguished). The word *august* still means "distinguished" when the second syllable in the word is stressed.

The last four months all contain number prefixes: *September, sept* (seven); *October, oct* (eight); *November, nov* (nine); *December, dec* (ten). As you can see, the number roots are wrong! How did the ninth, tenth, eleventh, and twelfth months get the elements of seven, eight, nine, and ten?

Until 153 B.C. the new year was celebrated in March, so the months corresponded to the correct numbers. Then a change in the calendar left these months with the wrong meanings.

Learning Strategy

Word Elements: Numbers and Measures

Every word element in this chapter has a meaning of number or measurement. A list of the prefixes for the first ten numbers is given below. Although you won't be studying all of them in this chapter, you will find this list a handy reference for textbooks and everyday reading. English uses these number prefixes frequently; in fact, we are still making new words from them.

Prefix	*Meaning*	*Example Word*
*uni-	one	unidirectional (in one direction)
*mono-	one	monologue (speech by one person)
*bi-	two	bidirectional (in two directions)
*di-, du-	two	diatomic (made up of two atoms)
*tri-	three	trio (a musical group of three)
quad-, quar-	four	quartet (a musical group of four)
quint-, quin-	five	quintet (a musical group of five)
sex-	six	sextet (a musical group of six)
sept-	seven	septet (a musical group of seven)
oct-	eight	octet (a musical group of eight)
nov-	nine	novena (a prayer offered for nine days)
*dec-	ten	decade (ten years)

*You will study these word elements intensively in this chapter.

To test your understanding of these number word prefixes, fill in the blanks in the following sentences.

a. A duplex is an apartment with _____ floors.

b. A trilingual person speaks _____ languages.

c. A quadruped is an animal that walks on _____ feet.

d. When a mother has quintuplets, _____ children are born.

e. Sextuple means to multiply by _____ .

f. If something is produced in septuplicate, there are

_____ copies of it altogether.

(*Answers:*   a. 2   b. 3   c. 4   d. 5   e. 6   f. 7)

All the word elements you will study in this chapter are either number prefixes *(uni-, mono-, bi-, di-, tri-, dec-, cent-)* or measurement roots and prefixes *(ambi-, ann, integer, magn-, meter).*

Element	Meaning	Origin	Function	Chapter Words
				Part 1
uni-	one	Latin	prefix	unanimity, unilateral
mono-	one; single	Greek	prefix	monarchy, monopoly
bi-	two	Latin	prefix	bilingual, bipartisan
di-, du-	two	Greek; Latin	prefix	dilemma, duplicity
tri-	three	Greek; Latin	prefix	trilogy, trivial
dec-	ten	Greek; Latin	prefix	decade, decimate
				Part 2
cent-	hundred	Latin	prefix	centennial, centigrade
ambi-, amphi-	both; around	Latin; Greek	prefix	ambiguous, ambivalence
ann, enn	year	Latin	root	annals, perennial
integer	whole; complete	Latin	root	disintegrate, integrity
magn-, mega-	large	Latin; Greek	prefix	magnanimous, magnitude
meter, -meter	measure	Greek; Latin	root suffix	metric, symmetrical

This chapter presents a large number of word elements for study, twelve in all. However, since the number prefixes follow a clear pattern, you will find them easy to learn. They are arranged in order of the numbers they represent, rather than in alphabetical order. The first six are discussed below.

Prefixes

Part 1

uni- (one)

The Latin prefix for one, *uni-*, is used in many English words. To *unite*, for example, is to make several things into one. *Unisex* clothing uses one design that is suitable for both men and women.

The *unicorn* was a mythical animal of great grace and beauty. Named for its one horn, it was supposed to have the legs of a deer, the tail of a lion, and the body of a horse. It is often represented as white with a red head and a horn of white, red, and black. Certainly, this animal would have had an interesting appearance!

mono- (one, single)

The Greek prefix for one, *mono-*, is usually joined to Greek combining roots. For example, *monogamy* is marriage to one person. A *monologue* is a speech given by one person. *Mono-* is also used to form many technical words used in scientific fields.

bi- (two)

The Latin prefix for two, *bi-*, forms words such as *bifocals*, glasses that contain two visual corrections. When the *bicycle* was invented in the 1860s, it was named for its two wheels.

di-, du- (two)

This Greek prefix for two is often used in scientific and technical words, so you will find it useful in your college courses. For example, the word *dichromatic* refers to animals that change their colors in different seasons and, therefore, have two colors.

tri- (three)

A *triangle* is a three-sided figure. A *tricornered* hat has a brim turned up on three sides. A *tricycle* has three wheels.

dec- (ten)

The *decimal* system uses the base ten. The common word *dime*, a tenth part of a dollar, is also taken from the prefix *dec* .

Words to Learn

Part 1

uni-

1. **unanimity** (noun)   yōo′nə-nĭm′ə-tē

From Latin: *uni-* (one) + *animus* (soul) (When people agree, they seem to have one soul.)

complete agreement

Few political issues receive **unanimity** of opinion.

The nation demonstrated **unanimity** in opposing the aggressor's threat.

In a surprising display of **unanimity,** every city council member voted to ban parking on Main Street.

▶ *Related Word*
unanimous   (adjective)   The winner of the 1996 Miss Jefferson City contest was the judges' *unanimous* choice.

2. **unilateral** (adjective)   yōō′nə-lăt′ər-əl

From Latin: *uni-* (one) + *latus* (side)

arbitrary; one sided; relating to only one side or part

Without consulting Congress, the U.S. President made a **unilateral** decision to invade the small country.

Students and faculty were angered when the dean of student services made a **unilateral** decision to ban all smoking from campus.

mono-

3. **monarchy** (noun)   mŏn′ər-kē   plural: monarchies

From Greek: *mono-* (one) + *arkein* (rule)

a state ruled by a king, queen, or emperor

Morocco is a **monarchy.**

NOTE: Rule in a monarchy is hereditary and passes from parent to child, usually in the male line.

▶ *Related Word*
monarch (noun)   One *monarch,* Henry VIII of England (1491–1547), was married six times.

Although *monarchs* once held absolute power, there are now many constitutional *monarchies,* or governments that limit the power of kings. Bhumibol Adulyadej, the constitutional monarch of Thailand, has provided stable leadership by supporting democratic institutions and thwarting the efforts of military leaders to seize power. Adulyadej has little power but enormous influence.

---

4. **monopoly** (noun)   mə-nŏp′ə-lē

From Greek: *mono-* (single) + *pōlein* (to sell) (When only one company or person can sell something, a monopoly exists.)

exclusive possession or control

Some states have a **monopoly** on the sale of liquor.

▶ *Related Words*
monopolistic (adjective)   England once maintained *monopolistic* control over the sale of salt in India.

monopolize (verb)   The teenager *monopolized* the family telephone.

bi-

5. **bilingual** (adjective)   bī-lĭng′gwəl

From Latin: *bi-* (two) + *lingua* (tongue, language)

having or speaking two languages

Children can easily become **bilingual,** but adults have more difficulty learning a second language.

The **bilingual** prayer book was printed in Hebrew and English.

▶ *Related Word*
bilingualism (noun)   Oswaldo's *bilingualism* was useful when he vacationed in Mexico.

A large number of people in both Canada and the United States are *bilingual*. Many Canadians speak French and English. In the United States, the most widely spoken languages, after English, are Spanish, Vietnamese, Hmong, Cantonese, Cambodian, Korean, Laotian, Navajo, Tagalog, and Russian.

---

6. **bipartisan** (adjective)   bī-pär′tə-zən

From Latin: *bi-* (two) + *pars* (part)

supported by members of two parties

Both Republicans and Democrats on the **bipartisan** committee worked on reforms for Social Security.

di-, du-

7. **dilemma** (noun)   dĭ-lĕm′ə

From Greek: *di-* (two) + *lēmma* (proposition) (A choice between two propositions or alternatives puts us in a dilemma.)

problem; difficult choice between equally bad things

Dorothy was faced with the **dilemma** of having either to drop the course or to flunk it.

At the start of the Civil War, Robert E. Lee, a talented general, was asked by President Lincoln to lead the Union (or northern) Army. Lee was faced with a *dilemma*. He opposed the withdrawal of the southern states from the Union and owned no slaves. However, he also felt deep loyalty to the southern state of Virginia. Lee turned down Lincoln's offer and eventually led the troops of the Confederacy (or south). Both choices in this dilemma led Lee to war. He is remembered as a great soldier and an honorable man.

---

8. **duplicity** (noun)   d$\overline{oo}$-plĭs′ə-tē

From Latin: *du*- (two) + *plicāre* (to fold or complicate) (A person who is involved in duplicity is not straightforward but is "folded in two ways.")

deceitfulness; double-dealing

> The spy's **duplicity** was revealed to a shocked nation.
>
> I was hurt by the **duplicity** of the boyfriend who cheated on me.

▶ *Related Word*
   duplicitous (adjective)   The *duplicitous* leader betrayed his allies.

tri-

9. **trilogy** (noun)   trĭl′ə-jē

From Greek: *tri*- (three) + *log* (word; to speak)

a group of three books, plays, or stories

> The *Cairo **Trilogy*** by Naghib Mafouz tells the story of a traditional Egyptian family in a country rapidly becoming modern.

10. **trivial** (adjective)   trĭv′ē-əl

From Latin: *tri*- (three) + *via* (road) (In Latin, *trivium* meant "where three roads meet," the public square where people would gossip.)

unimportant; silly

> Fashion is a **trivial** topic when compared to world peace.
>
> The teenager's fight with her friend upset her, but seemed **trivial** to her parents.

ordinary; commonplace

It was a **trivial** task for the experienced electrician to install the new plug.

▶ *Related Words*
    trivia (noun)   Stan was an expert on heavy metal music *trivia*.
    triviality (noun)   This *triviality* is not worth our attention.

dec-

11. **decade** (noun)   dĕk′ād′

From Greek: *dec-* (ten) (*Dekas* meant "group of ten.")

a ten-year period

    In a single **decade,** every farm in the county was replaced with suburban housing.

    Due to the demands of supporting a family, it took Mr. Markman almost a **decade** to complete his college degree.

12. **decimate** (verb)   dĕs′ĭ-māt′

From Latin: *dec-* (ten) (*Decimāre* meant "to take the tenth." This was the severe practice of killing every tenth soldier, chosen by lot, in order to punish a mutiny.)

To destroy or kill a large part of

    Starvation **decimated** the ship's crew.

    Hailstones **decimated** the farmer's crop.

▶ *Related Word*
    decimation (noun)   After its *decimation* by bombing during World War II, the Dutch city of Rotterdam was completely rebuilt.

Exercises

Part 1

■ *Definitions*

Match each word in the left-hand column with a definition from the right-hand column. Use each choice only once.

1. unanimity _____
2. dilemma _____
3. decade _____
4. monarchy _____
5. decimate _____
6. bilingual _____
7. trivial _____
8. unilateral _____
9. monopoly _____
10. trilogy _____

a. arbitrary
b. deceitfulness
c. unimportant
d. speaking two languages
e. supported by both sides
f. ten-year period
g. complete agreement
h. three books or plays
i. to destroy most of something
j. control by one person or company
k. problem
l. a state ruled by a king

■ *Meanings*

Match each word element to its meaning. Two of the choices in the right-hand column must be used twice.

1. uni- _____
2. di- _____
3. dec- _____
4. mono- _____
5. bi- _____
6. tri- _____

a. ten
b. three
c. one
d. two

■ *Words in Context*

Complete each sentence with the word that fits best. Use each choice only once.

a. unanimity   e. bilingual   i. trilogy
b. unilateral   f. bipartisan   j. trivial
c. monarchy   g. dilemma   k. decade
d. monopoly   h. duplicity   l. decimate

1. The three movies in one popular _____ include *Naked Gun, Naked Gun 2½: The Smell of Fear,* and *Naked Gun 33⅓: The Final Insult.*

2. This _____ matter is not worth my attention.

3. Until 1893, Hawaii was a(n) _____ ruled by a queen.

4. The man had a(n) _____ on all the business in town, and no one else could compete.

5. The _____ between 1960 and 1970 was marked by growing freedom in lifestyles and politics.

6. In an act of terrible _____ , the man betrayed his own brother.

7. The workers showed their _____ when all of them agreed to take a pay cut to save the company.

8. Lubna was faced with the _____ of living in extreme poverty or going to an unfamiliar country.

9. Without asking anyone's advice, the general made a

   _____ decision to attack.

10. Canadian Liberals and Conservatives alike supported the

   _____ measure.

■ *Using Related Words*

Complete each sentence by using a word from the group of related words above it. You may need to capitalize a word when you put it into a sentence. Use each choice only once.

1. decimation, decimated

   In Peru, the vicuña population has been _____ by hunters who kill the animals for their silky coats. To stop this

_____ , the Peruvian government once banned the sale of vicuña hair. Recently, however, the government has allowed people to cut the hair of the vicuña without killing it. This policy permits traders to make a living, while the vicuña population grows.

2. trivial, triviality

It might seem that the thumb is a _____ part of the human body. Yet this unique finger is hardly a

_____ . It enables us to grasp things in our hands and inspect them in a way that is unique in the animal world.

3. bilingual, bilingualism

Many people living in India are _____ . They speak both English and another language, such as Hindi, Telugu,

or Bengali. This _____ enables them to communicate in different areas of the country.

4. duplicity, duplicitous

There is no more shocking _____ than that of a general who betrays his own country. Entrusted with defending a fort during the American Revolution, Benedict Arnold prepared to betray it to the British. When his plans were discovered, he fled to

England. To this day the name of the _____ Arnold symbolizes a traitor.

5. monopolized, monopoly

For many years, one company had _____ long-distance telephone services. During the 1970s and 1980s, an antitrust suit determined that there was an illegal

_____ on this service. Now, the public is free to choose a long-distance carrier from among many different companies.

■ *Reading the Headlines*

This exercise presents five headlines that might appear in newspapers. Read each headline and then answer the questions that follow. (Remember that small words, such as *is, are, a,* and *the,* are often left out of newspaper headlines.)

MONARCH PURSUES TRIVIAL PASTIMES

1. Is the person a ruler? _____

2. Is the person spending time in valuable ways? _____

LOCAL GOVERNMENTS DISPLAY UNANIMITY IN DEALING WITH DILEMMA OF ILLEGAL DRUG SALES

3. Do the governments agree? _____

4. Is the problem easy to solve? _____

DUPLICITY OF GENERAL LEADS TO DECIMATION OF TROOPS

5. Was the general an honorable man? _____

6. Did troops die? _____

IN UNILATERAL DECISION, DEPARTMENT HEAD CUTS BILINGUAL PROGRAMS

7. Did the department head consult others? _____

8. Will there be less education in two languages? _____

BIPARTISAN SUPPORT SHOWN FOR BREAKING UP A DECADE OF GOVERNMENT MONOPOLY ON SALES OF GRAIN

9. Did only one party support this? _____

10. Did many agencies control the sale of grain? _____

Word Elements

Part 2

Part 2 presents the last number prefix, *cent-*, as well as five roots and prefixes that refer to quantities.

cent- (one hundred)
:   The prefix *cent-* is used in many common words. A *century* is a period of one hundred years. A *cent* is a coin worth one-hundredth of a dollar.

ambi-, amphi- (both; around)
:   These prefixes have two meanings. The meaning of "both" occurs in the word *ambidextrous,* meaning "able to use both hands." The meaning of "around" is found in *amphitheater,* a theater with seats on all sides of, or around, the stage. This prefix comes from ancient Greek and Latin: *amphi-* is the Greek form; *ambi-* is the Latin form.

The common word *ambitious* is derived from the Latin verb *ambīre* (to go around). In ancient Rome, an ambitious person was a candidate who "went around" asking people to vote for him. Now, of course, an ambitious person is one who desires achievement.

---

ann, enn (year)
:   An *annual* event occurs every year. At times, *ann* is spelled *enn,* as in the word *perennial.*

integer (whole; complete)
:   This root can refer to numbers, as in the English word *integer,* which means a whole number without a fraction value. Thus, 3 is an integer, but 3.5 is not. In Latin, *integer* also describes a "whole" person, who does not have serious character flaws. Such a person is said to have *integrity.*

magn-, mega- (large)
:   To *magnify* something is to make it bigger. Recent books have appeared about *megatrends,* meaning large trends in society. A *megalopolis* is a region including several large cities. *Magn-* is the Latin spelling; *mega-* is the Greek spelling.

meter, -meter (measure)
:   This element often appears as a root but can also be used as a suffix. One word using *meter* as a root is *metronome,* an instrument for measuring musical time. The element *-meter* is used as a suffix in the words

thermometer, an instrument for measuring heat, and *speedometer,* an instrument for measuring speed.

Words to Learn

Part 2

cent-

13. **centennial** (noun)   sĕn-tĕn′ē-əl

    From Latin: *cent-* (one hundred) + *ann* (year)

    one-hundred-year anniversary; a period of one hundred years

    > Residents celebrated the **centennial** of the city's founding.

The *quincentennial,* or 500th anniversary, of the first voyage of Christopher Columbus to the Americas was celebrated in 1992. (Note that *quin* means 5 and *cent* means 100.) Financed by Spanish royalty, Columbus set off to find a path to India. Instead, he landed in the Americas, reaching San Salvador, Cuba, and Haiti in 1492.

Although Columbus is often credited with "discovering America," it should be remembered that the Americas were first populated many thousands of years before by ancestors of the Native Americans who crossed from Russia over the Bering Strait.

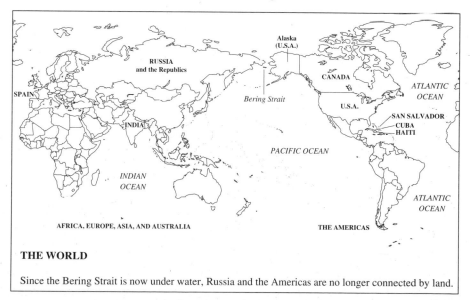

THE WORLD

Since the Bering Strait is now under water, Russia and the Americas are no longer connected by land.

14. **centigrade** (adjective)   sĕn′tĭ-grād′

From Latin: *centi-* (one hundred) + *gradus* (step)

referring to a temperature scale based on one hundred degrees

> A temperature of 35 degrees **centigrade** would indicate summer heat.

> Many signs now display outdoor temperatures in both the **centigrade** and Fahrenheit scales.

NOTE: 1. The *centigrade* scale is also referred to as *celsius.* 2. In the *centigrade* scale, 0° marks the freezing point of water and 100° marks its boiling point. In the Fahrenheit scale, named for its founder, Daniel Fahrenheit, water freezes at 32° and boils at 212°.

ambi-, amphi-

15. **ambiguous** (adjective)   ăm-bĭg′yo͞o-əs

From Latin: *ambi-* (around) + *agere* (to lead) (When something is ambiguous, two meanings are equally possible, and a person is led around rather than "straight toward" the meaning.)

not clear; having two or more meanings

> The **ambiguous** test item was difficult to answer.

▶ *Related Word*
>   **ambiguity** (noun) (ăm′bĭ-gyo͞o′ə-tē) The *ambiguity* of my mother's answer left me confused.

The great linguist Noam Chomsky has pointed out the *ambiguity* of the sentence: They are flying planes. This sentence can mean either "The planes are meant for flying" or "Those people are flying the planes."

16. **ambivalence** (noun)   ăm-bĭv′ə-ləns

From Latin: *ambi-* (both) + *valēre* (to be strong) (A person who is ambivalent about something has two equally strong feelings about it.)

existence of mixed or conflicting feelings

> The child felt **ambivalence** toward the roller-coaster ride, which inspired both excitement and fear.

▶ *Related Word*
>   **ambivalent** (adjective) Ajay was *ambivalent* about the difficult, but valuable, course.

3. ambi-, amphi- _____

4. cent- _____

5. meter _____

6. ann _____

c. both; around

d. large

e. year

f. whole

■ *Words in Context*

Complete each sentence with the word that fits best. Use each choice only once.

a. centennial   e. annals   i. magnanimous
b. centigrade   f. perennial   j. magnitude
c. ambiguous   g. disintegrate   k. metric
d. ambivalence   h. integrity   l. symmetrical

1. Finding good childcare is a(n) _____ problem for working mothers.

2. The _____ message could be interpreted in several different ways.

3. The _____ loser congratulated the winner of the election.

4. The _____ of the scientific society meetings are kept in the library.

5. When it is zero degrees _____ , it is cold outside.

6. Paper will _____ into a powder if it becomes too dry.

7. A person of great _____ can be easily trusted.

8. The tall skyscraper was a building of great _____ .

9. Patrick's _____ about going to college made him delay putting in an application.

10. Arizona was admitted to the United States in 1912 and will celebrate

its _____ in 2012.

■ *Using Related Words*

Complete each sentence by using a word from the group of related words above it. You may need to capitalize a word when you put it into a sentence. Use each choice only once.

1. magnanimous, magnanimity

The great baseball player Lou Gehrig remained _____ even when illness forced him to retire at age 35. In a farewell

speech at Yankee Stadium, he displayed _____ rather than bitterness when he said, "Today I am the luckiest man in the world." He died two years later of what is now sometimes called Lou Gehrig's disease.

2. disintegrate, disintegration

The earth has been hit many times by meteorites from outer space.

Chondrites, one type of meteorite, _____ rapidly

in our harsh weather. This _____ has prevented scientists from knowing exactly how many have landed on our planet.

3. ambivalent, ambivalence

Although the First Amendment ensures freedom of speech in the

United States, many citizens have some _____ toward it. For example, should free speech protect the rights of child pornographers? Should it be legal to yell "Fire" in a crowded

theater? In response to these _____ feelings, and to protect the public, some limits have been placed on the rights granted by this amendment.

4. ambiguity, ambiguous

Nothing is more annoying than _____ directions.

When giving directions, make sure there is no _____ in them.

5. symmetry, symmetrically

The ancient Greeks produced some of the greatest architects in the world. In Athens, the Acropolis temple, a temple dedicated to the goddess Athena, stands as a great architectural achievement. The Greeks perfected a series of decorated columns, which were

arranged _____ . _____ was often used in Greek architecture.

■ *Reading the Headlines*

This exercise presents five headlines that might appear in newspapers. Read each headline and then answer the questions that follow. (Remember that small words, such as *is, are, a,* and *the,* are often left out of newspaper headlines.)

GUIDELINES FOR CELEBRATION OF CITY CENTENNIAL ARE AMBIGUOUS

1. Will the city celebrate its one hundredth anniversary? _____

2. Are the guidelines clear? _____

ANNALS OF STATE SENATE REVEAL AMBIVALENCE ABOUT INCOME TAX

3. Did people look in the records? _____

4. Are the state senators totally against an income tax? _____

CONVERSION TO CENTIGRADE SCALE A PERENNIAL ISSUE IN THE U.S.A.

5. Does the scale involve temperature? _____

6. Is the issue a constant one? _____

ALLIANCE DISINTEGRATES AFTER INTEGRITY OF LEADER IS QUESTIONED

7. Is the alliance continuing? _____

8. Is the honesty of the leader being questioned? _____

MAGNANIMOUS LEADER FORGIVES INSULT OF CONSIDERABLE MAGNITUDE

9. Is the leader noble? _____

10. Was the insult small? _____

Chapter Exercises

■ *Practicing Strategies: New Words from Word Elements*

See how your knowledge of word elements can help you understand new words. Complete each sentence with the word that seems to fit best. Use each choice only once.

a. amphibious
b. bipolar
c. centimeter
d. decapods

e. dioxide
f. integrate
g. magnify
h. monorail

i. monotint
j. photometer
k. trimester
l. uniform

1. A(n) _____ is a picture with tints of one color.

2. A(n) _____ is often used in photography to measure light.

3. Magnets are _____ and have both a positive and a negative charge.

4. Since lobsters and shrimps have ten legs, they are _____ .

5. A(n) _____ aircraft can land on both land and water.

6. A(n) _____ system divides the academic year into three terms.

7. If you _____ something, you make it bigger.

8. Some trains move on a(n) _____ , or single rail.

9. If you _____ one thing with another, you form the two into a whole.

10. Things that are _____ all have the same, or one, appearance.

■ *Practicing Strategies: Combining Context Clues and Word Elements*

Combining the strategies of context clues and word elements is a good way to figure out unknown words. In the following sentences, each italicized word contains a word element that you have studied in this chapter. Using the meaning of the word element and the context of the sentence, make an intelligent guess about the meaning of the italicized word. Your instructor may ask you to check the meaning in your dictionary when you have finished.

1. The gracious room, beautiful furniture, and pleasant music all contributed to the *ambience* of the restaurant.

   Ambience means _____ .

2. Using a microscope, we looked at the *unicellular* life forms.

   Unicellular means _____ .

3. The Jewish religion was the first to practice *monotheism* and to reject the worship of many gods.

   Monotheism means _____ .

4. The *tripartite* system of U.S. government consists of executive, legislative, and judicial branches.

   Tripartite means _____ .

5. Some people believe that they can prevent illness by taking *megadoses* of Vitamin C.

   Megadoses means _____ .

■ *Practicing Strategies: Using the Dictionary*

Read the following definition and then answer the questions below it.

> **sham** (shăm) *n.* **1.** Something false or empty that is purported to be genuine; a spurious imitation. **2.** The quality of deceitfulness; empty pretense. **3.** A person who assumes a false character; impostor: *"He a man! Hell! He was a hollow sham!"* (Conrad). **4.** A decorative cover made to simulate an article of household linen and used over or in place of it: *a pillow sham.* —*adj.* Not genuine; fake: *sham modesty.* —*v.* **shammed, sham•ming, shams.** —*tr.* To put on the false appearance of; feign. —*intr.* To assume a false appearance or character; dissemble. [Perh. dial. var. of SHAME.] —**sham'mer** *n.*

1. What four parts of speech does *sham* function as?

   _____

2. Which common word in the dictionary key contains a vowel pro-

   nounced like the *a* in *sham*? _____

3. Which writer is used to help define *sham*? _____

4. What is the past-tense verb form of *sham*? _____

5. Give the number and the part of speech of the definition that best fits this sentence: "The *sham* on our sofa protected it from dirt."

   _____

■ *Companion Words*

Complete each sentence with the word that fits best. Choose your answers from the words below. You may use each word more than once.

Choices: of, into, toward

1. U.S. citizens were shocked by the duplicity _____ spy Aldrich Ames.

2. Defeated South African President F. W. de Klerk was magnanimous

   _____ the winner, Nelson Mandela.

3. The meeting disintegrated _____ a shouting match.

4. We are shocked by the magnitude _____ the federal deficit.

5. The ambiguity _____ her response left us confused.

■ *Writing with Your Words*

This exercise will give you practice in writing effective sentences that use the vocabulary words. Each sentence is started for you. Complete it with an interesting phrase that indicates the meaning of the italicized word.

1. In a *monarchy,* _____

_____ .

2. If we *decimate* the world's rainforests, _____

_____ .

3. He showed his *integrity* by _____

_____ .

4. I feel *ambivalent* toward _____

_____ .

5. One example of a *trivial* problem is _____

_____ .

6. One *perennial* concern of society is _____

_____ .

7. During the next *decade,* I hope that _____

_____ .

8. There is *unanimous* agreement that _____

_____ .

9. When another person started to *monopolize* my date's attention, I

_____ .

10. Converting to the *metric* system would _____

_____ .

Passage

Julius Caesar—Hero or Villain?

Although the famous Roman Julius Caesar died over two thousand years ago, his legend lives on in the **annals** of history. Some historians see him as a power-hungry villain. Others feel he was a reformer whose brutal assassination almost destroyed Rome. **(1)** However, there is **unanimity** of opinion on one issue: Caesar was the towering figure of his age.

Born about 100 B.C., Caesar came from a poor but noble family. At the time, the rulers of Rome were divided into two parties. The aristocratic party wanted to keep power in its own hands. The radical party wanted the support of the people, many of whom had lost their lands and were living in poverty in Rome. Caesar joined the radical cause.

To be successful, a Roman leader had to conquer new lands and help expand the republic. **(2)** Caesar made conquests of great **magnitude. (3)** He **decimated** resisting forces in Gaul (now Belgium and France) and added this territory to the Roman empire. He invaded England, where he met strange tribes who painted their bodies and worshiped trees.

Caesar was anxious to tell the Romans of his conquests. The books he wrote included a brief statement summarizing his military career: "Veni, vidi, vici." (I came, I saw, I conquered.)

(4) A **decade** of conquest gained Caesar considerable political power. He had formed a ruling "triumvirate" in 60 B.C. with Crassus and Pompey. After Crassus's death, Caesar and Pompey became rivals. **(5)** At first, Caesar felt **ambivalent** about attacking his former friend. The fact that Pompey was married to Caesar's daughter deepened the **dilemma.** However, after some thought, Caesar decided to take decisive action.

In the first act of the conflict, Caesar crossed the Rubicon River in 49 B.C. to challenge Pompey. (To this day the phrase *crossing the Rubicon* means to take an irreversible step.) **(6)** Caesar's victory over Pompey is recorded in a **trilogy,** *Commentary on the Civil War*. His triumph gave him a **monopoly** on Roman leadership, and he took the title of "dictator."

Despite his busy career, Caesar took time for several romantic interests, among them the Egyptian queen Cleopatra. Caesar aroused consid-

Julius Caesar was a unique and towering figure.

erable disapproval when, ignoring his own wife, he invited Cleopatra to Rome.

In his short time as dictator, Caesar accomplished many reforms. He extended Roman citizenship to the whole of Italy. **(7)** He improved the **disintegrating** condition of farming by giving land to soldiers who had served under him. His **integrity** in keeping promises to his soldiers gained him the loyalty of poorer citizens. However, Caesar's reform of the calendar had the most long-lasting effects. He replaced an inaccurate calendar with the improved Julian version. **(8)** In a somewhat more **trivial** action, he named the month of his birth, July, after himself.

(9) Unfortunately, Caesar was a victim of the **perennial** problem of successful people: the jealousy of others. **(10)** Caesar had shown **magnanimity** in not executing old enemies, but they now started to plot against him. Jealousy increased as some thought he might establish a **monarchy,** crowning himself as emperor. One nobleman, Cassius, was particularly angry over his own loss of power. Cassius plotted to assassinate Caesar, and week by week his list of treacherous conspirators grew. The day of Caesar's murder was planned for March 15, 44 B.C., called the Ides of March.

Legend records that Caesar was warned to "beware the Ides of March," but decided to face his fate. The assassins gathered on the floor of the Senate building. When Caesar entered, they attacked him with daggers. Caesar resisted until he realized that, in a terrible act of **duplicity,** his close friend Brutus had turned against him. "Et tu, Brute?" (You too, Brutus?) was his expression of anguish as he submitted to his murderers.

■ *Exercise*

Each numbered sentence below corresponds to a sentence in the Passage. Fill in the letter of the choice that makes the sentence mean the same thing as its corresponding sentence in the Passage.

1. However, there is _____ of opinion on one issue.
   a. division   b. evidence   c. agreement   d. history

2. Caesar made conquests of great _____ .
   a. helpfulness   b. difficulty   c. importance   d. violence

3. He _____ resisting forces in Gaul.
   a. helped   b. greeted   c. fought   d. destroyed

4. A _____ of conquest gained Caesar considerable political power.
   a. ten-year period   b. three-year period   c. twenty-year period
   d. two-year period

5. At first, Caesar felt _____ about attacking his former friend.
   a. guilty   b. hopeful   c. enthusiastic   d. conflicted

6. Caesar's victory is recorded in _____ .
   a. a book   b. two books   c. three books   d. ten books

7. He improved the _____ conditions of farming.
   a. poverty-stricken   b. unjust   c. worsening   d. terrible

8. In a somewhat more _____ action, he named the month of his birth, July, after himself.
   a. heroic   b. dishonest   c. personal   d. unimportant

9. Unfortunately, Caesar was a victim of the ———— problem of successful people: the jealousy of others.
   a. small   b. constant   c. serious   d. noticeable

10. Caesar had shown ———— in not executing old enemies.
    a. stubbornness   b. pride   c. forgiveness   d. weakness

■ Discussion Questions

1. Why was Caesar considered a great soldier?

2. Why do you think Caesar was (or was not) a great leader?

3. Would you have voted to make Caesar an emperor? Why or why not?

E NGLISH I DIOMS

Money

Since numbers and measures are often used in relation to money, the idioms for this chapter concern wealth. A person without any money is referred to as *broke*. To lose all your money is to *lose your shirt*. Not to have enough money is to be *caught short*. People who have been cheated out of money have been *taken to the cleaners* or *ripped off*. Such people may be forced to *live from hand to mouth*, meaning that they have only enough to cover their immediate needs, without any savings for the future.

When a person quickly goes from poverty to wealth, he or she goes *from rags to riches*. That person has a lot of money or is *in the money*. A rich person might *live high on the hog*, in great comfort, and with the best of everything. We could say that the person is *on easy street*.

A rich man or woman who refuses to spend money is often called a *cheapskate*. Kate Robinson inherited five million dollars from her parents but spent only about $80 per year. When she died in 1920, her furniture was stuffed with money. Since then, anybody who has money, but will not spend it, has been called *Cheap Kate* or, in more modern English, a *cheapskate*.

10

Word Elements: Thought and Belief

Our ability to think and our system of beliefs helps to define us as human beings. The importance of thought is apparent when we reason through a difficult problem in school or at work. The things we believe to be morally right affect our behavior. Part 1 of this chapter presents word elements about thought and belief. Part 2 presents prefixes we use when we do *not* believe something. These are prefixes of negation. Finally, several idioms will be discussed in this chapter. An idiom carries a different meaning from what we believe it to have when we first hear it.

Chapter Strategy: Word Elements: Thought and Belief

Chapter Words

Part 1

cred	credibility	*ver*	veracity
	creed		verify
	incredulity		veritable
fid	defiant	*-phobia*	acrophobia
	fidelity		claustrophobia
	fiduciary		xenophobia

Part 2

de-	delude	*Idioms*	behind the eight ball
	destitute		get to first base
	deviate		give carte blanche
non-	nonchalant		hold out an olive branch
	nondenominational		star-crossed
	nondescript		tongue-in-cheek

Did You Know?

Animal Words of Thought and Belief

For thousands of years, animals have played an important part in human beliefs. Primitive human beings knew and admired many types of animals. Often our ancestors tried to give themselves the powers of the animal world. To acquire the speed of a deer or the power of a lion, humans often dressed up in their skins and imitated the animals' movements and cries. These customs have contributed words to modern English. The feared ancient warriors of what is now Norway covered themselves in bear *(ber)* skin shirts *(serkr†* and rushed madly into battle, killing all within sight. From this custom, we derive the phrase *to go berserk,* or crazy.

Many great civilizations worshiped gods in the forms of animals. In ancient Egypt, the goddess Taurt was thought to have the head of a hippo, the back and tail of a crocodile, and the claws of a lioness. In some parts of Egypt, people worshiped cats, crocodiles, and baboons. All three animals have been found carefully preserved as mummies in special cemeteries.

In modern times, some animals retain important places in religion. Traditional Hindus hold one type of cow, the East Indian humped zebu, to be sacred. Since these cows symbolize the riches given by the gods to the Earth, Hindus are forbidden to kill these animals or control them in any way. The cow has come to be identified as a national symbol of modern India. These beliefs have resulted in the English expression *sacred cow,* meaning a belief that is too well established to be challenged.

Some religions have also involved animals in specific rituals. More than two thousand years ago, the ancient Jews chose one goat to symbolize people's sins against God. This goat was released into the desert wilderness, symbolically carrying with it the sins of the people. Although this custom has vanished, the English word *scapegoat* still means someone who takes the blame for another.

The thought processes that connect human beings and animals also remain strong in everyday English. Many of our expressions compare human behavior to that of animals. For example, to *parrot* means to repeat, as a parrot repeats familiar words. To *horse around* means to play, as horses do in a field. A man who is nagged by his wife is called *henpecked,* recalling the behavior of female chickens. When we do something wonderful, we may *crow* about it. We may *eat like pigs* (greedily) or disappoint our host by *eating like birds* (eating little). The generally bad reputation of the rat has given us the phrase *to rat on,* meaning to turn someone in or "squeal" on someone. There are hundreds of word and phrases that reflect our human thoughts about animals.

Can you identify the human meanings given to these common animal expressions?

1. hogwash

2. sitting duck

3. pigeonhole

4. crabby

5. puppy love

6. birdbrain

(*Answers:*   1. nonsense; silly talk   2. an easy target to hit   3. to identify as something very specific, to limit to one thing   4. in a bad mood   5. childish, youthful love   6. a stupid or foolish person)

Learning Strategy

Word Elements: Thought and Belief

The first part of this chapter concentrates on word elements relating to thought and belief. Three roots are presented: *cred* (believe), *fid* (faith), and *ver* (truth). Part 1 also introduces the suffix *-phobia* (fear of). Part 2 of this chapter presents two important prefixes with negative meanings. We use them when we do *not* believe in something. *Non* means "not." *De-* also has a negative sense, indicating "removal from" or "down."

Element	Meaning	Origin	Function	Chapter Words
				Part 1
cred	believe	Latin	root	credibility, creed, incredulity
fid	faith	Latin	root	defiant, fidelity, fiduciary
ver	truth	Latin	root	veracity, verify, veritable
-phobia	fear of	Greek	suffix	acrophobia, claustrophobia, xenophobia
				Part 2
de-	removal from; down	Latin	prefix	delude, destitute, deviate
non-	not	Latin	prefix	nonchalant, nondenominational, nondescript

Word Elements

Part 1

Information on the roots and the suffix for Part 1 is presented below.

cred (believe)

The root *cred* is used in many English words. When we do not believe something, we may call it *incredible*. *Credit* is granted to a customer because merchants believe that they will be repaid.

fid (faith)

The English word *faith* is taken from this root. Because dogs are thought to be faithful companions to human beings, they have traditionally been given the name of *Fido*, meaning "faithful."

ver (truth)

The root *ver* means "truth." A *verdict*, the judgment of a jury, is made up from the root *ver* (truth) and the root *dict* (say). Even that much-used word *very*, meaning "truly" or "really," comes from *ver*.

-phobia (fear of)

As a suffix, *-phobia* describes a strong or illogical fear of something and often forms words that are used in psychology. For example, *nyctophobia* is a fear of the dark. The base word *phobia* also means "fear."

According to Greek mythology, Phobos was the son of Ares, the god of war who was similar to the Roman god Mars. Greek warriors sometimes painted the likeness of Phobos on their shields, hoping that the enemy would run merely at the terrifying sight of his picture.

Words to Learn

Part 1

cred

1. **credibility** (noun)   krĕd′ə-bĭl′ə-tē

   From Latin: *cred* (believe)

   believability; ability to be trusted

> The frequent appearance of Gallup poll results in the media has given these surveys **credibility** with the public.
>
> Our adviser on bridge building lost his **credibility** when we realized he was not an engineer.

▶ *Related Word*

   credible (adjective)   (krĕd′ə-bəl)   The police accepted Susan's *credible* account of the accident.

2. **creed** (noun)   krēd

From Latin: *cred* (believe) (*Crēdo* meant "I believe.")

set of beliefs or principles

> The U.S. juror's **creed** states, "I am a seeker of truth."
>
> Five duties, reciting the words of witness, prayer, charity, fasting, and pilgrimage, are central to the **creed** of the Muslim religion.

NOTE: Creed often refers to a formal system of religious or moral beliefs.

3. **incredulity** (noun)   ĭn′krə-dōō′lə-tē

From Latin: *in-* (not) + *cred* (believe)

disbelief; amazement

> Spanish explorers of the 1500s expressed **incredulity** at the excellent sanitation standards of the Incas and Aztecs.
>
> Reports of the respected citizen's crime were met with **incredulity** by his neighbors.

▶ *Related Word*

   incredulous (adjective)   (ĭn-krĕj′ə-ləs)   People were *incredulous* when told that the boy had survived for three years alone in the forest.

People are often *incredulous* when told that flying in an airplane is safer than driving. However, here are the odds of dying due to various causes (published in Krantz, *What the Odds Are*).

Car crash: 1 in 125
Lightning strike: 1 in 9,100
Skin cancer: 1 in 22,409
Dog attack: 1 in 700,000
Airplane crash: 1 in 4,600,000

fid

4. **defiant** (adjective)   dĭ-fī′ənt

From Latin: *dis-* (not) + *fid* (faith)

refusing to follow orders or rules; resisting boldly

> The **defiant** teenage boy disobeyed school rules by refusing to cut off his ponytail.

> **Defiant** people demonstrated against the military government.

NOTE: Since this word begins with *de,* we might expect it to have the sense of "down." However, the Latin word had a *dis-* prefix, which became *de-* as the word *defiant* went through the French language.

▶ *Related Words*
defiance (noun)   The sergeant's *defiance* shocked his superiors.

defy (verb) (dĭ-fī′)   The Islamic woman *defied* the tradition of her country by not wearing a chador.

5. **fidelity** (noun)   fĭ-dĕl′ə-tē

From Latin: *fid* (faith)

faithfulness to obligation or duty

> Kock Fee showed his **fidelity** to his family by raising the money to bring them from Hong Kong to Canada.

exactness, accuracy

> Compact disc players reproduce music with excellent **fidelity.**

6. **fiduciary** (adjective, noun)   fĭ-doo′shē-ĕr′ē

From Latin: *fid* (faith) (You need to have faith in the person who handles your money.)

pertaining to money or property held for one person (or several people) by others (adjective)

> A retirement fund's board of directors has the **fiduciary** responsibility of managing the money for the fund's investors.

a person holding money for another (noun)

> Under the guidance of the **fiduciary,** the inheritance grew.

ver

7. **veracity** (noun)   və-răs**ʹ**ə-tē

From Latin: *ver* (truth)

truth; accuracy

> Birth records confirmed the **veracity** of the man's claim to be 100 years old.

▶ *Common Phrase:*
  veracity of

8. **verify** (verb)   věr**ʹ**ə-fī

From Latin: *ver* (truth) + *facere* (to make)

to determine the truth or accuracy of

> Before Tawio's loan was approved, a bank officer called to **verify** that he was employed.

> Long-distance truck drivers must **verify** that they rest four hours for every five hours that they drive.

> People often use a dictionary to **verify** a word's meaning.

▶ *Related Word*
  verification (noun)   Scientists obtain *verification* of their results by repeating experiments.

9. **veritable** (adjective)   věr**ʹ**ə-tə-bəl

From Latin: *ver* (truth)

unquestionable, being truly so

> The food show was a **veritable** gold mine of ideas for the student chefs.

almost; nearly; very similar to

> Our 98 cable channels provide a **veritable** feast of TV programs.

NOTE: Veritable is usually used in the phrases of "a veritable _____" or "the veritable _____ ."

-phobia

10. **acrophobia** (noun)   ăk′rə-fō′bē-ə

From Greek: *acros* (highest) + *-phobia* (fear)

fear of heights

> Because she suffered from **acrophobia,** Mrs. Robinson could not visit a friend who lived on the thirty-second floor of a high-rise.

▶ *Related Word*
acrophobic (adjective)   Marck's *acrophobic* attacks prevented him from riding on Ferris wheels.

11. **claustrophobia** (noun)   klôs′trə-fō′bē-ə

From Latin: *claustrum* (enclosed space) + Greek: *-phobia* (fear)

fear of closed or small spaces

> Mr. Stevens's **claustrophobia** caused him to panic when he was stuck in an elevator.

> Denicia felt **claustrophobic** in her small office.

12. **xenophobia** (noun)   zĕn′ə-fōb′ē-ə

From Greek: *xenos* (stranger) + *-phobia* (fear)

fear or hatred of foreigners or foreign things

> Because of rising **xenophobia** in the small country, war broke loose between Muslims and Christians.

> Because of his **xenophobia,** the senator wanted to pass laws that would prohibit immigration into the country.

▶ *Related Word*
xenophobic (adjective)   The *xenophobic* man refused to travel to foreign countries.

What do the following phobias refer to?

1. microphobia

2. ergasophobia

3. arachnophobia

(*Answers:*   1. fear of germs   2. fear of work   3. fear of spiders)

Arachnophobia

Exercises

Part 1

■ Definitions

Match each word in the left-hand column with a definition from the right-hand column. Use each choice only once.

1. verify _____

2. claustrophobia _____

3. credibility _____

4. veracity _____

a. set of beliefs

b. rebellious

c. faithfulness

d. ability to be believed

e. fear of truth

5. creed _____

6. fiduciary _____

7. xenophobia _____

8. defiant _____

9. acrophobia _____

10. fidelity _____

f. disbelief

g. fear of strangers

h. to determine truth or accuracy

i. fear of small spaces

j. fear of heights

k. a person holding money for another

l. truth

■ *Meanings*

Match each word element to its meaning. Use each choice only once.

1. cred _____

2. -phobia _____

3. fid _____

4. ver _____

a. faith

b. fear

c. truth

d. believe

■ *Words in Context*

Complete each sentence with the word that fits best. Use each choice only once.

a. credible
b. creed
c. incredulity
d. defiant

e. fidelity
f. fiduciary
g. veracity
h. verify

i. veritable
j. acrophobia
k. claustrophobia
l. xenophobia

1. The cheap film did not reproduce colors with _____ , so the bride's dress looked green in the photograph.

2. The _____ soldier refused to obey the army's rules.

3. The art dealer tried to _____ that the painting was really the work of the famous artist.

4. My aunt's _____ made her distrust anyone from a foreign country.

5. At first, Yuzuko expressed _____ when she was told she had won the lottery.

6. His _____ made him nervous when he was accidentally locked in the closet.

7. The lawyers expected the jury to believe the story of the

   _____ witness.

8. Charity and forgiveness are central to the _____ of Christianity.

9. The board of a company has a _____ responsibility to manage the money of stockholders.

10. The paintings in our attic proved to be a _____ treasure of old family portraits.

■ *Using Related Words*

Complete each sentence by using a word from the group of related words above it. You may need to capitalize a word when you put it into a sentence. Use each choice only once.

1. defied, defiance

   A man of great conscience who _____ his own government, Sempo Sugihara is credited with saving more than 2,000 Jews from murder during the Holocaust. Because he was the Japanese diplomat to Lithuania, people begged him for visas that would allow them to go to Japan and escape the Nazis. In

   _____ of government orders and at risk to his own life, Sugihara signed the visas as fast as he could write. His memory is revered by humanitarians everywhere.

2. acrophobia, acrophobic

   The 200-foot-high Mackinac Bridge, in Michigan, inspires

_____ in many people, who cannot bear to look down into the water. Some cry or get dizzy. Fortunately, officials

are available to drive the cars of _____ people, who usually shut their eyes during the journey.

3. incredulity, incredulous

People often react with _____ when told that they

can be hypnotized. A person often remains _____ until he or she has tried it. Hypnosis has many uses, including helping people to stop smoking, but it should be attempted only by an expert.

4. verification, verified

Several reports have _____ that falls from high altitudes need not be fatal. In 1990 a Soviet newspaper reported that a woman survived a three-mile fall after a mid-air plane colli-

sion. There has also been _____ of an incident in which a flight attendant fell six miles to the ground—and lived.

5. credibility, credible

Are some old houses haunted? The editors of the *Old House Journal* have received 27 case histories of haunting, giving it new

_____ . Reported incidents included ghostly noises, rushes of cold air, and the actual appearances of ghosts. The intelligence and thoughtfulness behind these reports make them

quite _____ . By the way, most of these owners are delighted to be sharing their homes with these spirits.

■ *True or False?*

Each of the following statements contains one or more words from this section. Read each sentence carefully and then indicate whether you think it is probably true or probably false.

____   1. A defiant teenager obeys all of her parents' rules.

____   2. An acrophobic person would enjoy the view from a high–flying airplane.

_____   3. A claustrophobic person would panic in a tiny closet.

_____   4. A person with xenophobia would have great credibility in dealing with foreigners.

_____   5. "It is now the year 3025" is a statement of veracity.

_____   6. A man who could multiply 70 numbers in his head would be a veritable genius at mental arithmetic.

_____   7. People should verify a fiduciary agent's honesty.

_____   8. Prayer is a part of the creed of most religions.

_____   9. We would express incredulity if we heard that there was a traffic jam during rush hour in a big city.

_____   10. Fidelity is a desirable quality in a friend.

Prefixes

Part 2

Part 2 of this chapter presents two very common prefixes that have a negative meaning: *de-* means "removal from" or "down"; *non-* means "not." Both prefixes are used in thousands of English words.

This Words to Learn section also presents several idioms. These phrases involve our thoughts and beliefs, for an idiom does not carry the meaning we believe it to carry when we first hear it.

de- (removal from; down)

   The prefix *de-* has various meanings. In some English words it has the sense of "removal from." For example, when we *decontaminate* something, we remove the contamination or impurities from it. When people *deforest* land, they remove trees from it. *De-* can also mean "down." When we *depress* a button, we push it down. When something *declines*, it "goes down."

non- (not)

   The prefix *non-* simply means "not." *Nonsense* is something that does not make sense. A *nonjudgmental* person is one who does not make judgments. *Non-* often combines with base words (roots that can stand alone as English words).

Words to Learn

Part 2

de-

13. **delude** (verb)   dĭ-lo͞od′

    From Latin: *de-* (bad) and *lūdere* (to play) (*Delūdere* meant "to deceive, to mock.")

    to mislead; to cause someone to think something that is false

    > The false prophet **deluded** people into thinking the world would end by New Year's Day.

    > Teenagers who **delude** themselves into thinking that they cannot die sometimes take terrible risks.

    ▶ *Related Word*
    delusion (noun)   (dĭ-lo͞o′zhən)   The mentally ill person suffered from the *delusion* that aliens were sending her messages.

    In the days when travel was more difficult, radio sports announcers often could not attend games played in cities away from their homes. Instead, they got news of each play from telegraph wires and "announced" the game over the radio. By providing sound effects such as cheering and the cracking of a baseball bat, announcers *deluded* listeners into thinking that they were hearing eyewitness accounts.

    ---

14. **destitute** (adjective)   dĕs′tə-to͞ot′

    From Latin: *de-* (down) + *stat* (placed)

    without money; poor

    > The **destitute** mother could not afford to feed her baby.

    NOTE: Destitute is a very strong word that means "entirely without resources; broke."

    ▶ *Related Word*
    destitution (noun)   The man's *destitution* forced him to live on the street.

15. **deviate** (verb)   dē′vē-āt′

From Latin: *de-* (removal from) + *via* (road) (*Dēviāre* meant "to go away from the road.")

to vary from a path, course, or norm

> Hikers who **deviate** from the trail risk getting lost in the woods.
>
> Topol **deviated** from tradition when he refused to let his family arrange a marriage for him.

▶ *Common Phrase*
deviate from

▶ *Related Words*
deviant (adjective)   (dē′vē-ənt)   Many mentally ill people show *deviant* behavior. (*Deviant* means "odd in a negative way.")

deviation (noun)   My father's *deviation* from his low-cholesterol diet endangered his health.

non-

16. **nonchalant** (adjective)   nŏn′shə-länt′

From Latin: *non-* (not) + *calēre* (to be warm) (Many people feel physically warm when they get angry. Therefore, someone who is nonchalant, "not warm," does not feel angry or concerned.)

unconcerned; carefree

> With a **nonchalant** toss of the covers, John declared that he had made the bed.
>
> Maria's **nonchalant** attitude toward paying bills ruined her credit rating.

NOTE: Nonchalant can be a somewhat negative word, indicating that someone should care but does not.

▶ *Related Word*
nonchalance (noun)   The soldier displayed *nonchalance* in the face of danger.

17. **nondenominational** (adjective)   nŏn′dĭ-nŏm′ə-nā′shə-nəl

From Latin: *non* (not) + *nomen* (name) (Something "not named" is not associated with any one "group," or religion.)

not associated with one specific religion

> The **nondenominational** hospital chapel welcomed people of all faiths.

18. **nondescript** (adjective)   nŏn'dĭ-skrĭpt'

From Latin: *non-* (not) + *de-* (down) + *script* (write) (Something nondescript cannot be written down because it is hard to describe.)

not distinct; difficult to describe because it lacks individuality

> Stores in the **nondescript** shopping mall all looked alike.
>
> The spy's **nondescript** appearance allowed her to escape detection.

Idioms

19. **behind the eight ball**

at a disadvantage; in a hopeless situation

> Because she missed the first four sessions of the class, Isabella felt that she was **behind the eight ball.**

In eight ball, a pocket billiards game, the object is to hit all the numbered balls into the pockets at the side of the table before trying to sink the eight ball. If the ball you are shooting at is located *behind the eight ball*, your shot is blocked, and you are likely to lose the game.

20. **get to first base**

do the first thing successfully

> If you want to **get to first base** in a job interview, dress neatly.

In baseball, you must run to first base, second base, third base, and then to home plate in order to score. If you cannot even *get to first base*, then you will never score, or get to home plate.

21. **give carte blanche**   kärt blänsh'

From French: a blank document

to give full, unrestricted power

> The Chief of Staff was **given carte blanche** to see the President at any hour.
>
> Sue Ellen's father **gave** her **carte blanche** to spend money.

A *carte blanche* was originally a piece of paper with nothing but a signature on it, used when an army surrendered. The defeated leader would sign his name, and the victor could then write in the terms of surrender.

22. **hold out an olive branch**

make an offer of peace

> The army leader **held out an olive branch** to the rebels when he offered to release captured prisoners.

According to the Bible, God punished the wicked world by sending a flood. However, God chose to save one good man, Noah, along with his family and one pair of each type of animal on Earth. Noah floated in an ark for the forty days of the flood. When the waters went down at last, a dove flew from the boat and brought back an *olive branch* as a symbol of God's peace. Today, both the dove and the olive branch have come to symbolize peace.

23. **star-crossed**

doomed to a bad fate; unlucky

> My cousin was a **star-crossed** traveler whose planes were always delayed.
>
> Both families opposed the **star-crossed** marriage.

For centuries, people of many cultures have believed that the astrological position, or placement, of the stars at a person's birth determined the person's future. A *star-crossed* person was born under unfavorable astrological influences. Shakespeare described the famous lovers Romeo and Juliet as *star-crossed,* or destined to a bad fate.

24. **tongue-in-cheek**

jokingly; insincerely; without really meaning something

> Mom made a **tongue-in-cheek** threat to force children who left dirty clothes on the floor to do the family wash for the next ten years.
>
> The short classical music compact disc featuring only well-known tunes had the **tongue-in-cheek** title "Classical Music for People Who Hate Classical Music."

NOTE: At one time, people indicated that they didn't mean what they were saying by pushing one of their cheeks out with their tongue.

The ice cream manufacturing company Ben and Jerry's Homemade, Inc., launched a *tongue-in-cheek* campaign for a chief officer, titled "Yo I'm Your CEO." People were invited to apply by submitting a box top of the ice cream and a 300-word essay. Applications came from children who nominated their parents, and pets that nominated their owners. Superman also applied. Just in case this *tongue-in-cheek* approach didn't work, however, the company also used an executive search firm.

Exercises

Part 2

■ Definitions

Match each word or phrase in the left-hand column with a definition from the right-hand column. Use each choice only once.

1. destitute _____

2. tongue in cheek _____

3. hold out an olive branch

_____

4. nonchalant _____

5. give carte blanche _____

6. behind the eight ball _____

7. get to first base _____

8. star-crossed _____

9. delude _____

10. nondenominational _____

a. unlucky

b. looking ordinary

c. to mislead

d. to vary from a path

e. at a disadvantage

f. to give full power

g. to do the first thing successfully

h. to make a peace offer

i. without money

j. not limited to one religion

k. unconcerned

l. jokingly; insincerely

■ Meanings

Match each prefix to its meaning. Use each choice only once.

1. de-_____   a. away from; down

2. non- _____   b. not

■ Words in Context

Complete each sentence with the word or phrase that fits best. Use each choice only once.

a. delude   e. nondenominational   i. give carte blanche
b. destitute   f. nondescript   j. held out an olive
c. deviate   g. behind the eight ball   branch
d. nonchalant   h. get to first base   k. star-crossed
                                               l. tongue-in-cheek

1. To make peace, the parents finally _____ to the son they had not spoken to in years.

2. I'll never _____ in a vocabulary course if I don't study.

3. Everybody knew that Raul was simply making a _____ comment and did not really mean what he said.

4. The _____ woman looked like everyone else.

5. The _____ team always seemed to lose its games.

6. Don't _____ yourself into thinking that success is just a matter of luck.

7. If you _____ from the safety procedures for disposing nuclear waste, you can cause a serious accident.

8. The _____ charity helped people of all faiths.

9. The wealthy owner could _____ to the decorator to spend whatever money was needed to redo the penthouse.

10. The _____ mother did not seem to care about how her child did in school.

■ *Using Related Words*

Complete each sentence by using a word from the group of related words above it. You may need to capitalize a word when you put it into a sentence. Use each choice only once.

1. destitute, destitution

   Homeless and _____ , Joe Long was spending another lonely day when he spied a car on fire. Rushing to the scene, he heroically pulled two people from the flames, saving their lives

   A grateful public has now saved him from _____ by gifts of money and the offer of a job.

2. nonchalance, nonchalant

   It is important to wear a life preserver when boating. Unfortunately, many people show _____ toward their own safety by forgetting this simple precaution. Such a

   _____ attitude may cause a tragic accident.

3. deviant, deviate

   Cultures _____ from each other in their social conventions. In the Middle East, people stand close together when they talk. The lack of distance often makes North Americans and Europeans uncomfortable. In Japan, looking at a person directly can be offensive, so North Americans and Europeans must learn to avoid eye contact when visiting that country. Such social cus-

   toms are not _____ , but simply reflect cultural differences.

4. delusions, deluded

   In the 1600s, people in Holland started to buy tulip bulbs for investment, causing prices to rise in a fever of "tulipmania." Because

   of the bulbs' popularity, people were _____ into thinking that prices would rise forever. Some had such

   _____ about the value of tulips that they invested everything they had in the flowers. When, after a few years, prices collapsed, many people were financially ruined.

■ *True or False?*

Each of the following statements contains one or more words or phrases from this section. Read each statement carefully and then indicate whether you think it is probably true or probably false.

_____   1. A star-crossed career might leave a person destitute.

_____   2. A nondescript building looks very different from most other buildings.

_____   3. People hold out an olive branch in the hope of peace.

_____   4. A Catholic religious service is nondenominational.

_____   5. Tongue-in-cheek statements reflect true feelings.

_____   6. Getting to first base means that all of your efforts will be completed.

_____   7. A competitive athlete would be nonchalant if she felt she was behind the eight ball in her hopes to qualify for the Olympic Games.

_____   8. Most people would enjoy being given carte blanche.

_____   9. It is not honest to delude others.

_____   10. Deviation from an assigned path can cause problems for an airplane.

Chapter Exercises

■ *Practicing Strategies: New Words from Word Elements*

See how your knowledge of prefixes, roots, and suffixes can help you understand new words. Complete each sentence with the word that seems to fit best. Use each choice only once.

a. aerophobia	e. depopulated	i. nonskid
b. affidavit	f. detoxify	j. phobic
c. credentials	g. discredited	k. verily
d. demote	h. nonprofit	l. very

1. Somebody who is fearful is _____ .

2. A(n) _____ organization is not organized to make money.

3. A(n) _____ surface prevents people from slipping.

4. A(n) _____ is a written statement made in good faith.

5. To *promote* means to move up; to _____ means to move down.

6. The fear of winds and breezes is _____ .

7. If you can no longer believe in somebody, that person has been

   _____ .

8. Since something poisonous is toxic, when we remove poison, we

   _____ .

9. People present _____ so that you will "believe" in their qualifications.

10. A place becomes _____ when people move out.

■ *Practicing Strategies: Combining Context Clues and Word Elements*

Combining the strategies of context clues and word elements is a good way to figure out unknown words. In the following sentences, each italicized word contains a word element that you have studied in this chapter. Using the meaning of the word element and the context of the sentence, make an intelligent guess about the meaning of the italicized word. Your instructor may ask you to check the meaning in your dictionary when you have finished.

1. Because of *zoophobia,* the man would not go near animals.

   Zoophobia means _____ .

2. The *credulous* child was easy to fool.

   Credulous means _____ .

3. Truckers carrying *nonflammable* chemicals need not fear fire.

   Nonflammable means _____

   _____ .

4. Because of the hot sun and lack of water, Moqui's body became *dehydrated*.

   Dehydrated means _____ .

5. The *deciduous* trees were bare of leaves in winter.

   Deciduous means _____ .

■ Companion Words

Complete each sentence with the word that fits best. Choose your answers from the words below. You may use each word more than once.

Choices: from, into, of, a, himself

1. People who deviate _____ the norm often make new discoveries.

2. The veracity _____ your statement cannot be questioned.

3. The man deluded _____ into thinking that he could successfully work four jobs at once.

4. My teacher is _____ veritable treasure trove of information on word origins.

5. Don't delude yourself _____ believing silly superstitions.

■ Writing with Your Words

This exercise will give you practice in writing effective sentences that use the vocabulary words. Each sentence is started for you. Complete it with an interesting phrase that also indicates the meaning of the italicized word or words.

1. According to my personal *creed* of conduct, _____

   _____ .

2. The *nondescript* building _____

_____ .

3. The *defiant* rebel _____

_____ .

4. I can never *get to first base* when I try _____

_____ .

5. *Fidelity* is _____

_____ .

6. My day became a *veritable* disaster when _____

_____ .

7. I would like to have *carte blanche* to _____

_____ .

8. I was surprised that he remained *nonchalant* when _____

_____ .

9. I felt *behind the eight ball* when _____

_____ .

10. I would be *incredulous* if I saw _____

_____ .

Passage

The Origins of Superstitions

Why is the number thirteen considered unlucky? Why do people who spill salt throw some over their shoulder? Are black cats evil? Can a mirror steal your soul? No scientist has **verified** these superstitions, yet many people once believed them without question. How did they originate?

The number thirteen has long been considered unlucky. According to legend, thirteen pins can make a dead spirit haunt a living person. A magician makes a doll that represents a living person and pierces it with thirteen needles. The doll is then placed on a grave, and a dead soul supposedly rises and haunts the unfortunate person represented by the doll.

(1) Thirteen was also believed to be a central number in the **creed** of witches. These supposedly evil souls were thought to **defy** God and to swear **fidelity** to the devil. Thirteen was the ideal number for a witches' coven, or meeting.

Many people considered Friday an unlucky day of the week because it was the day on which Christ was crucified. When Friday coincides with the thirteenth of the month, we get an especially unlucky day. However, other Fridays have also been known to bring misfortune. **(2)** On Friday, May 10, 1886, a financial panic in London, known as Black Friday, left many people **destitute.**

Unlike the number thirteen and Friday, salt was considered lucky. Because salt was used to preserve food, people believed that it would drive away bad spirits. However, spilling salt was thought to invite evil spirits. **(3)** In fact, dropping a salt container could make a **nonchalant** diner suddenly become frantic. There was only one way to avoid disaster: the diner had to take some salt into his right hand (the side of his lucky spirit) and throw it over his left shoulder (the side of his unlucky spirit). **(4)** Any **deviation** from this procedure would invite the invasion of the unlucky spirit, who was always lurking on the left.

Cats have held a special place in our superstitions. The mysterious ability of cats to survive falls from high places led the Egyptians to believe that they had nine lives. In fact, the Egyptians worshiped cats.

(5) In contrast, cats have had a rather **star-crossed** fate in Europe. The fact that cats' eyes reflect light in the dark caused European people of the Middle Ages to think they were evil spirits. Cats were often pictured as witches' companions, and some people thought that, after seven years' service, a cat might even become a witch. Since black was the color of the devil, black cats inspired especially intense fear. God-fearing people walking at night might see a black cat cross their path. **(6)** Certain that they had seen a devil, they would break into a **veritable** panic. A cat that crossed from left to right was particularly frightening.

People often made ridiculous claims about cats. For example, in 1718 a man named William Montgomery claimed that two elderly women had been found dead in their beds on the morning after he had killed two noisy cats. **(7)** Montgomery **deluded** himself into thinking that the cats had been these women in disguise.

Such attitudes could lead to vicious persecution. Women who owned cats might be persecuted for witchcraft. Women of strange appear-

Cats have a special place in our superstitions.

ance were most likely to be accused; **(8)** however, at times, even quiet, **nondescript** women were accused of being witches.

A less harmful, though no less silly, superstition revolved around mirrors, which many people believed had magical powers. Perhaps you remember Snow White's stepmother asking her magical mirror: "Mirror, mirror on the wall. Who's the fairest one of all?" The ancients believed that breaking a mirror would bring seven years of bad luck, avoidable only if the pieces were quickly buried. The seven-year figure was given by the Romans, who thought that the human body renewed itself every seven years. Others believed that a mirror broke because bad spirits appeared in it. Throughout history, people have feared that a mirror would steal the weak soul of a sick person or a newborn. **(9)** Of course, this idea had no **veracity,** yet some people would not allow infants to see a mirror until they reached one year of age.

(10) Most modern people are **incredulous** when told of these superstitions. Yet some of us still believe that they have **credibility.** An occasional high-rise lacks a thirteenth floor; the numbers simply skip from twelve to fourteen. Some people throw salt over their left shoulders, even if it is a **tongue-in-cheek** gesture or they no longer know why they are doing it. Perhaps you know somebody who shivers with fright when a black cat crosses a path at night and flashes its fiery eyes. Whatever the origin of superstitions, it's clear that some haunt us, even today.

■ *Exercise*

Each numbered sentence below corresponds to a sentence in the Passage. Fill in the letter of the choice that makes the sentence mean the same thing as its corresponding sentence in the Passage.

1. Thirteen was also believed to be a central number in the _____ of witches.
   a. great charm   b. bad character   c. belief system   d. bad luck

2. A financial panic known as Black Friday left many people _____ .
   a. fearful   b. insane   c. poor   d. unhappy

3. In fact, dropping a salt container could make a _____ diner suddenly become frantic.
   a. calm   b. hungry   c. horrified   d. pleasant

4. Any _____ from this procedure would invite the invasion of the unlucky spirit.
   a. change   b. benefit   c. rumor   d. noise

5. In contrast, cats have had a rather _____ fate in Europe.
   a. unlucky   b. fortunate   c. unusual   d. religious

6. Certain that they had seen a devil, they would break into a _____ panic.
   a. dreadful   b. sudden   c. slight   d. true

7. Montgomery _____ himself into thinking that the cats had been these women in disguise.
   a. helped   b. fooled   c. advised   d. frightened

8. Even quiet, _____ women were killed as witches.
   a. peaceful acting   b. warm-hearted   c. very religious
   d. ordinary looking

9. Of course, this idea had no _____ .
   a. support   b. faith   c. belief   d. truth

10. Most modern people are _____ when told of these superstitions.
    a. unbelieving   b. amused   c. surprised   d. horrified

■ *Discussion Questions*

1. Why were infants not allowed to see mirrors?

2. Why did so many people think cats have supernatural powers?

3. Would you be comfortable living on a thirteenth floor? Why or why not?

> ◀ **E**NGLISH **I**DIOMS
>
> ### *Animals*
>
> This section adds more animal idioms to those presented in the "Did You Know?" section of this chapter. An *ugly duckling* is a child who is physically unappealing. The phrase is taken from one of Hans Christian Andersen's fairy tales, in which an ugly duckling becomes a beautiful swan. In addition, a *lame duck* is a political official who is completing a term after someone else has been elected.
>
> Butterflies are also used in idioms. People who are nervous often *have butterflies in their stomach,* perhaps because of the movement they feel there. When we tell people to *hold your horses,* we want them to slow down. Also, "dark" horses in a race are ones little is known about, so they are not expected to win. Thus, an unknown or unfavored political candidate is called a *dark horse.*
>
> Dogs appear in many different idioms. People who are out of favor because they have done something wrong are *in the dog-house.* When a situation gets very bad, we say it has *gone to the dogs.* When we refer to the brutality of our world, we say, *"It's a dog-eat-dog world."*
>
> A *wolf in sheep's clothing* pretends to be a good person but is actually bad. To *keep the wolf from the door* is to keep out hunger or starvation.
>
> In the 1890s, cartoonist Francis "Red" Tulane, a radical, wrote a comic strip featuring overworked, exploited mice and a fat, unsympathetic cat who was their boss. Today a rich, unsympathetic person is known as a *fat cat.*

CHAPTER

Word Elements: The Body and Health

In the past hundred years, medical scientists have learned much about how the human body works. As a result, they have developed new methods to prevent and treat health problems. Children can be immunized against once-dreaded diseases, including polio, measles, smallpox, and tetanus. Since 1900, life expectancy in the United States has risen from 47 years to 74 years. The word elements in this chapter deal with the human body and health. Part 1 presents four roots; Part 2 presents four prefixes. Although these word elements are commonly used in the sciences and health professions, they also form words that you will meet in your general reading.

Chapter Strategy: Word Elements: The Body and Health

Chapter Words

Part 1

audi	audit	ped	expedite
	auditory		impede
	inaudible		pedigree
patho, -pathy	empathy	spec, spic	auspicious
	pathetic		conspicuous
	pathology		introspection

Part 2

a-, an-	anarchy	bio-, bio	biodegradable
	anonymous		biopsy
	apathy		symbiotic
bene-	benefactor	mal-	malady
	beneficial		malevolent
	benign		malpractice

Did You Know?

How Did Snacks Originate?

Health specialists constantly advise us to eat spinach, broccoli, and carrots. Yet modern life is filled with food that may not be as healthy as spinach but tastes good and is easily available in packaged form. Such snacks are sometimes called "junk food." Despite this negative label, most of us are far more likely to snack on a package of potato chips or nachos than on a raw carrot. The popularity of junk food shows that it is likely to be with us for a long time, so let's see how some of the names originated.

The potato chip was invented in the 1860s. According to one story, Chef George Crum once had an annoying customer who kept complaining that the french fries were too thick. Finally, Mr. Crum cut the potatoes into very thin slices, and the potato chip was born. According to another account, the potato chip was invented by settlers of Spanish descent living in large haciendas in California. In any event, the first potato chip factory was founded in 1925.

In 1896, Leo Hirschfield, an Austrian immigrant, invented a chewy candy and gave it the nickname of his childhood sweetheart, Tootsie. This was the Tootsie Roll. In the 1940s, the daughter of Charles Lubin gave her name to Sara Lee cakes and desserts.

The ice cream cone was invented in 1904 at the St. Louis World's Fair. Ernest A. Hamwi, a Syrian immigrant, was selling *zalabias,* wafers that could be rolled up. When a person at the ice cream booth next to him ran out of plates, Hamwi substituted his rolled-up wafers, and the ice cream cone was created.

In the early 1900s, eleven-year-old Frank Epperson accidentally invented the popsicle by leaving a sweet drink out overnight in the cold. The liquid froze around the stick that had been used to stir it. Epperson originally called his invention the Epsicle, but the name was later changed to the more appealing "popsicle."

M & M's got their name from the initial letters of the last names of Forrest Mars and Bruce Murrie. The candies first became popular during World War II among soldiers, who could eat them without making their trigger fingers sticky. Fifty years later, M & M's remain a popular snack.

Learning Strategy

Word Elements: The Body and Health

With the many advances in medicine and the life sciences during the twentieth century, more and more scientific words have been made from the word elements in this chapter. Part 1 presents four common roots; Part 2 presents four common prefixes.

Element	Meaning	Origin	Function	Chapter Words
				Part 1
audi	hear	Latin	root	audit, auditory, inaudible
patho, -pathy	feeling, suffering; disease	Greek	root; suffix	empathy, pathetic, pathology
ped	foot	Latin	root	expedite, impede, pedigree
spec, spic	look	Latin	root	auspicious, conspicuous, introspection

Part 2

a-, an-	without	Greek	prefix	anarchy, anonymous, apathy
bene-	good, well	Latin	prefix	benefactor, beneficial, benign
bio-, bio	life	Greek	prefix; root	biodegradable, biopsy, symbiotic
mal-	bad, harmful	Latin	prefix	malady, malevolent, malpractice

Word Elements

Part 1

The four roots in Part 1 are explained in more detail below.

audi (hear)
> Our *auditory* nerves enable us to hear. The word root *audi* is used also in such words as *audience,* a group of people who "hear" a performance, and *auditorium,* a place where crowds gather to "hear" a performance.

patho, -pathy (feeling, suffering; disease)
> The root *patho* has two meanings, both stemming from ancient Greek. First, *patho* can mean "feeling, suffering," as in the word *pathos,* meaning "a feeling of pity." A second meaning of *patho* is "disease," as in *pathologist,* a doctor who diagnoses disease, and *psychopath,* a person with a diseased mind. The spelling *-pathy* is used for the suffix form. For example, *sympathy* means suffering along with the sorrows of another.

ped (foot)
> *Ped* is found in such words as *pedal,* a control operated by the foot, and *quadruped,* an animal with four feet. Some words made from *ped* reflect society's scorn for the lowly foot. *Pedestrian,* which refers to people who travel by foot, is also used to describe something that is dull or ordinary.

spec, spic (look)
> The root *spec* is used in such words as *inspect,* "to look at carefully," and *despise,* to "look down on" or scorn someone. Glasses used to improve vision are called *spectacles.* Finally, the word *spy,* a person who secretly looks at the actions of others, may also be derived from *spec.*

Words to Learn

Part 1

audi

1. **audit** (noun, verb)   ô′dĭt

   From Latin: *audit* (hear)

   examination of financial accounts by an outside agency (noun)

   > Companies registered on public stock exchanges must submit their accounts for a yearly **audit.**

   > An **audit** revealed that the company was financially sound.

   to examine accounts (verb)

   > The accountant **audited** the records of several small businesses.

   to attend a class without receiving credit (verb)

   > I **audited** Spanish 103 so that I could practice the language.

   ▶ *Related Word*
   > **auditor** (noun)   The *auditor's* report revealed that the company had made a large profit. (*Auditor* means financial analyst.)

   NOTE: At one time, official examinations of financial accounts were held in public so that all could hear. In modern times, however, such examinations are done in written form.

2. **auditory** (adjective)   ô′də-tôr′ē

   From Latin: *audi* (hear)

   referring to hearing

   > **Auditory** standards for car alarms are needed so that neighborhoods are not disturbed.

   Animals often have well-developed and sensitive *auditory* systems. In 1994, an okapi (a relative of the giraffe) collapsed and died from stress caused by unusual noise. Three hundred yards away, an opera company was rehearsing Wagner's heroically loud *Tannhäuser.*

3. **inaudible** (adjective)   ĭn-ô′də-bəl

From Latin: *in-* (not) + *audi* (hear)

not able to be heard

> Pigeons can hear low-frequency tones that are **inaudible** to human beings.

NOTE: The opposite of *inaudible* is *audible,* meaning "capable of being heard."

patho, -pathy

4. **empathy** (noun)   ĕm′pə-thē

From Greek: *em-* (in) + *-pathy* (feeling, suffering)

understanding of or identification with another person's feelings

> The woman who had been crippled as a child had **empathy** for those with physical handicaps.
>
> When children identify with characters in books, they develop **empathy** for others.

▶ *Common Phrase*
empathy for

▶ *Related Words*
empathic (adjective)   (ĕm-păth′ĭk)   Mr. Heishema's *empathic* comments helped us face the death of our grandfather.
empathize (verb)   We *empathize* with your problems.

NOTE: How does *empathy* differ from *sympathy?* Sympathy means to feel sorry for another person. However, if we have empathy, we can actually identify with or experience the feelings of another human being.

5. **pathetic** (adjective)   pə-thĕt′ĭk

From Greek: *patho* (feeling, suffering)

pitiful; arousing pity

> The injured bird made a **pathetic** attempt to fly.

6. **pathology** (noun)   pă-thŏl′ə-jē

From Greek: *patho* (disease) + *-logy* (study of)

the study of disease

The science of **pathology** was greatly enhanced when the microscope came into general use.

disease and its cause; symptoms of disease

The **pathology** of cystic fibrosis is being studied by scientists.

▶ *Related Words*
pathological (adjective) (păth′ə-lŏj′ĭ-kəl) He was a *pathological* liar. (*Pathological* can mean mentally ill.)

pathologist (noun) The *pathologist* examined the murder victim, hoping to find clues about the crime.

A *pathologist* is a medical doctor who investigates body tissue samples (biopsies) for disease. Pathologists also do autopsies, or examinations of bodies, to determine the cause of death. Do you know what these medical doctors do?

1. oncologist

2. ophthalmologist

3. cardiologist

(*Answers:* 1. doctor specializing in cancer 2. doctor specializing in the eye 3. doctor specializing in the heart)

---

ped

7. **expedite** (verb) ĕk′spə-dīt′

From Latin: *ex-* (out) + *ped* (foot) (*Expedīre* meant "to free a person's feet from fetters or chains.")

to speed up; to accomplish quickly

The fax machine and E-mail have **expedited** modern communication.

▶ *Related Word*
expedition (noun) (ĕk′spə-dĭsh′ən) In 1497–1499, Vasco da Gama made the first European *expedition* around the southern tip of Africa. (*Expedition* means "journey.")

NOTE: Do not confuse *expedite* with *expedient* (which means "convenient").

8. **impede** (verb)   ĭm-pēd′

From Latin: *im-* (in) + *ped* (foot) (*Impedīre* meant "to entangle.")

to hinder; to block

> The ice on the road **impeded** our progress.

▶ *Related Word*
> **impediment** (noun) (ĭm-pĕd′ə-mənt) Because stairs are an *impediment* to wheelchairs, ramps have been built in many public buildings.

9. **pedigree** (noun)   pĕd′ə-grē′

From Latin (*ped*) through Old French: *pie* (foot) + *de* (of) + *grue* (crane) (In a pedigree or family tree, an outline shaped like a crane's foot was used to show the different generations.)

ancestry; certificate of ancestry

> The prince's **pedigree** showed that his ancestors included many kings of Greece.

Zoos that need to purchase a lion look carefully at the animal's *pedigree*. Because zoo scientists hope to bring new genes into the breeding pool, they search for animals that are not related to other lions held in the zoo. Most valuable are lions whose *pedigrees* show that they are only a few generations removed from the wild.

---

spec, spic

10. **auspicious** (adjective)   ô-spĭsh′əs

From Latin: *avis* (bird) + *spic* (look, watch)

favorable; promising success

> An increase in employment is an **auspicious** sign for the economy.
>
> Suleyma's **auspicious** first concert promised a great singing career.

The ancient Romans believed that since the flight of birds was close to the heavens, it could easily be guided by the gods. Thus, birds were watched as signs or omens. A man who was trained to observe flight patterns was called an *auspex*. When any matter of importance was being considered, the *auspex* decided whether the signs given by birds were *auspicious*.

---

11. **conspicuous** (adjective)   kən-spĭk′yoo-əs

From Latin: *con-* (closely) + *spec* (look)

easy to notice; attracting attention

> The important announcement was posted on doors, in hallways, and in other **conspicuous** places.

▶ *Related Word*
conspicuousness (noun)   I was embarrassed by the *conspicuousness* of my sister's low-cut dress.

12. **introspection** (noun)   ĭn′trə-spĕk′shən

From Latin: *intro-* (within) + *spec* (look)

self-examination of one's thoughts and feelings

> After a near-death experience, people may engage in **introspection** about their life goals.

▶ *Related Words*
introspect (verb)   People often *introspect* about their feelings before they marry.
introspective (adjective)   Poets are *introspective* people.

Exercises

Part 1

■ Definitions

Match each word in the left-hand column with a definition from the right-hand column. Use each choice only once.

1. audit ___e___

2. introspection _____

3. expedite _____

4. inaudible _____

5. pedigree _____

a. identification with another person's feelings

b. to hinder

c. noticeable

d. favorable

e. referring to hearing

f. pitiful

6. pathetic ___f___

7. empathy ___d___

8. impede ___b___

9. conspicuous ___c___

10. auspicious ___a___

g. to speed up

h. examination of financial accounts

i. not able to be heard

j. self-examination of one's thoughts

k. study of disease

l. record of ancestry

■ *Meanings*

Match each word element to its meaning. Use each choice only once.

1. patho ___c___

2. spec ___b___

3. audi ___d___

4. ped ___a___

a. foot

b. look

c. feeling, suffering; illness

d. hear

■ *Words in Context*

Complete each sentence with the word that fits best. Use each choice only once.

a. audit	e. pathetic	i. pedigree
b. auditory	f. pathology	j. auspicious
c. inaudible	g. expedite	k. conspicuous
d. empathy	h. impede	l. introspection

1. The perfect score on Anne's first test was a(n) _____ sign for her performance in the course.

2. Consuelo's _____ helped her understand her own feelings.

3. The brightly lit, large store was _____ on a street filled with dark buildings.

4. To _____ answers to consumer questions, the company has installed a "hot line" that operates 24 hours per day.

5. The ear is part of the body's _____ system.

6. Mothers of older children often feel _____ for parents traveling with infants.

7. The _____ children gathered food from garbage bins.

8. Carrying a heavy load will _____ your ability to run.

9. The sound was so far away that it was _____ to us.

10. Scientists have found that the _____ of mental illness often has a chemical basis.

■ *Using Related Words*

Complete each sentence by using a word from the group of related words above it. You may need to capitalize a word when you put it into a sentence. Use each choice only once.

1. impeded, impediments

There are many _____im,_____ to government approval of unusual foods in the United States. Recently, scientists developed the Flavr-Savr, a tomato that can be shipped without spoiling. This genetically altered food had to be approved by the Federal Drug Administration. The thoroughness of the testing

_____ release of the product for several months, but ensured consumer safety.

2. pathological, pathologist

Physicians are now able to freeze cancerous tumors that cannot

be removed by surgery. After a _____ has determined that a tumor is malignant, it is located through ultrasound techniques. Then liquid nitrogen is injected to freeze the tumor.

This process destroys the _____ tissue without harming healthy organs.

3. expedite, expedition

In 1911, two teams set out to be the first to reach the South Pole. Battling through the freezing, unknown land, each tried hard to

_____ its progress. Norwegian Roald Amundsen's

_____ reached the pole first. The British explorer Robert Falcon Scott reached it a month later, but on the return journey his team perished in the cold.

■ *Say It Again*

Each sentence below contains two or three vocabulary words. Read the sentence and then decide which of the three sentences listed after it has the same meaning.

_____   1. The empathy the couple shows for the pathetic child is an auspicious sign for the success of the adoption.

    a. The couple's feelings of identification with the pitiful child are a favorable sign for the success of the adoption.

    b. The couple's feelings of helpfulness for the lovely child are a good sign for the success of the adoption.

    c. The couple's feelings of identification with the small child are a good sign for the success of the adoption.

_____   2. Scientists have determined the pathology of the auditory nerve that makes soft sounds inaudible.

    a. Scientists have determined the disease of the sick nerve that makes soft sounds loud.

    b. Scientists have determined the disease of the nerve of hearing that makes soft sounds impossible to hear.

    c. Scientists have determined the loudness of the nerve of hearing that makes soft sounds important to hear.

_____   3. The company's growth was impeded by the auditor's unfavorable report.

    a. The company's growth was hindered by the financial analyst's unfavorable report.

    b. The company's growth was made sympathetic by the government's unfavorable report.

c. The company's growth was hindered by the government's unfavorable report.

_____ 4. The champions in the dog's pedigree were listed in conspicuous print.

a. The champions in the dog's list of competitors were listed in noticeable print.

b. The champions in the dog's ancestry were listed in noticeable print.

c. The champions in the dog's ancestry were listed in unreadable print.

Word Elements

Part 2

Part 2 concentrates on four prefixes that are often used in words about the body and in the health sciences.

a-, an- (without)
The words *amoral* and *immoral* help us understand the prefix *a-, an-* by contrasting it with *im-* (meaning "not"). An *immoral* person is *not* moral: this person has a sense of right and wrong, yet chooses to do wrong. An *amoral* person is *without* morals: such a person has no sense of right or wrong. The prefix *a-* is used in many medical words, such as *aphasia* (loss of speech) and *anesthetic* ("without feeling," referring to chemicals that make patients unconscious during operations).

bene- (good; well; helpful)
Bene- is used in such words as *benefit* (something that is helpful) and *beneficiary* (one who receives help or money from another).

bio-, bio (life)
The prefix *bio-* is used in the word *biology,* "the study of living things." You may have taken a biology course in school. *Biochemistry* deals with the chemistry of living things. A word you have already studied in this book, *autobiography,* includes *bio* as a root.

mal- (bad; badly; harmful)
The prefixes *mal-* and *bene-* are opposites. *Mal-* is seen in the word *malpractice,* or "bad practice." Doctors and lawyers may be sued for malpractice. In 1775, the playwright Richard Sheridan coined the word *malaprop* as a name for his character, Mrs. Malaprop, who used words that were not appropriate (or "badly appropriate"). One of her mala-

propisms is "He's the very pineapple of politeness." (She should have used the word *pinnacle*.)

Words to Learn

Part 2

a-, an-

13. **anarchy** (noun)   ăn′ər-kē

    From Greek: *an-* (without) + *arkhos* (ruler)

    political confusion; disorder; lack of government

    The ruler fled, leaving the country in a state of **anarchy.**

    Anarchy resulted when no one could control the rioting and looting.

    ▶ *Related Word*
    anarchist (noun)   The *anarchist* planted bombs in public places.

14. **anonymous** (adjective)   ə-nŏn′ə-məs

    From Greek: *an-* (without) + *onoma* (name)

    not revealing one's name; of unknown identity

    The famous tune "Greensleeves" was written by an anonymous composer.

    An **anonymous** letter revealed where the treasure was hidden.

    ▶ *Related Word*
    anonymity (noun)   To protect the *anonymity* of the child in the adoption fight, the newspapers referred to him as "Baby Richard."

15. **apathy** (noun)   ăp′ə-thē

    From Greek: *a-* (without) + *-pathy* (feeling)

    lack of emotion, feeling, or interest

    Public **apathy** resulted in a low voter turnout at the election.

    Ms. Nguyen's **apathy** toward the race changed to enthusiasm when she saw that her son was winning.

▶ *Related Word*

apathetic (adjective)   (ăp′ə-thĕt′ĭk)   The teenager was interested in rock music but *apathetic* toward schoolwork.

bene-

16. **benefactor** (noun)   bĕn′ə-făk′tər

beneficiary

From Latin: *bene-* (well) + *facere* (to do)

a person who gives financial or other aid; a donor

> The local art **benefactor** bought several paintings for her city's museum.

17. **beneficial** (adjective)   bĕn′ə-fĭsh′əl

From Latin: *bene-* (well) + *facere* (to do)

helpful; producing benefits

> A low-fat diet is **beneficial** to your health.

> Playing video games is **beneficial** to children's motor skills.

18. **benign** (adjective)   bĭ-nīn′

From Latin: *bene-* (well) + *genus* (birth) (*Benignus* meant "well-born, gentle.")

kind; gentle

> Santa Claus is a **benign,** fatherly figure.

not containing cancer cells

> Fortunately, my uncle's tumor was **benign.**

NOTE: The antonym, or opposite, of *benign* is *malignant.*

bio-, bio

19. **biodegradable** (adjective)   bī′ō-dĭ-grā′də-bəl

From Greek: *bio-* (life) + Latin: *de-* (down) + *gradus* (step)

capable of being chemically broken down by natural biological processes

> **Biodegradable** golf tees are now being made of cornstarch.

NOTE: Biodegradable substances break down into natural elements.

As our society becomes increasingly concerned about excessive waste, the word *biodegradable* has become more popular. Many companies now claim that their products are biodegradable. However, the word, strictly interpreted, should mean "not harmful to the environment." Paper, for example, is biodegradable in small amounts, but if too much is thrown away, the excess will not be broken down and may harm the environment. Food may be biodegradable, but if it is buried in a landfill, it will often be preserved rather than being naturally reprocessed. Claims are made by companies that certain plastics are biodegradable. However, many of these plastics simply break down into smaller particles and cannot be transformed into naturally occurring elements. The best way to ensure a healthy environment is to produce less garbage by recycling and reusing products.

---

20. **biopsy** (noun)   bī′ŏp′sē

From Greek: *bio-* (life) + *opsis* (sight)

the study of living tissue to diagnose disease

> The **biopsy** showed that the mole was not cancerous.

NOTE: To diagnose disease with a *biopsy*, a doctor will cut away a small piece of living tissue and inspect it under a microscope.

The words *biopsy*, *benign*, and *pathology* are often used in the diagnosis of cancer. If cancer is suspected, a doctor will take a *biopsy* of cell tissue, which is then examined for the presence of *pathology* (by a *pathologist*). If the biopsy shows the tumor to be *benign*, it is harmless. If the tumor is *malignant* (note the *mal-* prefix), it is harmful and must be treated.

---

21. **symbiotic** (adjective)   sĭm′bē-ŏt′ĭk

From Greek: *sym-* (together) + *bio* (life)

living interdependently; referring to a relationship where two organisms live in a dependent state

> Peanut plants have a **symbiotic** relationship with the nitrogen-fixing bacteria that live on their roots.

> The **symbiotic** relationship between the sisters was so strong that when one died, the other soon died too.

NOTE: Symbiotic relationships can be either biological or social. If they are social, *symbiotic* can be a negative word.

▶ *Related Word*
  symbiosis (noun) (sĭm′bē-ō′sĭs) The two types of microbes lived in *symbiosis.*

mal-

22. **malady** (noun) măl′ə-dē

From Latin: *mal-* (badly) + *habēre* (to keep) (*Mal habitus* meant "ill-kept, in bad condition.")

disease; bad condition

> Chicken pox is a contagious **malady.**

NOTE: *Malady* can describe a nonphysical bad condition. One might say, for example, "The *malady* of discontent spread throughout the land."

Some genetically caused *maladies* have affected American history. The inherited madness of King George III weakened him and encouraged the American colonies to revolt in 1776. In addition, George Washington may have suffered from a genetic defect that prevented him from having children. Washington's lack of a son may have been a factor in his refusal to become "king of America," as his soldiers wanted him to do. His malady may also have accounted for his hot temper and hatred of authority, traits that made him difficult to live with but an excellent general.

---

23. **malevolent** (adjective) mə-lĕv′ə-lənt

From Latin: *mal-* (bad) + *volens* (wishing)

ill-willed; evil; filled with hate

> The **malevolent** owner starved his pet dog.

▶ *Related Word*
  malevolence (noun) The ruler showed his *malevolence* by using poison gas against his own people.

24. **malpractice** (noun)   măl-prăk′tĭs

From Latin: *mal-* (bad) + *practice*

failure of a professional to give proper services

> After the physician left surgical pins inside her arm, the woman accused him of **malpractice.**

> The lawyer was accused of **malpractice** when she missed a client's important court date.

Exercises

Part 2

■ Definitions

Match each word in the left-hand column with a definition from the right-hand column. Use each choice only once.

1. malevolent ___k___
2. malady ___j___
3. beneficial ___g___
4. apathy ___f___
5. symbiotic ___l___
6. biopsy ___e___
7. anarchy ___c___
8. benefactor ___i___
9. biodegradable ___b___
10. benign ___d___

a. failure to give proper services
b. capable of being broken down by natural processes
c. political confusion
d. not containing cancer cells
e. study of living tissue
f. lack of feeling
g. helpful
h. keeping an identity secret
i. donor
j. illness
k. evil
l. living interdependently

■ *Meanings*

Match each word element to its meaning. Use each choice only once.

1. a- ___d___

2. mal- ___a___

3. bio- ___c___

4. bene- ___b___

a. bad

b. good

c. life

d. without

■ *Words in Context*

Complete each sentence with the word that fits best. Use each choice only once. You may need to capitalize some words.

a. anarchy
b. anonymous
c. apathy
d. benefactor

e. beneficial
f. benign
g. biodegradable
h. biopsy

i. symbiotic
j. malady
k. malevolent
l. malpractice

1. _____ resulted when ten thousand people rioted in the streets.

2. The doctor performed a(n) _____ on a small sample of my skin tissue.

3. _____ about one's surroundings increases garbage on the street.

4. A careful physician is rarely accused of _____ .

5. We were happy to learn that my mother's tumor was _____ .

6. The _____ criminal deliberately released poison into the water.

7. Researchers find that plants are _____ to the quality of indoor air.

8. In past centuries, a wealthy _____ would often support an artist or musician.

9. Most people try to use _____ containers that will not cause harm to rivers and streams.

10. Anne's _____ kept her in bed for a week.

■ *Using Related Words*

Complete each sentence by using a word from the group of related words above it. You may need to capitalize a word when you put it into a sentence. Use each choice only once.

1. apathy, apathetic

   The U.S. public follows some tragedies closely but treats others

   with only _____ . Manute Bol, an NBA player, has used the streets of Washington, D.C., to protest the slaughter and starvation in his native Sudan. He hopes that his protests will

   make the public less _____ and that citizens will urge the U.S. government to send help to his people.

2. malevolence, malevolent

   If you slice into a tomato, are you a _____ person?

   Do we show _____ when we forget to water plants? Malcolm Wilkins, an English botanist, claims that plants have feelings and produce crackling noises inaudible to the human ear when they are hurt.

3. symbiotic, symbiosis

   Human beings live in _____ with the bacteria that

   line their digestive tracts. In a _____ arrangement, humans supply a home for the bacteria, and the bacteria help to digest food. When people take antibiotics, they can destroy these bacteria and cause temporary indigestion.

4. anarchy, anarchists

In the past, some political theorists felt that without an all-power-

ful government there would be _____ . They feared the power of citizens who, if given freedom, could become

_____ . However, many successful modern governments have shown that people in a democracy can run an effective government.

5. anonymous, anonymity

In former years, mothers who gave up children for adoption often

preserved their _____ . In addition, parents who adopted children were unknown to the birth mother. Today, how-

ever, there is a trend away from _____ adoption.

■ *Say It Again*

Each sentence below contains two or three vocabulary words. Read the sentence and then decide which of the three sentences listed after it has the same meaning.

____   1. The malevolent ruler displayed apathy toward the anarchy in the streets.

a. The cruel ruler displayed a lack of interest toward the confusion in the streets.

b. The sick ruler displayed a lack of feeling toward the difficulty in the streets.

c. The cruel ruler displayed anger toward the confusion in the streets.

____   2. The anonymous benefactor donated a million dollars for research into a puzzling malady.

a. The wealthy donor gave a million dollars for research into the puzzling mistreatment.

b. The unknown professional gave a million dollars for research into the puzzling illness.

c. The unknown donor gave a million dollars for research into the puzzling illness.

_____ 3. Since the psychiatrist encouraged symbiotic relationships between patients and herself, other doctors accused her of malpractice.

a. Since the psychiatrist encouraged sick and confused relationships between patients and herself, other doctors accused her of cruelty.

b. Since the psychiatrist encouraged close, dependent relationships between patients and herself, other doctors accused her of giving bad treatment.

c. Since the psychiatrist encouraged independent relationships between patients and herself, other doctors accused her of giving bad treatment.

_____ 4. The benign presence of my grandfather had a beneficial effect on our family party.

a. The kindly presence of my grandfather had a confusing effect on our family party.

b. The kindly presence of my grandfather had a helpful effect on our family party.

c. The sickly presence of my grandfather had a helpful effect on our family party.

Chapter Exercises

■ *Practicing Strategies: New Words from Word Elements*

See how your knowledge of word elements can help you understand new words. Complete each sentence with the word that fits best. Use each choice only once. You may need to capitalize some words.

a. antipathy
b. asocial
c. atonal
d. audiotape
e. audition
f. benediction
g. biohazard
h. malaria
i. malfunctioning
j. malodorous
k. pedicure
l. spectator

1. A tape one listens to is a(n) _____ .

2. At a(n) _____ , people "hear" you in order to determine if you should be hired for a performance.

3. People once thought that "bad air" caused the disease _____ .

4. A(n) _____ person would not attend many parties.

5. _____ describes feelings "against" others, or hatred.

6. A _____ may harm living things.

7. Something not working well is _____ .

8. A _____ is a blessing, or "good words."

9. A _____ looks at a performance or display.

10. In a(n) _____ , one's feet and toenails receive cos-
    metic care.

■ *Practicing Strategies: Combining Context Clues and Word Elements*

Combining the strategies of context clues and word elements is a good
way to figure out unknown words. In the following sentences, each italicized word contains a word element that you have studied in this chapter.
Using the meaning of the word element and the context of the sentence,
make an intelligent guess about the meaning of the italicized word. Your
instructor may ask you to check the meaning in your dictionary when
you have finished.

1. A virus is the *pathogen* of polio.

   Pathogen means _____ .

2. A *maladroit* person often drops items and bumps into things.

   Maladroit means _____ .

3. A person's *biorhythms* control the timing of urges to eat and sleep.

   Biorhythms means _____ .

4. No bacteria can infect a patient in an *aseptic* operating room.

Aseptic means _____ .

5. The shape of the object was *pediform.*

Pediform means _____ .

■ *Practicing Strategies: Using the Dictionary*

Read the following definition. Then answer the questions below it.

> **gap** (găp) *n.* **1.a.** An opening in a solid structure or surface; a cleft or breach.   **b.** A break in a line of defense.   **2.** An opening through mountains; a pass.   **3.** A space between objects or points; an aperture.   **4.** An interruption of continuity.   **5.a.** A conspicuous difference or imbalance; a disparity.   **b.** A problematic situation resulting from such a disparity.   **6.** A spark gap.   **7.** *Comp. Sci.* An absence of information on a recording medium, often used to signal the end of a segment of information.   **8.** *Electron.* The distance between the head of a recording device and the surface of the recording medium. —*v.* **gapped, gap•ping, gaps.** —*tr.* To make an opening in.   —*intr.* To be or become open. [ME < ON, chasm.]

1. After *gap* was first recorded in Old Norse, in which language was it next used? _____

2. Give the number and the part of speech of the definition of *gap* most used in computer science. _____

3. What is the third-person-singular form of *gap* when used as a verb?

   _____

4. Give the number and the part of speech of the definition that best fits this sentence: "There was a ten-minute gap in our videotape."

   _____

5. Give the part of speech of the definition that best fits this sentence: "We gapped a hole in the wall." _____

■ *Writing with Your Words*

This exercise will give you practice in writing effective sentences that use the vocabulary words. Each sentence is started for you. Complete it with an interesting phrase that also indicates the meaning of the italicized word.

1. Exercise is *beneficial* because _____

_____ .

2. The *malevolent* person _____

_____ .

3. The racehorse's *pedigree* _____

_____ .

4. People are too *apathetic* about _____

_____ .

5. If your intentions are *benign,* _____

_____ .

6. If you want to *expedite* progress, _____

_____ .

7. The *pathologist* _____

_____ .

8. From my *auditory* sense, I could tell _____

_____ .

9. The *pathetic* child _____

_____ .

10. Traffic movement on the freeway was *impeded* because _____

_____ .

Passage

The Disease That Science Eliminated

It started with a fever and developed into a rash. Soon, sores appeared all over the body. Many sufferers died from damage to their hearts, livers, and lungs. This was smallpox, the most destructive disease in human history.

Today, when so many diseases can be prevented or cured, it may be difficult for modern people to feel **empathy** for the people that smallpox attacked. There was no cure, and one in four who got the disease died from it. **(1)** Those who survived were forever marked, for smallpox left **conspicuous** scars called "pocks." Smallpox was also highly contagious; everything a sick person touched could carry the disease. Often, sick people were "quarantined," or separated, from healthy ones. **(2)** This meant that **pathetically** ill people were sometimes left alone with no one to care for them.

(3) Smallpox struck people of all classes, including those with royal **pedigrees.** Two princes died of it in 1700 and 1711, ruining the alliances that depended upon their marriages. It killed King Louis XV of France in 1774.

In the 1600s and 1700s, smallpox changed history in the Americas by wiping out much of the Native American population. Since the disease had been newly introduced by Europeans, Native Americans had little resistance to it. When first exposed, they died in great numbers. In at least one shameful incident, a smallpox epidemic was started deliberately when **(4) malevolent** Jeffrey Amherst, an English soldier, sent infected blankets to Native Americans.

The defeat of this deadly disease is one of medical science's great triumphs. **(5)** First steps were taken in China over a thousand years ago, when **anonymous** physicians protected people by giving them the disease deliberately. To do this, material from a pox sore of an infected person was introduced into a healthy person. If this procedure was done carefully, the receiver usually developed a **benign** version of the **malady** but would then be protected from smallpox for life. By 1700, this practice had spread throughout Asia and the Mideast. It was brought from Turkey to England in the early 1700s. Although the method protected many people, it was not always safe, for some receivers developed severe smallpox and died.

Then, in 1796, Edward Jenner, an English doctor, made an important discovery. Jenner had noticed that milkmaids never seemed to get smallpox. **(6)** He reasoned that through their contact with cows, they got a related but relatively **benign** disease, called "cowpox," which protected them from smallpox. To test this theory, on May 14, 1796, Jenner took a small sample of a cowpox sore from the finger of Sarah Nelmes, a milk-maid, and applied it to a sore on eight-year-old James Phipps. James developed a very slight infection—and never contracted smallpox. Because cowpox came from cows, which were named *vacca* in Latin, Jenner called this procedure a "vaccination."

(7) As Jenner treated more people, he became certain of the **beneficial** effects of vaccination. **(8)** He was eager to publish his findings, but the Royal Society **impeded** his efforts by rejecting his paper. Finally, to **expedite** publication, Jenner printed the results himself.

Even after the publication of Jenner's findings, public reaction remained **apathetic,** especially in large cities. Jenner located no volunteers for vaccination in a three-month search of the London area. Although the method was soon endorsed by physicians and used often in the English countryside, Londoners did not commonly undergo vaccination until the middle of the next century. **(9)** In fact, an **audit** of the "Bills of Mortality," or record of deaths in London, shows smallpox to be a common cause of death until the 1840s.

Resistance to vaccination lasted even longer in France and Germany, where opponents accused physicians of **malpractice** for deliberately introducing disease into a healthy person. Ministers objected to doctors interfering with "God's will" by preventing disease. However, others in these countries trusted Jenner's method. The French emperor Napoleon had his entire army vaccinated in 1805.

In the Americas, rapid adoption of vaccination was an important factor in the population growth of the New World. People in both English and Spanish colonies made wide use of the method.

Jenner lived to see honors and awards, as well as attacks and betrayals. Through it all, he remained dedicated to the cause of vaccination. He worked so hard on its behalf that he had no time to earn money practicing medicine. Although he died a poor man, this **benefactor** left a great legacy to the world.

A century after Jenner's death, smallpox vaccination was practiced almost universally, and fewer and fewer people contracted the disease. **(10)** In the second half of this century, the number of cases decreased every year, an **auspicious** sign for world health. The last case was reported in 1977.

Today, all that remains of the smallpox virus are two small samples—one in the United States and one in Russia. The samples are being kept alive in case they are needed for scientific study. Otherwise, the once-deadly killer of mankind has vanished from the earth.

■ *Exercise*

Each numbered sentence below corresponds to a sentence in the Passage. Fill in the letter of the choice that makes this sentence mean the same thing as the corresponding sentence in the Passage.

1. Smallpox left _____ scars.
   a. harmless   b. sick   c. huge   d. noticeable

2. _____ ill people were sometimes left alone.
   a. Very   b. Dangerously   c. Totally   d. Pitifully

3. Smallpox struck those with royal _____ .
   a. powers   b. ancestries   c. wealth   d. dependence

4. _____ Jeffrey Amherst sent infected blankets.
   a. careless   b. evil   c. thoughtful   d. ill

5. _____ physicians protected people.
   a. Intelligent   b. Kind   c. Helpful   d. Unknown

6. They got a related but relatively _____ disease.
   a. short   b. gentle   c. strong   d. pitiful

7. Jenner became certain of the _____ effects of vaccination.
   a. helpful   b. noticeable   c. sad   d. fast

8. The Royal Society _____ his efforts.
   a. speeded   b. ignored   c. inspected   d. blocked

9. A(n) _____ of the "Bills of Mortality" shows smallpox to be a common cause of death.
   a. examination   b. publication   c. official record   d. accusation

10. This was a _____ sign for world health.
    a. noticeable   b. bad   c. favorable   d. reasonable

■ Discussion Questions

1. Why was the word *vaccination* taken from *cow*?

2. What were some of the ways that smallpox changed history?

3. Name three other diseases that can now be prevented by vaccination.

◀ ENGLISH IDIOMS

Food

Perhaps because of the importance of food to our health, many widely used English idioms contain references to cooking and things we eat. A sensitive, difficult issue is called a *hot potato*. When we are in difficulty, we are *in hot water*. Ideas that are not fully thought out are often called *half-baked*.

People who feel strong and energetic are *feeling their oats*. However, when we are disgusted with something, we are *fed up* with it, and when we lose our tempers, we *boil over*.

Other expressions refer to the birds we eat. To ruin or destroy one's hopes or plans is to *cook one's goose*. *Duck soup* refers to something easily done, and "That test was duck soup" refers to an easy test.

Idioms also refer to fruits and vegetables. To *go bananas* and to *go nuts* both mean to go crazy. One's *salad days* refer to the days of one's youth.

To *take with a grain of salt* means not to take seriously. To *cry over spilt milk* means to complain about something that can no longer be prevented.

The butter of the yak, a relative of the ox, had great value to the people of Tibet. When they wanted to please someone, they presented tubs of the butter as a present. Today, to *butter up* means to flatter.

CHAPTER

12

Word Elements: Speech and Writing

This chapter presents word elements about speech and writing, the two major forms of human communication. The first part of the chapter contains three elements related to speech; the second part gives two elements related to writing. Part 2 also presents three pairs of words that people often confuse in speech and writing and helps you learn to use these confusable words correctly.

Chapter Strategy: Word Elements: Speech and Writing

Chapter Words:

Part 1

dict	contradict	*voc, vok*	advocate
	dictator		invoke
	edict		revoke
log, -logy, loq	colloquial		vociferous
	ecology		
	loquacious		
	monologue		
	prologue		

Part 2

-gram, -graph,	demographic	*Confusable Words*	affect
-graphy,	epigram		effect
graph	graphic		conscience
scrib, script	inscription		conscious
	manuscript		imply
	transcribe		infer

353

Did You Know?

Shortening English

Human beings seem to like short words. The most widely used English words all have four or fewer letters. Listed from number one to ten, they are *the, of, and, a, to, in, is, you, that,* and *it.*

In fact, when an English word is used frequently, it is often shortened, or *clipped.* Many people now refer to *television* as *TV* and *telephone* as *phone.* Most students use the word *exam* to refer to an *examination. Fax,* as in *fax machine,* has been shortened from *facsimile.*

Some words were clipped so long ago that we may have difficulty remembering the original word. The word for a common malady, *flu,* was clipped from *influenza.* A *bus* was once called an *autobus,* and signs for *autobuses* can still be seen in Scotland. The word *caravan* has been replaced by *van.*

Although *flu, bus,* and *van* are relatively modern shortenings, some clippings date back several hundred years. In the 1500s, Italian comedies featured a foolish character named *Pantaloon* who wore an unfashionable, loose-fitting garment to cover his legs. This piece of clothing became known as *pantaloons,* a word shortened to *pants* in the 1800s. For centuries, when people parted, they said *God be with you* to each other. Four hundred years ago, this was shortened to *goodbye.*

A relatively modern way to shorten expressions is to form an *acronym,* a series of words that are replaced by their initial letters. For example, *laser* stands for *light amplification by simulated emission of radiation. Radar* was created from the initials of *radio detection and ranging.*

Acronyms have been coined to describe many aspects of American life. In business, a Certified Public Accountant is called a *CPA. BASIC* is a computer acronym for *Beginner's All-purpose Symbolic Instruction Code.* In sports, a *scuba* diver uses a *self-contained underwater breathing apparatus.* If an athlete sprains a muscle, *"rice,"* meaning *rest, ice, compression,* and *elevation,* is often prescribed.

Acronyms have also been devised for lifestyles. *Dinks* are *double incomes, no kids,* or childless couples who both work outside the home. The 1990 U.S. census counted the number of *POSSLQs,* or unmarried *persons of the opposite sex sharing living quarters.* Even political views have acronyms. People who favor reforms, until they are personally affected, are referred to as *nimbys,* or *not in my back yard.*

Although most acronyms are designed to shorten expressions, at least one organization using an acronym takes a long view of things. The project *Longstop* (*Long*-term gravitational *stability test of the outer planets*) has charted the movements of our solar system one million years into the future.

Learning Strategy

Word Elements: Speech and Writing

Human beings are skilled communicators. Not surprisingly, we have many word elements that deal with communication in oral and written form. Part 1 of this chapter concentrates on speech, and Part 2 deals with writing.

Element	Meaning	Origin	Function	Chapter Words
				Part 1
dict	speak	Latin	root	contradict, dictator, edict
log, -logy, loq	word; study of; speak	Greek; Latin	root; suffix	colloquial, ecology, loquacious, monologue, prologue
voc, vok	voice; call	Latin	root	advocate, invoke, revoke, vociferate
				Part 2
-gram, -graph, -graphy, graph	write	Latin; Greek	suffix; root	demographic, epigram, graphic
scrib, script	write	Latin	root	inscription, manuscript, transcribe

Word Elements

Part 1

The word roots for Part 1 are explained below in more detail.

dict (speak)

This root appears in several common words. *Dictation* is something spoken by one person and copied down by another. *Diction* is the clearness and quality of one's speech.

Speech is now a key element of popular music. *Rap*, which uses speaking instead of singing, is one of the most creative and important developments in current music. Its roots come from African chanting, spoken blues, the performances of James Brown, and the *toasts* of Jamaican disk jockeys. Rhythm and beat are important to rap. Lyrics often deal with current social issues, and some rap groups are extremely controversial. Popular performers include Dr. Dre and Snoop Doggy Dog.

-logy, log, loq (word; study of; speak)

To be *eloquent* is to speak well. A *dialogue* is speech, or a conversation, between two or more people. However, the suffix *-logy* means "study of." You may have taken courses in *biology* (the study of living things), *psychology* (the study of the mind), or *anthropology* (the study of human beings).

voc, vok (voice; call)

A record that contains the human voice speaking or singing is called a *vocal* recording. *Vocabulary*, meaning "things spoken by the voice," or "words," also comes from *voc*. You will not confuse this root with the other word roots in this chapter if you remember to associate it with the word *voice*.

Words to Learn

Part 1

dict

1. **contradict** (verb)   kŏn′trə-dĭkt′

   From Latin: *contra-* (against) + *dict* (speak)

   to say or put forth the opposite of something

   > It is not wise to **contradict** your boss in public.

   > Although the facts **contradicted** his personal beliefs, the newscaster faithfully reported what he had seen.

   > Unfortunately, the evidence gathered from the experiment **contradicted** the scientist's theory.

   ▶ *Related Words*
   contradiction (noun)   Research into the benefits of vitamins has yielded *contradictory* results.

contradictory (adjective) There is *contradictory* evidence about the benefits of removing asbestos from buildings.

Oxymorons are *contradictions* of language, or statements in which one word seems to contradict another. A few examples are *jumbo shrimp, killing with kindness, dull shine,* and *whole half.*

---

2. **dictator** (noun)   dĭk′tā-tər

From Latin: *dict* (speak) (A dictator is a ruler who speaks with power; whatever the ruler says is done.)

a ruler with total authority

> Joseph Stalin, former **dictator** of the Soviet Union, ordered several million people into gulags, or prison camps.

▶ *Related Word*
  dictatorial (adjective)   (dĭk′tə-tôr′ē-əl)   The club president's *dictatorial* manner ensured that he lost the next election.

3. **edict** (noun)   ē′dĭkt′

From Latin: *e-* (out) + *dict* (speak)

an order or decree

> An **edict** of the Soviet Union once required all citizens to carry passports stating their residence and ethnic group.
>
> There was a city **edict** prohibiting pets in high-rise buildings.

log, -logy, loq

4. **colloquial** (adjective)   kə-lō′kwē-əl

From Latin: *com-* (together) + *loq* (speak) (When we "speak together" with friends, our speech is colloquial.)

informal conversation or expression

> The word *yeah* is a **colloquial** way of saying *yes.*

▶ *Related Word*
  colloquialism (noun)   The word "burned" is a *colloquialism* for "angry."

5. **ecology** (noun)   ĭ-kŏl′ə-jē

From Greek: *oikos* (house) + *-logy* (study of) (Ecology is concerned with the environment, the "home" or "house" in which we all live.)

the study of the relationship of living things and their environment

> The growth of tourism has threatened the **ecology** of several western states.

▶ *Related Words*
  ecological (adjective)   (ĕk′ə-lŏj′ĭ-kəl)   Acid rain has ruined the *ecological* balance of many lakes and ponds.

  ecologist (noun)   The *ecologist* investigated the effect of auto fumes on wildlife.

As human beings change their environment through industrial and technological advances, the science of *ecology* is increasingly needed to protect plant and animal life. The rain forests of South America, Africa, and Asia are being cleared to obtain lumber and provide farm land. Ecologists have demonstrated how this practice may lead to the extinction of forest animals. Even human life may be endangered, since the roots of forest trees help to hold water. When these trees are cut, water evaporates, causing dryness that kills plants and eventually leads to human starvation.

In 1987, scientists confirmed that there was a dangerous hole in the protective ozone layer that surrounds our atmosphere. This hole, centered over Antarctica, may indirectly cause skin cancer in humans and animals as well as have a dangerous warming effect on the Earth's temperature. Researchers feel that the ozone hole may be due to the use of industrial chlorofluorocarbons, which are sometimes used in aerosol cans, refrigerators, air conditioners, and some food containers.

---

6. **loquacious** (adjective)   lō-kwā′shəs

From Greek: *loq-* (speak)

very talkative

> My **loquacious** sister kept me on the telephone for over an hour.

▶ *Related Words*
  loquaciousness (noun)   Because of his *loquaciousness,* the politician loved to grant interviews to reporters.

7. **monologue** (noun)   mŏn′ə-lôg′

From Greek: *monos* (one) + *log* (speak)

a speech or performance by one person

> Dave Letterman is known for his amusing **monologues.**

8. **prologue** (noun)   prō′lôg′

From Greek: *pro-* (before) + *log* (speak)

the introduction to a play or book

> The author described the historical background of the book in the **prologue.**

an introductory event

> The assassination of Archduke Ferdinand of Austria was the **prologue** to World War I.

The *prologues* to many TV programs and movies have become famous. Can you identify what these introduce?

1. Faster than a speeding bullet, more powerful than a locomotive. . . .
2. Space, the final frontier. . . .
3. In a time long ago, in a galaxy far, far away. . . .

(*Answers:*   1. *Superman*   2. *Star Trek* (and sequels)   3. *Star Wars*)

---

voc, vok

9. **advocate** (verb)   ăd′və-kāt′; (noun)   ăd′və-kĭt

From Latin: *ad-* (toward) + *voc* (to voice, call)

to urge publicly; to recommend (verb)

> Members of Amnesty International **advocate** the protection of human rights and the prevention of torture.

a person who publicly urges a cause (noun)

> Maria was an **advocate** of equal rights for handicapped people.

▶ *Common Phrase*
advocate of

10. **invoke** (verb)   ĭn-vōk′

From Latin: *in-* (in) + *voc* (to call) (*Invocāre* means "to call upon.")

to call in assistance; to call upon

> The minister **invoked** the help of God in troubled times.
>
> The President **invoked** the aid of the National Guard to stop the rioting.

▶ *Related Word*
invocation (noun)   (ĭn′və-kā′shən)   The rabbi gave an *invocation*. (*Invocation* means "prayer.")

The Fifth Amendment of the U.S. Constitution states that those accused of a crime cannot be forced to testify against themselves. Thus, when asked to explain something that may injure their case or make them appear guilty, accused people may "*invoke* the Fifth Amendment" and refuse to answer.

---

11. **revoke** (verb)   rĭ-vōk′

From Latin: *re-* (back) + *vok* (to call)

to cancel or withdraw

> Judges often **revoke** the licenses of people convicted of driving drunk.

▶ *Related Word*
revocation (noun)   (rĕv′ə-kā′shən)   A country that violates human rights risks *revocation* of trade agreements with the United States.

12. **vociferous** (adjective)   vō-sĭf′ər-əs

From Latin: *voc* (voice) + *ferre* (carry)

crying out noisily; speaking loudly

> The **vociferous** crowd loudly cheered the returning hero.

▶ *Related Word*
vociferate (verb)   The people *vociferated* "Long live the king!"

Exercises

Part 1

■ Definitions

Match each word in the left-hand column with a definition from the right-hand column. Use each choice only once.

1. ecology _____
2. invoke _____
3. monologue _____
4. contradict _____
5. prologue _____
6. edict _____
7. colloquial _____
8. loquacious _____
9. dictator _____
10. advocate _____

a. person with sole power
b. informal
c. very talkative
d. order; decree
e. study of the relationship of life and environment
f. helpless
g. to call in for assistance
h. speech by one person
i. introduction to book or play
j. to recommend
k. to say loudly
l. to say something opposite

■ Meanings

Match each word element to its definition. Use each choice only once.

1. voc, vok _____
2. log, -logy, loq _____
3. dict _____

a. speak; study of; word
b. speak
c. voice; call

■ Words in Context

Complete each sentence with the word that fits best. Use each choice only once.

a. contradict
b. dictator
c. edict
d. colloquial

e. ecology
f. loquacious
g. monologue
h. prologue

i. advocate
j. invoke
k. revoke
l. vociferous

1. A library may _____ your card if you continue to lose books.

2. The small, poor country tried to _____ the aid of its rich neighbor.

3. The _____ had total control over her country.

4. When a mother and father _____ each other, a child may not know whose directions to follow.

5. Students should use formal rather than _____ English when they write term papers.

6. The _____ of the area was disturbed when a flood destroyed the food supply of the animals.

7. October's drop in stock prices was a(n) _____ to the economic problems of November.

8. The _____ woman talked throughout our card game.

9. I am a(n) _____ of more money for education.

10. The government issued a(n) _____ declaring that all citizens must be off the streets by 10 P.M.

■ *Using Related Words*

Complete each sentence by using a word from the group of related words above it. You may need to capitalize a word when you put it into a sentence. Use each choice only once.

1. vociferous, vociferated

Years ago, politicians _____ for several hours in each speech. Since no microphones were used, the candidate who had the loudest and strongest voice often won an election. Abraham Lincoln began a new style in 1863, when, following a

_____ two-hour speech by Edward Everett, Lincoln gave a 270-word presentation called the Gettysburg Address. This short speech is now considered one of the greatest addresses ever given.

2. dictator, dictatorial

Was Napoleon a _____ or an enlightened ruler?

He slaughtered those who resisted him in Italy with _____ savagery. Yet he extended the rights of citizens and created an excellent series of laws called the Napoleonic Code.

3. contradicted, contradictory

Animals may sometimes confuse us by using _____ body language. For example, a dog may wag its tail while growling.

The tail-wagging, a friendly action, is _____ by the threatening growl. At such times, one should approach a dog with caution.

4. revoked, revocation

At one time, plastic tubing for plumbing, or PVC, was banned from

use in many cities. Recently, the ban has been _____

in various areas. However, this _____ often does not cover high-rise buildings. Copper tubing for plumbing must still be used in many of these taller structures.

5. ecology, ecological

Global warming has a major effect on world _____ . Melting ice causes higher sea levels, and the wildlife that occupies shorelines and shallow water has difficulty surviving. Areas that once supported crops turn into deserts. As the earth warms, the

_____ balance is upset.

■ *True or False?*

Each of the following statements contains at least one word from this section. Read each statement and then indicate whether you think it is probably true or probably false.

_____   1. People often invoke the help of God during difficult times.

_____   2. "Yes" and "no" are terms that contradict each other.

_____   3. Government agencies advocate child abuse.

_____   4. The prologue of a play occurs before the play starts.

_____   5. A monologue involves several people.

_____   6. A child who broke his mother's rules might have privileges revoked.

_____   7. Dictators commonly rule in a democracy.

_____   8. People are usually loquacious when they vociferate.

_____   9. Ecological balance refers only to human life.

_____   10. A government edict would probably use colloquial language.

Word Elements

Part 2

The second part of this chapter presents two word elements that deal with the concept of writing. Then three pairs of confusable words, which college students often have trouble distinguishing, are introduced.

-gram, -graph, -graphy, graph (write)
This suffix has three spellings. It is spelled *-gram,* as in *telegram,* a written message sent by wires. (*Tele-* means "far.") The spelling *-graph* is used in *autograph,* a person's signature, or "self-writing." (*Auto* means "self.") Finally, the suffix can be spelled *-graphy,* as in *photography* (literally, "writing in light"). *Graph* can also function as a root.

scrib, script (write)

This root is found in many common words. A *script* is the written form of a television program, movie, or play. When small children make written marks, they often *scribble*. A *scribe* writes down the words of other people.

Words to Learn

Part 2

-gram, -graph, -graphy, graph

13. **demographic** (adjective)   děm′ə-grăf′ĭk

    From Greek: *demos* (people) + *-graph* (write)

    referring to the study of population characteristics

    > **Demographic** trends show that the world's population is rising.

    ▶ *Related Word*
    demography (noun) (dĭ mŏg′rə-fē) *Demography* reveals that an increasing number of people work in the field of high technology.

14. **epigram** (noun)   ĕp′ĭ-grăm′

    From Greek: *epi-* (on) + *-gram* (write)

    a short, clever saying, often in rhyme

    > Benjamin Franklin's **epigram** on the value of consistent work was "Little strokes fell great oaks."

15. **graphic** (adjective)   grăf′ĭk

    From Greek: *graph* (write) (*Graphe* meant "drawing, writing.")

    referring to drawings or artistic writing

    > My computer software can create charts, drawings, and other **graphic** displays.

    described vividly or clearly

    > The food critic described the delicious meal in **graphic** detail.

    > Charles Dickens's **graphic** description of abused and neglected children shocked the English public of the 1800s.

▶ *Related Word*

graphics (noun)   The Hyatt hotel chain had its *graphics* professionally designed.

scrib, script

16. **inscription** (noun)   ĭn-skrĭp′shən

From Latin: *in-* (in) + *script* (write)

carving or writing on a surface

> Many U.S. coins bear the **inscription** *E pluribus unum,* meaning "one from many."

> The Saudi Arabian flag bears an **inscription** from the Koran.

a signed message on a picture or in a book

> The **inscription** that the star wrote on his picture read "From R. Kelly."

▶ *Related Word*

inscribe (verb)   (ĭn-skrīb′)   The engraver *inscribed* the date of my college graduation on the ring.

> Atif, an excellent student who died in a car accident, is *inscribed* in his teacher's memory. (In this sentence, *inscribe* is used in a nonphysical manner.)

17. **manuscript** (noun, adjective)   măn′yə-skrĭpt′

From Latin: *manu* (by hand) + *script* (write)

the original text of a book or article before publication (noun)

> The author submitted his **manuscript** to several publishers.

> The **manuscript** of *The Life and Times of Fredrick Douglass* sold for several thousand dollars at a recent auction.

referring to writing done by hand (adjective)

> It took many years to master the beautiful **manuscript** lettering that was once used to write books.

Before printing was invented, scribes laboriously copied whole books. The *manuscripts* they created were often beautiful works of art, and they were quite expensive.

Johann Gutenberg invented modern printing in about 1450. The famous Gutenberg Bible was his first production. The printing process brought about a social revolution because it made books, and therefore knowledge, less expensive and more widely available.

NOTE: Manuscript writing (done with disconnected letters) is often distinguished from cursive writing (done with connected letters).

(18.) **transcribe** (verb)   trăn-skrīb′

From Latin: *trans-* (across) + *scrib* (write)

to make a complete written copy

> Court reporters **transcribe** every word of a legal proceeding.

to copy something into another form

> The piano concert was **transcribed** onto an audiotape.

▶ *Related Words*
  transcriber (noun)   The *transcriber* turned the dictation into a letter.
  transcription (noun)   The government made a *transcription* of the tapes recorded by former President Richard Nixon.

Confusable Words

19. **affect** (verb)   ə-fĕkt′

to have an influence on; to change

> Sunlight often **affects** people's moods in a positive way.

20. **effect** (noun)   ĭ-fĕkt′

a result

> Sunlight often has a positive **effect** on people's moods.

NOTE ON POSSIBLE CONFUSION: Try to remember that *affect* is usually a verb and *effect* is usually a noun, as in the following two sentences.

The great teacher *affected* my life.

The great teacher had an *effect* on my life.

(21.) **conscience** (noun)   kŏn′shəns

sense of right and wrong; moral sense

> **Conscience** dictates that we do not steal from others.

▶ *Related Word*
  conscientious   (adjective)   (kŏn′shē-ĕn′shəs)   *Conscientious* jury members listened attentively throughout the long trial.

22. **conscious** (adjective)   kŏn′shəs

aware; awake

> Because a local anesthetic was used, Nathan was **conscious** throughout the operation.

> The jury members were **conscious** of the importance of their decision.

NOTE ON POSSIBLE CONFUSION: Remember that *conscience* is a noun and *conscious* is an adjective, as in the following two sentences.

My *conscience* was bothering me.

I am *conscious* of my responsibility.

23. **imply** (verb)   ĭm-plī′

to suggest; to say something indirectly

> A soft smile and kindly voice **imply** that a person is pleased.

▶ *Related Word*
   implication (noun) (ĭm′plĭ-kā′shən) His *implication* was clear to us.

24. **infer** (verb)   ĭn-fûr′

to conclude; to guess

> I **infer** from your soft smile that you are pleased.

▶ *Related Words*
   inference (noun) (ĭn′fər-əns) The chemistry student drew an *inference* from the results of her experiment.
   inferential (adjective) (ĭn′fə-rĕn′shəl) This difficult problem requires *inferential* thinking.

NOTE ON POSSIBLE CONFUSION: A speaker or writer *implies;* a listener or reader *infers.*

Exercises

Part 2

■ *Definitions*

Match each word in the left-hand column with a definition from the right-hand column. Use each choice only once.

1. manuscript _____

2. graphic _____

3. transcribe _____

4. epigram _____

5. affect _____

6. inscription _____

7. conscience _____

8. imply _____

9. demographic _____

10. effect _____

a. aware

b. a sense of right and wrong

c. to make a complete written copy

d. to influence

e. to hint

f. short, witty saying

g. carving on a surface

h. original text of a book

i. to draw a conclusion

j. a result

k. referring to population statistics

l. referring to drawings or artistic writings

■ *Words in Context*

Complete each sentence with the word that fits best. Use each choice only once, and capitalize when necessary.

a. demographic   e. manuscript   i. conscience
b. epigram   f. transcribe   j. conscious
c. graphic   g. affect   k. imply
d. inscription   h. effect   l. infer

1. The _____ of the ancient book was a thousand years old.

2. _____ surveys reveal that many people in Canada speak both English and French.

3. It takes time to _____ a long tape into writing.

4. The cruel criminal did not have a(n) _____ .

5. The description of the cold weather was so _____ that we began to shiver.

6. I try not to let my busy social life _____ my ability to study.

7. I was not _____ of the fact that I had broken any rules.

8. The governor of Florida was concerned about the _____ of high-rise buildings on the ocean front.

9. The people of Florida will probably _____ from the governor's comments that high-rise buildings would not improve the ocean front.

10. "Man proposes, God disposes" is an example of a(n) _____ .

■ *Using Related Words*

Complete each sentence by using a word from the group of related words above it. You may need to capitalize a word when you put it into a sentence. Use each choice only once.

1. implied, infer

   The mayor's unhappy face and quiet manner _____

   that something was wrong, but we could not _____
   exactly what had happened. Later, we found out that the chief of police had resigned.

2. demography, demographic

   _____ shows that an increasing number of moth-

   ers of young children are working. This _____
   trend points to a need for high-quality and widely available child-care facilities.

3. inscriptions, inscribed

   Designed by Yale architectural student Maya Lin, the memorial for

   the Vietnam War is a long slab of black granite. _____
   in the surface are the names of all American soldiers who died in

battle. People throughout the United States come to see the

_____ honoring those who have fallen. Many visitors are moved to tears.

4. affect, effect

Which has a greater _____ on a person, heredity or environment? In the 1800s, scientists believed that heredity had a far greater influence. However, environment also has been shown

to _____ people strongly. For example, in a study done by Skeels in the 1930s, when children placed in an orphanage were given loving attention, their IQs increased dramatically.

5. consciences, conscientious

Early Protestant settlers in America were said to have had the

"Protestant work ethic." According to this, their _____ would bother them if they did not work hard enough. Thus, these

people were often _____ workers.

■ *True or False?*

Each of the following statements contains one or more words from this section. Read each sentence carefully and then indicate whether you think it is probably true or probably false.

____   1. Engaging in conversation has a positive effect on language development.

____   2. Religious training helps children to develop a conscience.

____   3. A transcription leaves many things out.

____   4. We are conscious when we sleep.

____   5. Epigrams are usually clever.

———　　6. Authors write manuscripts.

———　　7. A graphic description of pain might frighten a small child.

———　　8. Adding an inscription onto a new watch you were buying would probably affect the price.

———　　9. A demographic study might serve as the basis of taxation.

———　10. If you imply that others are stupid, you will make friends.

■ *Practicing Strategies: Combining Context Clues and Word Elements*

Combining the strategies of context clues and word elements is a good way to figure out unknown words. In the following sentences, each italicized word contains a word element that you have studied in this chapter. Using the meaning of the word element and the context of the sentence, make an intelligent guess about the meaning of the italicized word. Your instructor may ask you to check the meaning in your dictionary when you have finished.

1. Delivering a *eulogy* in his brother's honor, Winston said many wonderful things about him.

   Eulogy means _____ .

2. *Pictographs* were used by ancient civilizations.

   Pictographs means _____

   _____ .

3. At the *colloquium,* many people gave talks about the economy.

   Colloquium means _____

   _____ .

4. The *entomologist* specialized in ants, bees, and spiders.

   Entomologist means _____ .

5. The written word "t-o-y" has three *graphemes.*

   Graphemes means _____ .

Chapter Exercises

■ *Practicing Strategies: New Words from Word Elements*

See how your knowledge of word elements can help you understand new words. Complete each sentence with the word that seems to fit best. Use each choice only once.

a. biography   e. hologram   i. revocalize
b. describe   f. interlocution   j. scriptorium
c. dictate   g. phonograph   k. sociology
d. graph   h. prescription   l. travelogue

1. A(n) _____ is something that must be written out before you can get medicine. (*Pre-* means "before.")

2. A book written about someone's life is a(n) _____ .

3. The study of society is called _____ .

4. A(n) _____ record is "writing" made from sound. (*Phono-* means "sound.")

5. When we speak and others copy down our words, we _____ .

6. A spoken account of a trip might be called a _____ .

7. A(n) _____ is a three-dimensional written picture in which a whole object seems to appear.

8. A(n) _____ often displays numerical information as a drawing or in written visual form.

9. When we "voice something again," we _____ it.

10. Books were once written by hand in a _____ .

■ *Companion Words*

Complete each sentence with the word that fits best. Choose your answers from the words below. You may use each word more than once.

Choices: draw, of, on

1. The book contained a graphic description _____ violence.

2. We can _____ an inference from a speaker's implications.

3. A mother is often conscious _____ her baby's every movement.

4. I am an advocate _____ equal pay for equal work.

5. Weather often has an effect _____ people's decisions to travel.

■ *Writing with Your Words*

This exercise will give you practice in writing effective sentences that use the vocabulary words. Each sentence is started for you. Complete it with an interesting phrase that also indicates the meaning of the italicized word.

1. I am an *advocate* of _____

   _____ .

2. The *graphic* description _____

   _____ .

3. The *loquacious* employee _____

   _____ .

4. I have *contradictory* feelings about _____

   _____ .

5. According to the *edict,* _____

   _____ .

6. The *dictator* _____

   _____ .

7. The speaker *implied* _____

   _____ .

8. We *inferred* from the speech that _____

_____ .

9. I am *affected* by _____

_____ .

10. A *conscientious* worker _____

_____ .

Passage

The Man Who Did Not Cry Wolf

Centuries of folklore and tradition have expressed distrust and fear of wolves. We speak of starvation as "having the wolf at the door." It is the wolf who tricks the folktale figure Little Red Riding Hood. Finally, an evil person who appears to be innocent is called a "wolf in sheep's clothing."

Only a few brave people have ever tested these legends by observing wolves at close range. Farley Mowat was one such person. **(1)** The Canadian government was concerned that wolves were damaging the **ecology** of the Arctic by eating so many caribou that the animal was disappearing. Therefore, officials sent Mowat to see what **effect** hungry northern wolves were having on caribou herds. **(2)** In his book *Never Cry Wolf,* Mowat's description of a year living close to wolves **contradicts** the traditional image of the "big, bad wolf."

From the beginning, Mowat's encounters with wolves surprised him. Weaponless, he found himself at their mercy three times; although they could have killed him, they simply walked away. Even when he went into their territory, the wolves did not attack. **(3)** The **implication** was clear: the senseless viciousness of the wolf was largely in the human imagination.

Fascinated, Mowat was determined to observe the wolves at close range. He defined his own territory, lived in a tent, and watched them through a telescope. Mowat's wolf family consisted of a couple, "Georgie" and "Angeline," their wolf pups, and "Uncle Albert," a single male. They were affectionate and caring. The entire wolf den was organized around feeding the pups. Each afternoon, George and Uncle Albert went off to hunt, returning the next morning. **(4)** However, Angeline, apparently **conscious** of her responsibilities as a mother, stayed home to watch her youngsters.

Wolves vociferate together in high-pitched howls.

During family play, sometimes a pup's lively nipping and licking wore Angeline out, but the good-natured Uncle Albert was always ready to take her place. **(5)** Mowat gives a **graphic** description of wolf games of "tag," with Uncle Albert playing "it." Uncle Albert was also an effective, if unwilling, babysitter. All three adults carefully instructed the puppies in hunting.

At first, wolf calls disturbed Mowat. **(6)** The animals would come together and **vociferate** in high-pitched howls for several minutes, sending chills of fear down Mowat's spine. Gradually, he began to realize that wolves could communicate different messages. After listening to howls one day, Ooteck, Mowat's Eskimo companion, became greatly excited and rushed off. A few hours later, he returned with a host of visitors. How had Ooteck known where to find them? He had gotten the information from the wolves' howls. Another time, Ooteck claimed that two wolf packs, separated by many miles, announced the presence of caribou herds to each other.

As he continued to watch the wolves, Mowat began to wonder what they ate. For most of the year, the caribou were far away. How did the den support itself during this time? One day he watched Angeline trap twenty-three mice in one afternoon. Could it be that the great beast of the north could support itself by eating the lowly mouse?

To test the ability of a large animal to live on mice, Mowat used himself as a subject. For several months, he ate only mice, developing several recipes! He reported that this diet did not **affect** his health, and he remained as vigorous as ever. **(7)** He drew the **inference** that wolves could also live on a diet of mice.

Did wolves ever hunt caribou? Mowat found that the wolves hunted a few, mainly weak or old, caribou. By removing the animals that would find it hard to survive, the wolves actually strengthened the caribou herd. But if wolves were not killing the caribou, who was? Mowat decided that most were hunted by human beings.

(8) Mowat's experience with Arctic wolves was a **prologue** to efforts that aroused the public's **conscience** about the treatment of the animals. Soon after he returned from the wild, he began work on a **manuscript** to make people more aware of wolves. The resulting book, *Never Cry Wolf*, played an important part in saving the northern wolf, which, he estimated, numbered fewer than 3,000. **(9)** Mowat **invoked** the aid of wildlife organizations in preserving and increasing the wolf population. He urged the government to **revoke edicts** that gave rewards for dead wolves. **(10)** In response to the pleas of Mowat and other wildlife **advocates,** people are now taking steps to protect this valuable animal.

■ *Exercise*

Each numbered sentence below corresponds to a sentence in the Passage. Fill in the letter of the choice that makes the sentence mean the same thing as its corresponding sentence in the Passage.

1. The Canadian government was concerned that wolves were damaging the _____ of the Arctic.
   a. weather balance   b. environmental balance
   c. balance of power   d. balance of fur trapping

2. Mowat's description of a year living close to the wolves _____ the traditional image of the "big, bad wolf."
   a. draws on   b. denies   c. shows   d. supports

3. The _____ was clear.
   a. talk   b. moral   c. suggestion   d. singing

4. However, Angeline, apparently _____ of her responsibilities as a mother, stayed home to watch her youngsters.
   a. aware   b. because   c. forgetful   d. resentful

5. Mowat gives a(n) _____ description of wolf games of "tag."
   a. long   b. accurate   c. scientific   d. vivid

6. The animals would come together and _____ in high-pitched howls for several minutes.
   a. cry out   b. sing beautifully   c. ask for help   d. disturb others

7. He drew the _____ that wolves could also live on a diet of mice.
   a. conclusion   b. note   c. picture   d. explanation

8. Mowat's experience with Arctic wolves was a(n) _____ to efforts to make people more aware of wolves.
   a. climax   b. introduction   c. resistance   d. answer

9. He _____ the aid of wildlife organizations.
   a. hoped for   b. refused   c. dreamed about   d. called in

10. In response to the pleas of Mowat and other wildlife _____ , people are now taking steps to protect this animal.
    a. models   b. supporters   c. donors   d. leaders

■ Discussion Questions

1. What events first made Mowat suspect that wolves were not as vicious as people believed?

2. How do the wolves compare with human parents?

3. Killing wolves and selling their skins is one way for people who live in the Arctic to support themselves. Do you think the Canadian government should allow this? Why or why not?

◀ ENGLISH IDIOMS

Speech and Writing

Since language is used to express ideas, many English idioms contain concepts of speech and writing. To *talk back* means to answer rudely. To *talk down to* is to speak to somebody as if he or she were stupid. However, to *talk up* something means to make something appear to be good. When we *talk big,* we boast, or brag, possibly about something that is not true. When we *talk over* a problem, we discuss that problem for quite a while. To *talk* people *out of* something is to persuade them not to do it. For example, a person might talk a friend out of quitting college.

When we *talk through our hats,* we don't know the facts but make unsupported or untrue statements anyway. When a person *sweet talks* someone else, he falsely flatters that person. On the other hand, when he *talks turkey* he speaks the truth frankly, or *tells it like it is.*

Writing also plays a part in our idioms. To do something *to the letter* is to do it exactly. When we say *"It's nothing to write home about,"* we are saying that we are not enthusiastic about something.

To see the *handwriting on the wall* is to realize that disaster is coming. In the Bible, Belshazzar, king of Babylon, saw a hand appear at a feast and write on the wall a cryptic message that only the Jewish prophet Daniel could understand. The message predicted the destruction of Belshazzar's kingdom.

REVIEW

Chapters 9–12

■ Reviewing Words in Context

Complete each sentence with the word or phrase that fits best. Use each choice only once.

a. auditory
b. bilingual
c. biodegradable
d. biopsy
e. centennial
f. colloquial

g. conscious
h. dilemma
i. fiduciary
j. inaudible
k. inscription
l. metric

m. monologue
n. nondescript
o. symmetrical
p. trilogy
q. vociferous
r. hold out an olive branch

1. The _____ woman spoke Tagalog and English.

2. He faced the _____ of deciding which of two unpleasant people should go with him on his business trip.

3. The _____ people shouted and screamed in the streets.

4. The _____ system is used by scientists to measure temperature, weight, and length.

5. The _____ alarm flashed lights rather than making a noise.

6. We will _____ to our enemy in hopes of making peace.

7. A single actor gave a(n) _____ on an empty stage.

8. The hotel lobby was _____ , with furniture on both sides of the room in the same arrangement.

9. Paper is a(n) _____ substance that breaks down through natural processes.

10. She used _____ expressions that made us all aware that her talk was informal.

11. We are _____ that you are annoyed, and we will try to understand why.

12. The pathologist examined the _____ to determine if it contained cancer cells.

13. Her appearance was _____ ; however, we will always remember the wonderful speech that she gave.

14. The girl's uncle had _____ responsibility for the money that had been willed to her by her grandparents.

15. A _____ celebrates the hundred-year anniversary of the company.

■ *Passage for Word Review*

Complete each blank in the Passage with the word or phrase that makes the best sense. The choices include words from the vocabulary lists along with related words. Use each choice only once.

a. affect	e. conspicuous	i. given carte blanche
b. audit	f. destitute	j. incredulous
c. beneficial	g. deviation	k. malevolent
d. centigrade	h. effect	l. verify

Why My Stepfather Was Court-Martialed

In 1941, when my stepfather was drafted into the United States Army, he had no interest or experience in cooking. Therefore, he was

(1) _____ when he was told that, on a written test, he had displayed a talent for preparing food. Army officials offered him a six-week course in becoming a chef. My stepfather accepted because he was sure he would be able to eat lots of leftovers.

As things turned out, he got good grades in cooking school. He be-

came head chef of an army kitchen and was **(2)** _____ to run things as he wanted to.

All went well until he had to deal with spinach. Because spinach

contains several vitamins that are **(3)** _____ to human health, the army supplied it several times per week. Unfortunately, the soldiers simply refused to eat it. Even seeing spinach on their plates put them in a bad mood. After many hours spent cooking spinach, my stepfather realized that, at the end of the meal, he was throwing all of it away.

To save time and effort, he decided simply to dispose of the hated vegetable before it was cooked.

Unfortunately, one day a visiting army officer, passing through the camp, noticed a large, **(4)** _____ _____ pile of raw spinach in the garbage. Another officer was sent out to **(5)** _____ that the first officer had seen everything correctly. Then an army accountant made an official **(6)** _____ of the amount that was missing from the raw spinach supply. At the end of this investigation, the army accused my stepfather of destroying government property.

At his court-martial trial my stepfather told the army officers that his intentions had not been **(7)** _____ . Instead, he was simply trying to save the army the trouble of cooking the unwanted vegetable. Nevertheless, the army officers found him guilty and deducted five dollars from his pay for the next three months. Because he did not have much money, this loss of pay was enough to leave him **(8)** _____ for quite a while.

After the trial, however, one officer talked to my stepfather privately and told him that cooking spinach would **(9)** _____ the way that the army thought about the vegetable. Raw spinach was government property, but cooked spinach was considered garbage. In other words, if the spinach were cooked, it could be thrown out.

From then on, my stepfather cooked all the spinach and then immediately put it into a garbage can. By following this procedure without any **(10)** _____ , he kept everyone happy. The government did not have its property thrown out, and the soldiers did not have spinach on their plates.

■ *Reviewing Learning Strategies*

New words from word elements Below are some words you have not studied that are formed from classical word elements. Using your knowledge of these elements, write in the letter of the word that best completes each sentence. Use each choice only once.

a. accredited	e. biometrics	i. pedometer
b. aquaphobia	f. dictaphone	j. telepathy
c. audiologist	g. galvanometer	k. uniped
d. binary	h. malcontent	l. verdict

1. A(n) _____ is an animal that walks on one foot.

2. A(n) _____ is a specialist in the study of measuring hearing.

3. If you are not content, you are _____ .

4. Fear of water is _____ .

5. Named after Luigi Galvani, a pioneer in electricity, a

   _____ measures electrical current.

6. Sensing or feeling from far away is _____, since

   _____ means "far."

7. _____ is the branch of science that takes statistical data, or measurements, on living things.

8. We can believe in the skill of a doctor or dentist who is

   _____ .

9. A jury is said to "speak the truth" when it gives a _____ .

10. Something _____ consists of two parts.

Index of Words and Word Elements

Word elements are printed in italics.

Index of Key Terms